Where the Lion Roars

An 1890 African Colonial Cookery Book

I0142890

By

A. R. B. (Mrs A. R. Barnes)

EDITED BY

David Saffery

JEPPESTOWN

Published by Jeppestown Press,
10A Scawfell St, London, E2 8NG, United Kingdom.

First published as *The Colonial Household Guide*, by Darter
Brothers and Walton, Cape Town, South Africa, 1890.

Introduction and commentaries © Copyright David Saffery 2006

Cover design © Copyright Chris Eason 2006

Front cover features *Cottages at Karoo National Park*, by Gemma
Longman, 2006; www.flickr.com/photos/g-hat/. Back cover shows
Kitchen, Stellenbosch Village Museum, Stellenbosch, South Africa, by Mike
Wong 2006; www.flickr.com/photos/squeakymarmot/.
Both reproduced under CCPL:
http://creativecommons.org/licenses/by/2.0/legalcode

Original advertisements from contemporary sources including *The
Knobkerrie* and *Diamond News*, 1871-1885

ISBN: 0-9553936-1-2
       978-0-9553936-1-7

" 'Feed the Beast' is the counsel given by Du Maurier's experienced wife to the young friend who asks her how a husband may be kept at home. This little volume shows how it may be done in an immense variety of ways; it supplies also a good store of useful information and hints upon every description of domestic matters."

Cape Times, 1889, on the first edition of the *Colonial Household Guide*, by Mrs A. R. Barnes.

CAPE GOVERNMENT RAILWAYS
(MIDLAND SYSTEM).

Tenders for Refreshment Room,
NAAUWPOORT STATION.

Tenders are invited for One Year's Leave as from the 1st August next, of the Refreshment Room at Naauwpoort Station.

Sealed Tenders to be sent to the Undersigned, from whom further information may be obtained, not later than Noon, on the 25th proximo, marked on the outside, "Tenders for Naauwpoort Refreshment Room."

The highest or any Tender not necessarily accepted.

A. W. HOWELL,
Traffic Manager.

1890 PREFACE.

THE chief object of this book is to assist in their duties the housewives and mothers of the colony. Such persons have been greatly puzzled at times in taking up a book of cookery written in England to find something suitable for preparation with colonial materials; for this reason many such recipes as are usually met with in a ponderous volume have been rejected, while their place has been filled by others more in favour in the colony, the greater part of which have been fairly tried and found to answer well.

Nothing contributes so much to the discomfort of a home as badly or wastefully cooked food, and it is hoped the book will assist those who have had little or no opportunity of learning to cook until they find themselves in a home of their own; who yet, being apt to learn, may only need a little practical guidance to enable them to succeed.

The latter part of the book, on general household subjects, etc., will, it is believed, prove helpful to those who require such assistance.

The Second Edition of this work contains a large amount of further useful and special information, and many new recipes have been added. For the benefit of our Dutch housewives, it is still intended, if the circulation of this edition be successful, to publish it at an early date in Dutch, and with this object it is hoped many will endeavour to make "The Colonial Household Guide " extensively known.

KIMBERLEY, SOUTH AFRICA.

2006 PREFACE.

Mrs Barnes' *Colonial Household Guide* was only the third or fourth English-language cookery book ever to be published in Africa: the first, a pamphlet printed in Pietermaritzburg, was produced just 15 years or so before Mrs Barnes' guide to domestic management was published in 1889.

To a modern reader perhaps the most striking aspect of Mrs Barnes' work is that it identifies a cuisine and lifestyle that, barely three generations after the 1820 settlers arrived in South Africa from the United Kingdom, was already in many aspects distinctly different from that of the British middle classes. Like her contemporaries Miss A. G. Hewitt and Hildegonda Duckitt, Mrs Barnes revels in the use of local ingredients and unfamiliar techniques: her Plum Pudding No. 2 recipe casually suggests substituting an ostrich egg for the 12 hen's eggs otherwise required!

Other recipes display a refreshing familiarity with ingredients that have not historically formed part of the traditional British African settler repertoire—the fruity sourness of tamarind pulp in a curry, or the aroma of wood-smoke lending savour to sweet, buttery kernels of mealies.

This is definitely the cuisine of acculturation: British colonists adopting ingredients and cooking techniques from the indigenous population as well as from earlier generations of European settlers and the Malay and Indian slaves they imported. Mrs Barnes even recommends a traditional medicinal plant (the "Goonah", or Sour Fig (*Carpobrotus edulis*)) of the Khokhoi people as a remedy for a sore throat, and gives precise and matter-of-fact instructions for preparing a traditional African cow-dung floor.

For this reprinted edition I have chosen not to include Mrs Barnes' section on South African gardening, and the extended essay on poultry-rearing by the appropriately-named Mr Chick. I have also tidied up some printing errors and idiosyncratic spelling choices—for example, caraway for carraway, and replaced brede with the more common bredie. Apart from that, the work is as Mrs Barnes wrote it. I need hardly add that many of the household hints, child-rearing advice and medical advice do not accord with modern practice, and should not be followed: they should be viewed as historical curiosities and are given for interest only.

LONDON, UNITED KINGDOM

FRESH FISH
EVERY DAY.

READY CLEANED FISH,
AT LOW PRICES,
14, DARLING STREET
(ADJOINING MASONIC HOTEL),

Large Stock of Salt Fish always on Hand.

CAPE FISH COMP.
A. W. AYLES, Manager.

CONTENTS.

Contents

Contents

Contents

Contents

Contents

Contents

Contents

Contents

Contents

Contents

Contents

Contents

Contents

Part I. Introduction.

Coffee.

IT is a colonial custom to take a cup of coffee on rising in the morning; indeed, an old colonist would rather go without breakfast than miss it. With it, and a dry biscuit, he can be contented to leave his breakfast until some time later. The reason is obvious, for country people and farmers generally perform more work before breakfast in attending to their stock, etc., than during the remainder of the morning.

To have a satisfactory cup of coffee made, it should certainly be of the best quality. Coffee is better for being procured in its raw state. This done, carefully sort it, taking out all beans and other bad-coloured nibs, which are the principal cause of a bad flavour when it is made. Put the coffee into a shallow tin, or, if there be a small quantity to be roasted, into an old frying pan, over a fire, not too fierce, or it can be placed in a hot oven; but in each case it must be well stirred until the nibs are all through of a dark-brown, and not a black, colour. Some persons sprinkle a little salt over it whilst roasting.

With a small coffee mill it is easily ground; but those people in country parts who do not possess one get the coffee powdered by rubbing the nibs between two flat stones placed on the ground. Chicory should be sparingly added, not more than one teaspoonful to a cupful of the coffee.

The quantity of coffee to be used should be at the rate of a teacupful for six persons.

It is commonly made by being put into a coffee pot, with a pinch of salt, and covered with boiling water. Pour a little out, and throw some back again into the pot, once or twice, to cover the coffee scum. Afterwards let it settle for a minute or two; then it may be poured out gently without shaking the pot, and served with the addition of milk (warm milk being often preferred) and sugar. Sometimes a muslin or flannel strainer is fixed inside the top of the pot, and considered useful.

American mode of making coffee.

Allow a dessert spoonful of coffee to each coffee cup, put in an enamelled saucepan, break an egg over the dry coffee, and mix thoroughly; then pour on boiling water, and simmer twenty minutes, when the coffee will be clear, like tea, and quite free from grounds. There should be hot rich cream served with it, or whipped cream. It is not necessary to put an egg to each cup, although it improves the flavour, but there must be enough egg to wet the dry coffee, and keep it from scattering, or it will not be clear.

Cocoa.

Those people who do not care for, or who cannot take, coffee on early rising are often glad of a cup of cocoa.

Epps', Taylor's, or Cadbury's cocoa seems to be the easiest to digest, although many persons prefer Van Houten's cocoa, which requires less, being stronger.

Cocoa is easily prepared in a breakfast cup.

Take two good-sized teaspoonfuls, mix with the same quantity of boiling water or boiling milk smoothly into a thick paste. Fill up the cup with boiling water or boiling milk, stirring well whilst doing so.

If preferred with the boiling milk, it only requires the addition of some sugar.

Chocolate.

If this be purchased in cakes, scrape it fine with a knife, and for a breakfastcupful take about two good-sized teaspoonfuls; mix with a little hot water, and stir it into the boiling milk. Add a little sugar.

A pinch of powdered cinnamon added is agreeable to the taste of some folks.

Tea.

Keep this article well covered over, and do not allow it to get damp.

To avoid the opening of any large quantity more than is necessary, keep some at hand in a small suitable article.

The tea generally liked is Uillman's mixture, which, although dearer than Souchong[1], is of a far better flavour, and stronger.

In making, the water must at the time of pouring on the leaves be fast-boiling to extract the oil. The teapot should be warm to assist this purpose; it is easily made so by pouring through it a little hot water.

The quantity of tea to be used is a teaspoonful for each person and one over. This is a sufficient quantity, and rather less will do if the tea be strong and good.

A pinch of carbonate of soda may be added when the water is hard or brackish; but it must only be used sparingly, or the water being strongly flavoured the tea would be spoiled.

Always ask persons you are serving if they take milk and sugar in their tea, as there are many who prefer to have it without the one or the other, and the pleasure of giving satisfaction with a cup of tea should never be lost.

The Cape bush tea[2] is better when used alone for being made in an earthenware teapot; it requires being stewed awhile before using, and often a little of it is added to a cupful of other tea, and considered wholesome, many liking the addition of its flavour. This tea is now being extensively used in the colony.

---

[1] Lapsang Souchong
[2] *Rooibos* or bush tea

How to make tea.

With reference to the subject of brewing tea, most experts agree in the opinion that the water should only just boil—in fact, all the tasting of tea in merchants' offices is done on this principle, and, notwithstanding the experience of a doctor who has written in favour of water being boiled for many hours, there can be no doubt that the general practice adopted for so many years is the best. Thus, when the boiling water is poured on the tea, the infusion should take place for five or six minutes, as after that time a portion of tannin is extracted, which spoils the fine flavour of the tea, besides being injurious to the system. Thus the pernicious plan too often adopted at railway stations and restaurants of allowing the tea to stew cannot be too highly deprecated. There is no doubt that the wretched flavour of this so-called tea prevents the more general consumption of it by travellers, and tends to cause an unreasonable high price to be charged, which in itself is prohibitive to the poorer classes. Of course the time absorbed in drinking a cup of tea is a consideration when only a minute or two is allowed at a station, and the profit on beer and alcoholic liquors is so large that there is little desire to encourage the sale of tea. The tea at railway stations should be made as we have already indicated, and when properly infused the liquor should be put in another vessel, either glass or earthenware, and kept hot. It would thus be ready for travellers immediately on their arrival. The addition of milk would reduce its heat, so that it would be drinkable at once; the avoidance of the stewing process would remove one of the present great drawbacks to the quality of the railway tea; and while not, of course, being equal to the fragrance and flavour of a fresh brew, it would still have an attractive taste, instead of the repellent character of the decoction generally sold.

Kitchen Utensils.

Before proceeding to the task of what to cook, I would suggest for a small household what articles are really useful in ordinary cooking and for table use.

I will mention first, where a stove is not obtainable, a bake pot which is made of iron with a flat lid will be found to answer the purpose. It is used as an oven, fire being placed underneath and above the lid, which can be lifted up by the handle with an iron hook and replaced without letting the ashes fall inside. Meat, pastry, cakes, and bread may be well baked in them.

Meat, and all the articles to be baked, are better for being put first in a tin before being placed in the pot.

If care is taken it is astonishing how well articles of food can be cooked in the bake pot.

There is also another baking pot made of copper used in the colony for baking pastry, which answers well also.

But to refer to a stove, which is the most economical and cleanly apparatus for cooking for a small household, the "Queen", "Enchantress", "Mistress", and others are suitable for wood also, and a hot oven can be easily procured.

With such stoves there are usually several cooking utensils supplied, such as a tin for baking meat in the oven, a kettle, a round saucepan and meat boiler; but the other accompanying articles are not of much use, as they are too clumsy and heavy.

It is well to provide yourself with a good frying pan, two or three enamelled saucepans of small sizes, a preserving pan, a gridiron, two zinc or tinned bowls for washing crockery or mixing puddings, paste, etc., in, a meat chopper, two iron table spoons, and two common knives and forks for kitchen use to save better ones, a long-handled iron two-pronged fork for lifting joints of meat and hams from the boiler, a long-handled iron spoon, a tinned soup ladle; also, for kitchen use, a colander, a gravy strainer, a pair of bellows, a sieve, a combined nutmeg and bread grater, a flour dredger, a metal cake; also a blanc-mange mould, an egg boiler, egg whisk, and lastly a strong kitchen candlestick and mincing machine.

Of course several of these articles may be dispensed with if necessary, but are found very useful if procured, costing but little, and lasting years when taken care of.

In crockery, get a soup tureen and a ladle, which latter article is best for being made of metal, some vegetable dishes, which last longer and better for being purchased without handles, and with as little ornamental work on them as possible, a gravy boat, meat and pie dishes, dinner, soup, pudding, cheese, and dessert plates.

To avoid having on the table various patterns of crockery (for often the original one cannot be replaced when broken), purchase such an article as can always be obtained when required.

It is well to have a rolling pin and paste board, some patty pans, pastry cutters, bread tins if required, and a set of metal dish covers, for covering meat when being carried to table to keep it warm. Be careful always to have the steam dried from the inside of them at once after use, or they will soon rust.

A good table knife is indispensable to comfort, and the best in the end prove to be the cheapest. Rodger's cutlery marked with *** is good, and lasts well. Forks and spoons are far better for being made of a solid metal, and not plated, when clean them as much as you will you only make them look better, instead of wearing off the coating which is so soon removed in cheap plated articles. Metal forks and spoons manufactured by Page and marked on the back by a **B Rd** (registered) wear well.

When they are removed soiled from the table have them washed at once; they are far easier to clean then, and can be soon done with a small piece of damp chamois leather dipped into a little of Oakey's knife polish. The prongs of the forks are usually cleaned with a thin slip of wood laid inside the leather.

Before returning these things to their place see they are carefully dusted. Salt spoons are best for being made of ivory or bone.

Never have your knives thrown into hot water, for the blades only should be immersed, and our native servants, especially if left to themselves, soon ruin all knives, china, and glassware. China teacups and saucers are generally put by them all together into a dish tin or tub; then they do not hesitate to pour boiling water over them, and unless the crockery be previously boiled (as presently directed) crack go the cups, and these can be spoiled otherwise fast enough by the boiling tea being poured into them.

If they do not wash the cups in this way, they begin to do the greasy articles first, and then, adding a little more hot water, wash the china last; consequently, they are often greasy and smeared. It is usual for them during the process of washing up to use a great quantity of soap on their dish cloth, usually an unnecessary article where the things are in order judiciously cleansed, but if soap be required Hudson's soap powder mixed with a little hot water, and added to the tub, is the most cleanly and economical.

A soft towel is useful to dry the cups and small goods, and where plates and dishes can be rinsed in cold clean water, then placed in a rack to dry, much time is saved.

Stains from plates and pie dishes are easily removed by dipping the cloth into ashes, then rubbing them well. If this fails, a little moist salt will answer the purpose.

Before using china, glass, and crockery articles, wrap them around well with straw or rags, place them in a boiler of cold water, and let them remain over a gentle fire until they begin to boil, then remove them, and they are ready for use. If they are treated in this way when new, they are less likely to crack with rough usage.

Iron pots should be well scoured with wood ash, cleansed, turned upside downwards, and be left with their lids off.

Plated cruets should not be rubbed with knife polish. Wash them well with warm water, use a little of Oakey's silversmith's soap on a soft brush, and proceed with it to rub the dirty parts gently, rinse and dry thoroughly with a soft glass cloth. The bottles should be kept well polished, a few peas, tintacks, or small mealies[3] shaken well in the cleansing water of them will remove stains of their sediments.

Keep your cruets well filled, and your salt cellars moderately so. In putting mustard into the bottle, do not smear it all over the inside, as it then appears to be stale:

Take care all your glassware is bright and clean; it must always be polished well with a clean soft cloth. The appearance of a table is greatly spoiled if the glass be dull and smeary.

Colman's or Keen's mustard is the best for use; mix it rather thick with cold water; that which has been boiled is preferred, as least likely to ferment. Sometimes a little sauce is added; but if not well attended to it corrodes quickly on the spoon and plated top of the bottle. It is well to mix only a little mustard, and often.

Colonial folks are fond of pickles, hotchpotch, chutney, and other such condiments. Such things look better when placed in pickle glasses; but whenever the bottle is preferred on the table stand it first on a small tin. This rule also applies to jam tins, etc.

To Lay a Table.

In preparing a table for any meal care must be taken to have the different dishes placed as uniformly as possible, and no knives or forks so near the edge of the table as to be easily

---

[3] Mealies: southern African name for maize

knocked off. Be careful to keep the table cloth clean and neatly folded up after use.

All dishes of vegetables, meats, and fish, as well as butter dishes, salads, pastry, pickles, and fruits, must have their accompanying spoons, knives, or forks, or sometimes both, placed conspicuously near them, to assist in their being neatly served.

Serviettes or table napkins can be either rolled up, and placed in a ring at each person's place, or they can be folded in a variety of ways; sometimes the roll or piece of bread is laid inside it, or a piece of bread is placed at the left-hand side of each person, and more of it should always be obtainable near at hand. One tumbler and wine glass at the right-hand side of each person is generally sufficient for family use.

For an ordinary dinner table, place at the right-hand side of each person one table and one dessert knife, and when soup is to be taken one table spoon, and a fish knife if required.

At the left-hand side place one dinner fork, and when fish is served a fork for it also. Over each plate, whenever there is pudding or pastry, place a dessert spoon and fork, close together, the handle of the fork pointing the reverse way to the handle of the spoon, and the latter handle to the right.

A knife for cheese is generally placed between the fork and spoon.

For curry, as an entree, supply an extra dessert spoon and fork, so when it is to be served make this provision.

Champagne, claret, finger, or other glasses are to be in their places if required at the right-hand side.

For hot meals have well-warmed plates, and an extra quantity always near at hand to fall back upon. Never use the same plate for different classes of food. Always break, not cut, your bread, and never carry food to your mouth on a knife. If a fish knife be not supplied for fish, break off a crust of bread, using it in the left hand and the extra fork in the right when it is served.

At the table remember you are not the only one there, attend to the wants of others, and be ready to pass, if there be no waiter in attendance, such articles as may be required.

Draw your chair well under you, so as to give as much room as possible to any one passing behind you; as the waiter always removes the soiled plates, etc., from your left-hand side, move slightly aside to facilitate his movements. If you are not sure of the correct way to partake of any article of food wait awhile and watch others, and you will soon observe the readiest method.

There are some varieties of food which must be held by the hand, such as watercresses. There are many colonial fruits and vegetables which puzzle one at first how to handle and serve. For instance, the water melon, after the ends are cut off, is divided in just the same form as the divisions of an orange. The peel is served with it. A good way of cutting the melon, after removing each end, is to make diagonal incisions, backwards and forwards, deep into it, through the peel; then if it be pulled open, and stood on the dish upon its flat ends, it appears a pretty ornament to the table, especially if it be of a deep-rose colour.

Pineapples are served in round slices, the reverse way to the water melon, but with the peel. Avoid eating it too near the peel, or the lips become very tender, as they do also from the rind of the garden figs when they are not fully ripe.

Bananas and plantains should have the top point cut off; the hand holds the other end whilst the rind is peeled off in strips down it, and the fruit can be cut from the inside.

The pips of the pomegranate are scooped out with a spoon, sprinkled with sugar, and thus eaten. This fruit stains all the linen it touches very much, and is deceiving, for the stains do not appear until the article is washed. Mulberries stain everything at once, but these stains will wash out. Tea stains from the table cloth are far more difficult to remove than those of coffee; they have to be bleached out in the sun, or boiled with a solution of washing soda, or paraffin, one tablespoonful to one gallon of water.

Part II. Breakfast Dishes, Stews, etc.

The first meal to be thought of after early coffee is the breakfast, at which time more solid meat is consumed in the colony than is usual in England.

Boiled Eggs.

A plain boiled egg is usually liked, but it is too often boiled hard, through not having fast-boiling water for it and a quick fire whilst it is cooking. If the water be simply simmering the coldness of the eggs causes it to stop, especially if the fire be low. Whilst the eggs remain in the water they are hardening; then if they are left the usual time of three minutes after the water boils of course they are hard and spoilt. If eggs are dipped into cold water a moment after they are removed from the pot, the shells will pare away quite easily at the table.

Poached Eggs.

Poached eggs are simply eggs boiled in water without their shells. For this purpose a poaching pan, with round hollow wells fixed into it, specially designed for the purpose, may be bought. The water settles into these wells, and the shelled eggs are cooked in them until the yolks become firm, but not hard. A frying pan of water also answers the purpose, although the eggs retain a better shape when cooked in the wells. Fold a napkin small, place it on a plate or dish, with small nicely shaped pieces of dry toast on it, Remove the eggs carefully, placing one on each piece of toast, with a little pepper and salt sprinkled over each.

Memo. on Frying.

Before placing the meat into the frying pan see that the fat is thoroughly hot, and as soon as one side of the meat is well covered with it turn it over and cover the other side also. This will keep the gravy in the meat. In turning it over, which must frequently be done, place the fork into the skin, or the fat part of the meat, for the same purpose. Always add the salt when the meat is nearly finished cooking, or it too will extract the gravy, but the pepper can be used at any time for it. Cooking tongs are handy to turn the meat.

Ham and Eggs, or Eggs and Bacon.

Cut the ham or bacon into thin slices, take off the rind, have the frying pan covered at the bottom with hot fat, drop in the meat for a short time only, unless it be liked well cooked and crisp, then take it out, break each egg separately into a cup, keeping the yolk unbroken, turn the eggs into the pan, sprinkle lightly with pepper, and when they are nicely set, dish them up on to the ham or bacon with a kitchen slice, or a broad-bladed knife, to prevent their breaking, but divide each egg before attempting to do so. Eggs retain a better shape if fried in greased patty pans. Should the ham or bacon be preferred broiled, place on the gridiron over a very slow fire until ready, instead of frying it. Serve hot with poached eggs.

Curry and Rice.

Cut the meat up very small. Fresh uncooked meat is necessarily the best. Dredge it with flour, and place the meat in the bottom of a saucepan which has some melted fat in it, add some sliced onions, pepper and salt, and as much dry curry powder as is liked. Some people and children care for only sufficient to flavour it, whilst others like it very strong and hot. Cartwright's curry powder (Cape Town) is the best to be obtained in the colony. It is prepared from an old and valuable recipe.

Dissolve some tamarind in hot water, add its liquor, or if no tamarind is at hand a very small pinch of tartaric acid gives the same flavour. Stir all well together until the meat browns nicely, then add as much hot water as will cover the whole, put in the potatoes soon after if they are to be cooked with it, skim off all the fat, and proceed to boil until the meat is tender. If, when ready, the curry needs thickening, mix into a smooth paste a little maizena[4] or flour, and stir into it. Ascertain, before sending to table, if it is hot enough or sufficiently flavoured. Serve with boiled rice.

To Boil Curry—a Quicker Method.

Take of either cooked or uncooked mutton a sufficient quantity, cut it up small, place it in a saucepan, with some pared potatoes, sliced onions, and sufficient water to well cover it. Season with pepper and salt, add water in which some tamarind has been dissolved, and let the whole cook slowly until tender. It is well to add the potatoes sometimes, if they cook quickly, after the meat is on the fire awhile. When the meat is sufficiently cooked skim off all the fat, mix enough curry powder with a little water, add to the pot also some thickening, prepared of maizena or flour, mixed with water into a smooth paste. It is now ready for use, after boiling a few minutes longer to cook the thickening; meanwhile stir it to prevent its being burnt, as it will quickly do, after it is added. Place the curry on a dish with the rice all round it, or if the rice remaining has afterwards to be used for a pudding or anything else, put the curry into a vegetable dish, and the rice into another one, upon the table.

Boiled Rice.

Many people are most particular about the way this is prepared, the looser and lighter the grains are when cooked the better for them; whilst, on the other hand, our Dutch friends, who consume a large quantity every day, like it boiled soft and pressed down into a solid mass, and sometimes it is almost

---

[4] Maizena: a trade name for cornflour

tasteless when the salt is omitted. For boiling the grains loosely observe the following method: for about one and a half cupfuls of rice, washed well in two or three waters, have ready a saucepan, holding about one quart of fast-boiling water, which must have nearly a teaspoonful of salt dropped into it before the rice is added. Cover it up and let the water boil quickly again, then remove the lid, and as it continues to boil moderately fast give the saucepan a shake now and again, to prevent it sticking to the bottom. In about twenty minutes, or less, it will be ready for use, the water having boiled slowly away. Of course, to have both the curry and rice ready together, the former must be first prepared and nearly cooked before the rice is placed on the fire.

Hints on Cooking.

Always first ascertain what has to be cooked, reflect upon the time each article takes to get properly done, and then proceed with what should be first prepared, so that at the minute of the appointed time nothing is forgotten, or would have to be hastily prepared at the last moment to meet the emergency. A good cook should never be hurried and worried, but should contrive to prepare everything quietly and in order.

It is usual to think first of the meat required, as this generally takes longer than the vegetables.

Where there is much to be done, and a large quantity of pastry or baked puddings made, it is better, if the oven be small, to have it prepared and baked previous to the actual dinner, as it can generally be warmed, if necessary, whilst the meat is on the dining-room table.

Whilst the meat is cooking there is generally sufficient time to prepare the vegetables.

After a little practice this is easily performed; a small sharp knife for potatoes and small vegetables is the most useful, although colonial servants generally manage to get hold of the largest and bluntest one they can find; then they proceed to hack the vegetables to pieces, instead of paring them thin, keeping their proper shape.

A coloured servant needs careful watching whilst meat is boiling; for, unless she can see it going as hard as possible, she cannot, or will not, understand that it is cooking.

Sometimes, for the dinner, there are one or two kinds of sauces to be prepared, gravy, or melted butter required when dishing-up time comes. These should be thought of beforehand, and got ready whilst the vegetables are cooking; the plates and dishes must also be warmed, that there be no hurry, and consequently no risk of breakage just before meals.

Should a mother or a sister be the cook, it is quite possible for her, with a little management, to be ready and able to sit down at table as soon as the dinner is upon it. A few minutes to change a dress (which can then be protected for the time by a large apron) can always be obtained whilst the vegetables are cooking. It is not well that further duties keep her from the table, whilst others are partaking of the good things she has prepared; her comfort should also be studied, for cooking in hot and trying weather is most wearying.

Liver and Bacon.

To prepare this, take the liver of a small sheep's pluck, also the heart, from the other parts; then see carefully in the liver where the gall is seated; cut this out entire. If it breaks, it is often so bitter that the whole of the liver may be spoiled. Now proceed to cut up the liver into pieces, about two inches long, one inch wide; slice the heart into narrow lengths, down the top to the bottom; wash the meat well, dry in a towel, sprinkle with flour, pepper, and salt, and fry in a pan with fat, slowly, until it is well cooked. Remove and place in a vegetable dish, then fry some small thick pieces of bacon, and when ready mix them with the liver, pour some rich thickened brown gravy over it, and serve.

Liver with Onions.

Fry some sliced onions in some fat mixed with a small lot of sweet herbs, then remove the onion, and the fat must drain away from it. Place it in a gravy strainer; then it is easily done. Now have ready some small chopped pieces of liver, which, being seasoned, are to be fried quickly in fat; dish them up, place in a vegetable dish with the onions, cover with gravy, and send to table.

A large vegetable dish is better for sending food in to table when it has much gravy with it.

Steak and Onions, Fried.

Take a good-sized piece of steak, pepper and dredge it lightly with flour, place it in the hot fat of the pan and fry gently, frequently turning it over. Just before it is done sprinkle with salt, remove it and place in a warm place whilst the onions are frying.

They can be cut into rings whilst the meat is on the fire; when that is removed put them in the pan, season them, cover the pan over tightly with a plate a few minutes, which will keep in the steam and soften them; then remove the plate, make up a brisk fire, and stir them until they are tender and nicely browned. Put them over the top of the steak, pour the fat from the pan aside, now add a little hot water, and thicken with a half teaspoonful of maizena. Pour this over the steak and serve.

Stewed Steak.

Have ready some moderately sized, rather thick pieces of steak, without much fat, and some onions cut into rather thick rings. Place all in a saucepan, with cold water to cover, season with pepper, salt, and a little mushroom catchup[5], if

---

[5] Ketchup

liked, or with other sauce. Boil slowly, take off the fat, and thicken the gravy. Send to table tender and nicely seasoned.

Maizena, which is now so cheap, makes a far more palatable thickening for gravies; it is also quicker for use, as it mixes smoother and readier than flour, neither does it take so long to cook or lose its raw taste after it is added to the pot or pan.

Mutton Chops, To Fry.

A loin of mutton is often spoiled, either by chopping the meat down badly, thus leaving one loin with all the bones, and the other without its proper quantity, or by its not being jointed where it should be. It should be observed how many chops or divisions the loin naturally has; then cut it in pieces accordingly. If the butcher has not time to do it well, tell him to send you the meat entire; then cut it through the thin flank to the joint, and it is further easy to divide with a small chopper; turn the flank ends around the chops, and place them in the frying pan this way, after being seasoned with pepper. Fry rather slowly, that they may be tender and juicy. Sprinkle with salt just before they leave the pan, and serve with a nice brown gravy.

Broiled Chops.

Many persons relish chops better when they are broiled instead of being fried. For this a clear fire is necessary, and it must not be too fierce. Pepper the chops and place them on the gridiron, which often answers the purpose better on a stove when it is placed upside down. Turn the chops well, but avoid placing the fork into their lean parts. Sprinkle with salt lightly when they are nearly done, and spread a little butter over them before serving.

Grilled or Broiled Steak.

Take a thick piece, season with pepper, and cook it in the same way as the broiled chops, only serve it rather underdone.

Minced Meat.

The remains of a cold joint can be finely cut up, after removing all the skin and fat; then to it can be added two or three onions, also finely chopped. Stew gently in good gravy, add a little Worcester sauce or Yorkshire relish[6], and thicken it. Cut up a piece of toasted bread into three-cornered pieces, place them in the dish with the mince, and serve with some boiled, mashed potatoes.

Sausages.

Pork ones, especially, must be slowly and well cooked. If they are fried it is best to prick the skins with a fork in some places. This will prevent their bursting with the heat.

Beef sausages are nicer for being fried in butter, and a few onions fried make an agreeable addition to them. Send to table served in gravy. A few mashed potatoes are always a suitable addition to these small dishes.

Potato Chips.

Instead of mashed potatoes these are often served, as they are quickly prepared. Pare a few potatoes, cut them into thin slices, pepper and salt them, put them into a frying pan of hot fat, cover with a plate awhile, then remove it and stir them until they are sufficiently tender, then drain from the fat and serve.

---

[6] A liquid seasoning similar to Worcestershire sauce; well-known manufacturers included Hendersons and Goodalls.

Bubble and Squeak.

Some cold potatoes and boiled cabbage must be chopped fine, and mixed with some small slices of cold salt beef, previously cooked. Season vegetables slightly, and fry a few minutes.

Stewed Chops.

These must be prepared and cut in the same way as if for frying; they are then to be neatly placed in a saucepan, with the addition of some onions, cut in rings, not too thin. Season each chop separately with pepper and salt. A few potatoes are generally added. Cover with cold water, and boil very slowly for about an hour, thicken, and serve in a vegetable dish.

Irish Stew, or Haricot.

This can be made by using any part of uncooked meat, which must be cut up small and boiled slowly for a considerable time, with the addition of onions and any other vegetables which are procurable, also to be cut up.

Sometimes small, plain, suet or hard dumplings are added. The whole must be nicely seasoned, and if necessary slightly thickened before serving. The addition of a little sauce will often improve the flavour.

Tomato Stew.

Part of the fore-quarter of mutton, chopped and cut up small, makes this the best. Place the meat in a saucepan with a little butter, dredge with flour and seasoning, stir in some onions nicely cut up, and brown awhile; then have ready some tomatoes skinned and cut up; they are so juicy the stew may not require any water, but go on cooking until it is ready. Stir often, and skim off any fat before serving. In the absence of fresh tomatoes use tinned ones. These answer the purpose well. If all of the liquid of the tin is not required pour some away.

Rolled Steak.

Obtain 2 lb. beefsteak from the round in one piece. Take tablespoonfuls of bread crumbs, 1 teaspoonful catchup, 1 tablespoonful of butter, and 1 saltspoonful of salt, 2 tablespoonful mixed herbs, a little pepper, and 1 teaspoonful of Worcester sauce. Make a stuffing of these ingredients, spread it over the steak, roll it up, fasten each end with a skewer, and, if necessary, tie it round the centre with twine. Dredge it well with flour. Put 1 tablespoonful of butter into a frying pan, and brown the steak, after which put it into a stew pan with the remaining warm fat of the frying pan. Stir a little more flour into it, a half-pint boiling water, and a little more pepper and salt, a bay leaf or two (these are procurable at some of our chemists), and let the steak simmer until it is tender. Serve hot.

Rolled Pig's Tongue.

Into a broad slice of salt pork (the belly part is the best) lay a pickled pig's tongue. Cover the tongue with minced parsley, some sage leaves, and some finely cut onion. It can then be placed into a piece of calico, and securely tied into a roll. Boil it for four hours gently, and when quite cold remove it from the cloth, and serve in thin slices.

To Clean Tripe.

If it cannot be got already cleaned, first wash it with lukewarm water which has a little washing soda in it. After this, leave it all night in clean cold water which has a little buttermilk in it. Take it out and put it on to boil; when, as soon as it does, remove it from the water, scrape it well, cut it into convenient-sized pieces, and proceed to cook it.

Sheep's Feet, or Tripe.

These articles must be well cleaned, and stewed slowly for four or six hours in two separate waters. In the second water add some milk, some large onions, cut up into rather thick rings; some pepper and salt, with a small lump of butter. Thicken and serve in a vegetable dish. If this dish of food be required for breakfast, partly boil it the day before.

Pig's Feet.

Boil the pig's heart and liver until tender, then mince it small. When the feet are boiled sufficiently, which must be done in a separate water, put them into a stew pan with the liver, some gravy, a little thyme (that which is bottled will do, if none other), and stew them a few minutes longer. Put some very small pieces of dry toast around a dish, lay the feet inside of this, and pour the gravy, etc., into the centre of the dish.

Cow Heels.

See they are thoroughly clean, boil them some hours until tender. After they have boiled some time add some sliced onions, season, and serve with parsley and butter. This dish is wholesome and strengthening.

Meat Fried in Batter.

Have a batter ready of flour, a little salt, and baking powder, with eggs and milk mixed as thick as cream. Cut some slices of underdone mutton or beef, season, and dip them into the batter on both sides, and fry them until they are a light brown. Sometimes they are well relished for breakfast or supper.

Frikadels.

These are often prepared for breakfast, and when nicely made are very tasty. Any uncooked or cooked cold meat can be used. The usual way in preparing them is to cut up the meat small, season with pepper, salt, and a very little sauce, and add to it some cut-up onions which have previously boiled a few minutes, together with a few herbs and parsley. After adding a few bread crumbs and a well-beaten egg, the whole is well mixed and passed through a sausage machine. Then it is formed into balls, which are slightly flattened, dipped into a beaten egg and some flour, and they are ready to fry slowly in a pan of hot fat. Sometimes, if the meat be not tasty, a little ham is added, or a small quantity of St. Louis tinned corned beef answers the purpose; but if the latter be rather salt, be careful not to use much of it. Serve with a rich gravy.

Kidneys and Ham.

This makes a nice breakfast dish. Skin the kidneys, halve them longways, season a little, and fry slowly until they are well cooked, remove them, and fry a few thin slices of ham. When ready place the ham on a dish, kidneys above it, and serve with a nice gravy, seasoned with a little sauce.

Keokuk Toast.

Make a batter with 1 egg, 2 teaspoonfuls of milk, 1 tablespoonful of flour, pepper, and salt; have ready some slices of stale bread, which dip into, warm water; turn them over in the batter, and fry in hot fat until both sides are a rich brown.

Cleghorn and Harris.

Ham Toast.

Melt in a stew pan a small piece of butter till it. is browned a little. Put in as much of finely minced ham as will cover a large round of buttered toast, and add as much gravy as will make it moist. When quite hot, stir in an egg quickly with a fork. Place the mixture over the toast, which cut in pieces any shape you may fancy.

Cleghorn and Harris.

Stewed Ox Tail.

Cut the tail into pieces through the joints, set on the fire in a pot to boil slowly for three or four hours. Skim off all the fat; then add some seasoning, a little sauce, a few carrots cut into round thin slices, and an onion or two cut into rings. Thicken with a little fine sago, skim it again, and serve when the meat is nicely tender. Mashed potatoes to accompany the dish.

German Sausage.

Although usually served as it is, cut into thin slices; it is often liked, especially if rather stale, when fried for a few moments in a frying pan where a slice or two of nice bacon has been cooked. The bacon is then served with it.

Broiled Sheep's Kidneys.

Skin each kidney, cut them open enough to keep flat, sprinkle well with pepper and salt, dip them into butter melted, keep them open with a small skewer, and broil over a slow fire. Add a little Worcester sauce to a nice gravy in serving.

Scrambled Eggs on Toast.

Put a piece of butter into a frying pan, have some eggs lightly beaten, mixed with seasoning and chopped parsley. Stir this into the butter until it just sets, pour it on the toast, and serve.

Cupped Eggs.

Make 6 small rounds of toast, butter them, take 6 teacups and butter them, then sprinkle with bread crumbs, chopped parsley, and a little minced ham. Break an egg into each cup, put the cups into a saucepan till the eggs are quite pretty and white but not hard, turn them out gently on to the rounds of toast, and serve on a napkin with plenty of parsley about them.

Sylvia's Home Journal.

Mushrooms with Eggs.

Put into stew pan 1 oz. of butter, break 3 eggs into it, a little salt and pepper. To this add 2 tablepoonfuls of small mushrooms previously stewed; stir them together, and set them over the fire, continuing to stir until the whole is lightly set; have ready some small rounds of hot buttered toast, heap mushrooms and eggs on to them, and serve.

Cheese Soufflé.

Take 2 or 3 oz. of rather dry cheese finely grated, 4 pint milk, a spoonful or two of cream; put them into a dish with a very little cayenne pepper and salt, lightly beaten with the yolks of 3 eggs. The whites of the eggs are to be stirred in the last thing, after having been beaten into a stiff froth. The tin or dish in which it is to be baked must have about 2 oz. of butter melted in it. Then the soufflé must be baked in a steady oven for nearly one hour, and served.

Welsh Rabbits, or Rare-bits.

Melt in a frying pan a teaspoonful of butter, throw into it some cheese cut up fine, to which has been added a little mixed mustard, Worcester sauce, and a very little stout or beer. Have the toast hot, and spread the mixture over it.

Cabbage Bredie[7].

This is a favourite colonial dish, but it is rich, and not easily digested. Take some of the fore-quarter of mutton, cut it up small, place some butter in a saucepan, season it, and stir until the meat in it becomes a nice brown, then add the cabbage already sliced up into thin shreds. Stir and cook until tender; if a little water be necessary, add it; skim off the fat and thicken. Serve very hot.

Bean Bredie.

Prepare the meat as in the cabbage bredie, but instead of cabbage use some beans (French), cut into short pieces. Cook until ready, and serve hot.

For tomato bredie see tomato stew, which is prepared the same way.

Sasaatjes[8].

Cut all the meat off a leg of mutton into square bits; if fresh pork is handy add some pieces of it too; put the meat into a large deep dish, cut up a few small pieces of garlic, two red chillies, and strew it over the meat. After browning some sliced onions in a pan add to them a cupful of water, in which some tamarind has been well squeezed, and a little more than a tablespoonful of good curry powder has been mixed. When this mixture is cool throw it over the meat, then add a little sugar, and leave the dish with contents standing nearly a week. When the weather is cool it will keep even longer. Turn the meat carefully around each day with a spoon. When required for use string the meat on wire or wooden skewers, broil on the gridiron over an open fire, then take out all the pieces of garlic

---

[7] Bredie: an intensely-flavoured stew

[8] Usually spelt sosaties; the word comes from the same Malay root as *satay*

and chillies, and serve either with or without a gravy sauce poured over them. This is a favourite picnic dish, as the meat can be cooked out of doors, and is a nice relish.

To Make a Plain Omelet.

Ingredients: 6 eggs, 1 saltspoonful salt, ½ saltspoonful pepper, 4 lb. butter. Break the eggs into a basin, omitting the whites of three, and beat them up with the salt and pepper until extremely light; then add 2 oz. of butter, broken into small pieces, and stir this into the mixture. Put the other 2 oz. of butter into the frying pan; make it quite hot, and as soon as it begins to bubble whisk the eggs, etc., very briskly for a minute or two, and pour them into the pan; stir the omelet with a spoon one way until the mixture thickens and becomes firm. Then fold the edges over, so that the omelet assumes an oval form, and when it is nicely brown on one side and firm it is done. Hold the pan before the fire for a minute or two, and brown the upper side of the omelet with a salamander[9] or hot shovel. Serve expeditiously on a very hot dish. The flavour of this omelet may be very much enhanced by adding minced parsley, minced onions, or eschalot, or grated cheese, allowing a tablespoonful of the former and half the quantity of the latter to the above proportion of eggs. Shrimps or oysters may also be added, the latter to be scalded in their liquor, then bearded and cut into small pieces. Omelets are sometimes sent to table with gravy, which should be thickened with arrowroot or rice flour, and served in a tureen.

Mrs. Beeton's 1s. *Book of Cookery.*

Ham Omelet.

Ingredients: 6 eggs, 4 oz. of butter, 1 saltspoonful of pepper, 2 tablespoonfuls of minced ham. Mode: mince the ham

---

[9] A hot iron plate used to brown dishes

fine without any fat, and fry it for two minutes in a little butter; then make the batter for the omelet, stir in the ham, and proceed as in the recipe before. Do not add any salt to the batter. Serve out quickly without gravy. Cooked lean bacon or tongue may be used instead of ham.

Mrs. Beeton's 1s. Book of Cookery.

Kidney Omelet.

Ingredients : 6 eggs, 1 saltspoonful of salt, ½ teaspoonful of pepper, 2 sheep's kidneys, or 2 tablespoonfuls of minced veal, and 5 oz. of butter. Mode: skin the kidneys, cut them into small dice, and toss them into a frying pan in 1 oz. butter over the fire for two or three minutes. Mix the ingredients for the omelet, and when the eggs are whisked proceed as before.

Mrs. Beeton's 1s. Book of Cookery.

Oyster Omelet.

Stew 6 oysters in their own liquor, remove oysters, and thicken liquid with butter rolled in flour; season with salt, cayenne pepper, mix with it a teaspoonful of chopped parsley. Chop up oysters and add them to sauce; simmer gently until same thickens. Beat 3 eggs lightly with 1½ tablespoonfuls of cream, fry until they are delicately set; before folding over pour a few spoonfuls of mixture in centre; turn it carefully on a hot dish with balance of sauce around it. Serve immediately. If small oysters are used put them into the centre of the omelet whole, fold and serve with sauce around it.

From the Royal Baking Powder Company.

Tomato Omelet.

Skin 2 or 3 tomatoes, cut in slices, fry in butter; beat up some eggs to make omelet, season with salt and pepper; warm some butter in pan, put in eggs, stirring well to keep from adhering; mix in the tomatoes, turn out omelet on plate, doubling it in two. Another nice way is to roll up tomatoes in omelet, and serve with tomato sauce.

From the Royal Baking Powder Company.

Scotch Porridge.

Boil 3 pints water in saucepan with a teaspoonful of salt, mix very gradually into it whilst the water is fast boiling 1 lb. oatmeal, stir it constantly and continually for quarter of an hour, then pour it into soup plates, allow it to cool a little, and serve it with a cupful of milk to each person. It may be boiled with milk, but then it is rather rich for delicate stomachs. Some people like the oatmeal to simmer by the side of the fire for several hours, as they consider it far more digestible then.

Inquire Within.

Albert Sandwiches.

Take 3 eggs, a piece of butter the size of a walnut, a little grated cheese, a dash of salt and of cayenne pepper. Put all into a saucepan and stir over the fire until it thickens. Cut some round pieces of bread, fry them in butter until brown. Spread the paste over them. Have some nice ham or tongue grated to be strewn over them before serving.

Eggs Pickled in Vinegar

are a nice relish. They are boiled in their shells for ten minutes, peeled when cold, placed in a jar, and boiled vinegar spiced to taste poured over them. When discoloured they are ready for eating.

Scotch Haggis.

Boil a sheep's pluck[10], after well washing it; save the liquor. Pass through a sausage machine, or mince well, the

---

[10] Pluck: heart, liver and lights (i.e. lungs)

softest parts of the lights and the heart, and grate up best part of the liver, putting it all together into a basin. Have the bag of the stomach (already cleaned by the butcher), and after you have well washed it again put it on in cold water to boil a few minutes to contract it. Take 2 lb. of well-dried oatmeal, 2 lb. of well-chopped suet, and a medium-sized onion well chopped also, with 1 teaspoonful of salt and pepper. Mix into a stiff paste with some of the liquor the pluck was boiled in. When ready put this mixture into the stomach bag, keeping the smooth side of it inside, and after sewing up the opening boil it gently for 3 hours. It will be necessary to prick the haggis several times whilst cooking to prevent its bursting, and put a plate under it whilst boiling to prevent it sticking to the bottom of the saucepan.

Pork Brawn.

Cut a pig's head in half, rub well into it 2 good handfuls of coarse salt, and leave it all night. Next morning boil it slowly for 6 hours, and 1½ hours before it is finished put on to boil 2 pigs' tongues, a few sheep's feet, and 3 or 4 ears. At the end of this time remove from the fire, and draw out all the bones and other coarse parts. Proceed further to cut up all the meat into small pieces and season it. If you have a few slices of cold boiled tongue (ox) of a nice red colour (which can be produced by a little saltpetre being placed in the brine when pickled), put the slices around the mould in which the brawn is to be placed, and press the other meat firmly inside. Turn out the brawn the following day.

Mutton Brawn.

Wash a sheep's head after it has been cleaned, chop it up into small pieces, take 12 feet cleaned and chopped, put the whole into a large saucepan, and boil until the meat falls off the bones in as much water as will cover it; then take out the bones, and flavour with salt, pepper, and a few whole peppercorns;

give it one boil-up, and pour into basins or moulds to cool. It requires a steady fire when boiling. Ox head is done in the same way. The brawn will keep some time if kept air-tight, and it is very relishable.

MASONIC HALL,
ST. JOHN'S STREET.

BOMON'S
JUVENILE OPERA COMPY,

This (Wednesday) Evening,
Pirates of Penzance,
BY GILBERT & SULLIVAN,
WILL BE PRODUCED BY CHILDREN.

FULL ORCHESTRA.

New Scenery and Lime-light Effects·
New Costumes.

Conductor, MONS. BOMON· Manager Mr. HARRIS. Scenic Artist, Mr. LAPWORTH. Lime-light by Mr. O'CONNOR.

Doors open at 7.30 p.m. To commence at 8 o'clock. Reserved Seats, 4s.; Unreserved, 3s.; Gallery, 1s. 6d. Plan at DARTER'S, where Seats can be booked. Carriages may be booked for 10.30.

Part III. Fresh Fish, etc.

Railway communication has placed this article of food within reach of many who live remote from the coast. If it be forwarded sharp, being opened and the entrails taken out, salt having been placed inside of each fish, it may be found sweet and fresh even after a long journey if the weather be cool. When the scales of the fish are not already cleaned off, leave them to soak in clean water awhile; then they can be quickly removed with a short stout knife, holding the fish firmly by the tail the while. Take care of the sharp projecting bones, for a deep scratch or a piece broken off into the hand from one of them may bring about blood-poisoning.

Should the fish be for frying, after it is cleaned and the fins and end of the tail chopped off, it will be necessary to pass the knife across the fish, so as to divide it in parts as well as in pieces not too thick, for it must be well cooked, and not sent to table unless firm and brown. A small chopper will easily then divide the bones of the back. Now proceed to wash it well, and dry carefully in a clean towel; for if it or the fat in which it is fried be damp or contain any gravy in it, the fish will break in the frying pan. After well drying have a dish of flour handy, dip each piece well into it, then into another containing beaten egg, and lastly into another of grated bread crumbs; then after seasoning with salt and pepper, if the fat or oil in the pan be boiling hot, place in the fish, not too much at a time, and fry until it is well cooked and becomes a nice light brown. Of course the egg and bread crumbs can be omitted if necessary.

Fresh Fish, To Boil.

Instead of cutting the fish into such small pieces as for frying, the fish can often, if the pot be long enough, be boiled whole or otherwise cut into halves. Dry it well in a towel, roll in flour, and pin it up securely in a fine soft cloth. Have the pot

Fresh Fish, etc

fast boiling with a sufficient quantity of water to cover the contents when immersed. Before the fish is put in throw into the boiling water a sufficient quantity of salt, say about a dessertspoonful for 3 pints of water. Close the pot and keep it fast boiling for twenty minutes (or should it be very thick, allow a few minutes over), then dish up into a flat dish on a fish strainer, and pour over a little sauce; also serve with it more parsley and butter sauce. (See SAUCES.)

Fish Balls, No. 1.

Cold fresh fish can be worked up with mashed potatoes, herbs, bread crumbs, and a well-beaten egg into balls, and fried nicely brown. Take care to remove every fish bone before so doing. Anchovy sauce is a usual accompaniment to them, so is also the colonial hotchpotch blatyang[11] or chutney with fresh fish served in any form.

Fish Balls, No. 2.

A few sweet herbs, dried or fresh, some cold boiled potatoes, one or two eggs, a little milk, and a quarter of a pound of dripping. Flake the fish, remove all bones, mash the potatoes, and moisten with milk, adding pepper and salt to taste. White pepper should be used. Put in the fish, and the herbs, with onion finely chopped. Mix well together, beat the eggs, and combine well with the mixture; then form with the hand the balls or cakes into uniform size, melt the fat in a frying pan, and when it boils throw in the cakes, letting them remain till of a light golden brown; then drain, and serve on a napkin garnished with parsley.

---

[11] Blatjang, the Afrikaans and Malay word for chutney sauce

58

Curried Fish.

Take the pieces of cold well-fried fresh fish, and see they are perfectly sound and firm; notice how much of the best English vinegar it will take to cover the whole. A less quantity will not do. Put this vinegar into a clean saucepan with a good quantity of fine large onions, cut into rings, not too thinly. Let the onions boil in the vinegar until they are crisp, mix some curry powder sufficiently strong, adding some small quantity of maizena, but be careful to mix it with a little vinegar, not water. Boil a few minutes, stirring the while with a wooden spoon, and when the liquid is cold pour it over the fish, which must be put into an earthenware jar or wooden tub and covered over. It will then keep good for months.

The Baba[12].

In some parts of the colony this fish, almost without bones, during some seasons of the year is caught in the muddy banks of the rivers. Its flavour resembles that of an eel, being very rich. This fish is usually fried. Remove the head, cut the remainder into thin slices through the backbone, wash well, dry in a towel, sprinkle with pepper and salt, and fry, with or without egg and bread crumbs.

Soles, Fried.

We can now obtain these in various parts of the colony, but not being very plentiful we consider them a luxury. They are usually fried in oil. See that they are well cleaned, skin off their dark sides, and dry them thoroughly in a cloth. Have ready beaten egg and some grated bread crumbs, dip the fish into the former, then into the latter, season with pepper and salt, and fry until they become a light golden brown. Serve hot.

Sometimes a little lemon juice is squeezed over them.

---

[12] Baba: barbel (catfish)

59

Soles, Broiled.

Sprinkle the fish on both sides with a little pepper, salt, and lemon juice, rub it over with hot butter, sprinkle it with fine bread crumbs, and broil or bake in the oven.

Fresh Fish, Frozen.

English fresh fish is now sometimes brought to the colony preserved in ice; but as soon as it is thawed again it must be quickly cooked, or it will not be good.

Stewed Eels.

Wash them thoroughly clean in salt and water; dry carefully in a cloth. Cut them into pieces about three inches long, put them into a saucepan, which has some good meat gravy, with a little pepper, salt, and an onion; let them stew slowly from fifteen to twenty minutes; then take them out and keep them on a hot dish. Strain the gravy, add a little catchup and port wine, and thicken with a little maizena. Put the eels back in the gravy, boil them up, and serve with small pieces of dry toast.

Fried Eels.

Prepare as above, dip into egg and bread crumbs, and fry them in hot oil or fat until they are a light golden brown. Squeeze a little lemon juice over them, and serve with melted butter or parsley and butter. Garnish the dish with parsley.

Baked Fish.

A fish weighing from 4 to 6 lb. is a good size to bake. It should be cooked whole to look well. Make a dressing of bread crumbs, butter, salt, and a little salt pork or bacon cut fine (parsley and onions if desired). Mix this with one egg. Fill the body, sew it up; lay in a large dripper; put across the fish some strips of salt pork to flavour it. Put one pint of water and a little salt in pan. Bake an hour and a half. Baste frequently. After taking up fish thicken the cream gravy and pour over it.

Royal Baker and Pastrycook.

Oyster Stew.

Take the oysters with their liquor, adding a little water, if not sufficient liquor; one tablespoonful butter, pepper and salt to taste; cover the stew pan, place over fire, and then remove as soon as it boils. If milk be desired; the bottom of the soup plates should simply be covered with cold milk; then serve the stew.

NOTE. Many persons prefer oysters well done, in which case the stew should be boiled five minutes.

Tinned Oyster Stew.

Cut some onions into rings, put them over the fire in a small quantity of water to boil until tender. Pour off the water, add some pepper, salt, and a small lump of butter, with the contents of the oyster tin. Let the whole cook up, and boil a few minutes. Mix a little maizena with half teacupful milk, thicken, and after it has remained a minute or two longer it is ready to serve.

Part IV. Salt Fish Boiled and Broiled.

The smoked salt fish of the colony, and those fish imported from other countries, can be prepared for use in a variety of ways. If broiling is preferred, it is well generally to pour a small quantity of boiling water over the fish, especially the red-herring, leaving it to stand a minute or two, and then washing and drying with a clean towel before placing it on the gridiron; for often, unless freshly opened, they are generally too salt to eat otherwise. The imported dried cod, ling, smoked herrings, haddocks, and all suchlike fish are better for being well washed first. The Cape snoek[13], haddock, and other such fish, when freshly smoked, need only be wiped with a damp cloth before broiling.

In boiling such fish it is usual to throw away the first water and finish it in a second quantity. If you want to know the strength of its saltness, taste the liquor in which it is boiling. The boiled fish is eaten very hot, butter is generally spread over it at the table, or, if liked, anchovy or any other fish sauce can be substituted.

Dried Fish Pie (Sammys).

The remains of cold, salt, boiled fish are with a fork carefully removed with its skin and bone, and broken up into very fine particles; an onion chopped very small is added to it, with some cold potatoes, well mashed with plenty of butter, and some chopped parsley, with cayenne pepper to taste. The whole is then well incorporated, placed in a buttered pie dish, scored over with a fork, and baked until it is a light brown. Serve hot.

---

[13] *Thyrsites atun*—a Southern Hemisphere sea fish with coarse, tasty flesh

Salt Cod—French Mode of Cooking.

Boil a piece of salt cod in two separate waters; brown some butter, dredge in a little flour and a little sugar, and in this fry some slices of onions to a nice brown. Throw in a tablespoonful of vinegar, give a boil up, pour over the fish, and serve, garnished with parsley.

Salt Fish—Spanish Mode of Cooking.

Boil in plenty of water a piece of salt fish that has been in soak for at least twenty-four hours. When sufficiently boiled to allow of it, pick out all the flesh in small flakes and put it by. Slice very finely a couple of onions, fry them in salad oil until they begin to colour, add a little tomato sauce, a little pepper, and the salt fish. Let the whole simmer on a slow fire for a couple of hours, shaking the saucepan occasionally.

Pickled Fish.

Take a large fish of, say about 5 lb., well clean it, and remove large bones, cut it into small squares, then drain or dry it well. Have ready 1 oz. of ground allspice, ½ oz. pepper, 1½ oz. salt; mix this well together on a plate. Wash well 2 doz. bay leaves (they can be procured from the chemist), and into a clean dry jar place a layer of the fish, which must be sprinkled with the seasoning, then a layer of bay leaves, and this must be repeated until it is finished. Cover it with cold vinegar, and tie it down with a double layer of brown paper, and bake in a slow oven six or seven hours. It can be placed in the oven in the evening, but the first heat must bring it to boiling point; it can then gradually cool until morning. Mackerel is the best fish to use. Serve hot. It is a delicious preparation.

Part V. Tinned Fish.

Tinned Salmon.

This tinned fish is largely imported; but many persons spoil the appearance of it, as they do of other tinned preparations, by not opening the tin sufficiently large for it to be turned out whole. Tin-openers are procurable all over the colony at a very reasonable price, and one should always be obtained when possible, for with its help even a child can open any ordinary tin without one-half the usual labour otherwise. Always observe the directions accompanying each tin as to the best method of opening or using each article.

Turn the salmon out whole into a dish, or divide and lay it in two parts, showing the bone of the fish down the centre. It looks more real and relishable. A little white pepper should be lightly sprinkled over it, and a small quantity of good vinegar. If served in this way the change from so much meat is an agreeable relish.

Salmon Croquettes, No. 1.

Very often some of the cold salmon may remain unused; if so, it can be utilized in the following way: take a few boiled potatoes, add the salmon to it without its liquor, and a little pepper, salt, and an egg beaten up. Mash this all together, breaking the lumps, or pass the whole through a sausage machine. Roll it into the shape of thick sausages, dip into flour, and fry until a nice light brown. Serve hot.

Salmon Croquettes, No. 2.

One tin salmon, 2 raw eggs, 1 tablespoonful of butter, yolks of 2 hard-boiled eggs, 1 teaspoonful anchovy sauce, juice of 1 lemon; season with salt, pepper, a little mace and nutmeg, ½ cup crumbs. Mince the fish; work in the butter, slightly warmed, the powdered yolks, the seasoning, raw eggs, finally the crumbs. Make into rolls; shape well by rolling in a dish covered thickly with flour. Fry quickly in hot fat. Roll each when done for one instant upon a clean cloth to take off the grease. Lay squares of treble tissue paper-red, green, and white-upon a dish, fringing the ends, and serve.

Cleghorn and Harris Recipes.

Sardines, Curried.

Take a box of sardines and drain off all the oil into the frying pan. Add to this a dessertspoonful of curry powder previously mixed with cold water. Thicken the oil with a little maizena or arrowroot, first mixed with water. As soon as the curry and oil make a sauce about as thick as good melted butter the sauce is ready. Pour this over the sardines, and place them in the oven long enough for them to get heated through. When quite hot serve with slices of toast.

Salmon Pie.

A salmon pie is often a relish for breakfast or supper. Place the salmon without its liquor in the bottom of a buttered pie dish, sprinkle a little white pepper over it, the dish is then to be filled up with potatoes, which have been well mashed with butter. Score the top with a fork, glaze with an egg, and bake until it becomes a light brown.

Tinned Shrimps.

These make an agreeable change, but they must be well washed before being placed in the dish. Then send them to table with a little pepper and salt over them.

N.B. There are now such a variety of goods in tins—imported poultry, meat, puddings, fruits, vegetables, sausages, etc.—that it is well to get a list of them from your grocer; for in this country, where so little variety of food is produced, they become often very necessary to use.

Precautions in Using Canned Food.

In the use of canned food certain precautions must be observed. The food must be turned out of the can as soon as opened. Never on any account add vinegar, sauces, etc. to canned foods while they are in the tins, and if from forgetfulness it is done never allow such mixtures to remain in the cans an hour or so. Canned foods are put up as fresh as possible, and after they are opened will not keep as long as people generally think they will, with the exception of sardines, which may be kept several days. A person should use the same common sense in eating canned fruits, vegetables, and meats that is used in regard to food not canned.

Part VI. Roast Meats.

Roast Beef.

It is almost impossible to procure beef in some country places, nor can it be got in very small towns save now and again, for the meat is too much to be used whilst good, although the greater part of it may be consigned to the pickle. The sirloin is considered one of the choicest joints for roasting; it, or other roasting pieces, must first be slightly peppered and dredged with flour, as the latter makes it bake a nice brown. See that the oven is hot before the meat is put into it, or all the gravy will be drawn out of it, and the meat look white and tasteless. Have a little water in the bottom of the oven pan, and whilst the meat is cooking continue every few minutes to baste it well with some good dripping, turning the meat over from time to time with a fork, taking care to stick it into the end of the skin. Native servants will very seldom baste or turn the meat over; they do not like the trouble, so see that they do it. Sprinkle with salt about half an hour before the meat is ready. Beef is not usually cooked so much as mutton. Horseradish sauce is frequently served with it when procurable. A batter or Yorkshire pudding is also sometimes served, and many people like the potatoes baked (without skins) in the gravy and fat of the oven tin. If so, choose small ones, sprinkle them with salt, and keep them well basted and turned over whilst they are baking. Do not turn the fat of your oven tin over the meat, but pour this off, and in its place supply a rich brown gravy instead.

Leg and Shoulder of Mutton.

These are joints which are more used by small families than any other parts of meat. Prepare (after chopping through the knuckle and leg bone) in the same way for roasting as the last joint. Sometimes the leg of mutton is stuffed or forced with mince or sausage meat, and seasoned with herbs.

Lamb is roasted as other mutton, only the joints are different. The meat is divided into fore and hind quarters. It does not take so long to roast, and is served with mint sauce generally.

If the lamb is to be roasted, boil some cloves and cinnamon in water, and baste the lamb with it.

The saddle of mutton is the end of the back each side of the bone, but the backbone is not divided in the usual way of the carcase.

Roast Loin of Mutton.

Be careful that every joint of the backbone is well chopped through, so that it can readily be served in proper chops, for no joint is more annoying to carve at table than this one if not well prepared. A saw will nicely separate the joints. If a stuffing be liked, prepare it with bread crumbs, parsley, and other herbs, fine onion, salt, pepper, and mixed with a beaten egg; this is then rolled inside the loin, secured with skewers or fine twine, which can be removed before sending to table. Dredge the meat lightly with flour, season, and bake to a nice brown, well basting it while cooking. Roast or baked potatoes usually accompany this joint.

Roast Pig, No. 1.

Take a young pig. After thoroughly cleaning inside, rinse it out with table soda and water, then again with cold water, wiping it inside and out. Prepare the following dressing: 1 cupful crumbs, ½ onion (chopped), 2 teaspoonfuls of powdered sage, 3 tablespoonfuls melted butter, 1 saltspoonful salt, some pepper, ½ nutmeg (grated), and yolks of 2 eggs well beaten; moisten with ½ cup soup stock, stuff pig into its original size and shape, sew up, place in kneeling posture in dripping pan, tying the legs in proper position; dredge with flour, pour a little hot salted water in dripping pan, baste with butter and water three times as the pig warms, afterwards with gravy from dripping pan. When it begins to smoke all over rub every twenty minutes with rag dipped in melted butter. This will keep skin from cracking. Roast in moderate steady oven two hours. Place the pig upon a hot dish, surround with parsley and blanched celery tops, place a green wreath around neck and a sprig of celery in its mouth; skim and strain gravy, thicken with browned flour, boil up, add a glass of any good wine and juice of a lemon. Serve in a boat. In carving, cut off head first, split down the back, take off hams and shoulders, and separate the ribs.

From the Royal Baker and Pastrycook.

Roast Pig, No. 2—An Easier Method.

Clean pig and score it well all over with a sharp knife, as it is then much easier to carve. Pork sausage meat can be used for stuffing, bought from the butcher. Many prefer the stuffing without sage, and only have in addition a few onions finely chopped, and a little sauce may be added. Rub the pig well over with butter, and dredge well with flour; salt, and baste it well whilst baking, and see that it all becomes thoroughly well done and nicely browned. Bake three hours or longer. Place a potato in the mouth when preparing the pig. Pork must be served very hot and with a rich brown gravy.

Roast Leg of Pork.

Well sprinkle with pepper and salt, and score it well either before placing it in the oven or when it is half done. If liked, stuff with sage and onions. Serve with apple sauce.

Fat for Kitchen Use.

Get some suet, melt it down, skim carefully, and mix it with the fat of a large Cape sheep's tail[14] till it is sufficiently soft for kitchen use. A little lard may also be added. Be careful when mixing any other fat with it to see it contains no gravy, otherwise when carefully covered over it will keep good and ready for use a long time. If other fat to be added has gravy in it, or if it be discoloured, pour boiling water on it or melt it in the oven, skim, and when cool take off the top fat, and when it is re-melted and passed through a strainer you can add it to the other fat. A good cook is never without plenty of clean dry fat at hand in case of emergency.

---

[14] Sheep's tail fat was traditionally used in the Cape as a cooking fat

Part VII. Poultry and Game.

Wild Buck[15], To Roast.

This meat is better for being hung up, as long as desirable, as is also most meat, when the weather permits. It is well to rub a joint all over with pepper and flour, and then slip it into a bag of muslin before hanging up in a cool place. Under the branches of a shady tree is the best spot. When required for use soak it awhile in vinegar water, then take a sharp-pointed firm knife, and stick it deep into the fleshy part; into these incisions force small pieces of bacon, or, if not procurable, pieces of pork will answer well. Have plenty of fat in the baking tin where you place the meat, which must be nicely sprinkled over with pepper and a little salt. Baste well. Serve with a rich gravy, and place on the table black currant jelly or jam, a great improvement to its flavour.

Wild Buck, Stewed.

Cut the meat rather small, and add to it some fingers of bacon. Chop finely one or two small onions, and into a piece of muslin tie a few herbs (dried ones will do) with some cloves and allspice. Cover the whole in the pot with water, and let it boil for one and a half hours slowly. Remove the muslin, skim, thicken, and serve.

Roast Fowl.

Pluck the fowl[16], but if you require the feathers for pillows, cushions, etc., have all the small clean ones put aside at once for that purpose. It is a common habit to save time to dip

---

[15] Antelope

[16] This recipe can be made with any roasting chicken

the bird into hot water, as the feathers can be more readily removed, but this tends to make the fowl tough.

Singe the fowl before opening it whilst it is dry, then proceed to make a slit straight across the bottom of the breast bone underneath. Be careful to draw out the whole of the inside, with gizzard and liver complete. Care must be taken that the gall does not break in the liver, or it will be spoilt. Chop off the neck, sever the legs half-way down at the joints with a knife; take the gizzard, after removing the inside of it when it is opened, proceed to get the crop. By easing the skin around the neck, it can be gently and entirely drawn. If the giblets are boiled they add to the richness of the gravy, otherwise they can be fastened to the fowl with a skewer and roasted. Make a stuffing of the following: some bread crumbs, finely chopped onion, sweet herbs, small lumps of butter or bacon fat, a little minced bacon, with a little pepper and salt. Stuff the fowl with it, then push the leg ends under the breast bone through the two openings; turn the wings alike round over the top of the back, dredge the fowl well with flour, sprinkle with pepper and salt, and bake it until both sides are nicely browned, care being taken to keep it well basted. Serve with gravy.

Guinea fowls, pheasants, and many other of our small game can be prepared and roasted in almost the same way. Serve with good ham or bacon.

Boiled Fowl.

Prepare it in the same way as for roasting, but boil it if possible with a sweet piece of salt pork or bacon, or it could be cooked in the liquor in which a good ham has been boiled, if it be not too salt or discoloured. Skim the top off well, and boil slowly for about one hour and a quarter, or until the meat feels tender. Fowls having light feathers are best for boiling, as the flesh is whiter, whilst dark-feathered ones are richer for roasting. Send to table with the pork or ham and parsley and melted butter.

Roast Duck, No. 1.

Prepare in the same way as a fowl. Fasten a small skewer through the body, securing the legs firmly on each side. Sew, with a needle and cotton, the opening, to prevent the stuffing from slipping out. A ham, or piece of boiled bacon or pork, is generally served with it.

Roast Duck and Goose, No. 2.

Hang it till tender, stuff with bread crumbs, sage if liked, thyme, onion cut up fine, and mix with the yolk of an egg. To truss: cut the neck off, beat the breast bone rather flat with a rolling pin, draw the wings down by its side, and secure them with a skewer through the body. Place another skewer through the bottom of the legs, and sew up the body after it is stuffed. The skewers will remain firm in their places if a piece of string is tied to each end of them. They can be removed before sending to table. The liver, divested of the gall, and the gizzard, are to be tucked inside the wing. The bird must be well dredged with flour, and basted often. It is served with a nice brown gravy.

Roast Turkey.

Prepare and stuff the inside as any other fowl, only the breast requires to be stuffed too. It is usual to give a smart blow with the rolling pin and force down the breast bone where it is so pointed. Have the stuffing well mixed with butter and flavoured with sauce. Bake the turkey slowly, turning it over now and again during the process. Baste it well with fat to keep it tender and moist. Serve with a ham and rich brown gravy.

Boiled Turkey.

This has to be cooked the same way as a fowl, only longer time must be allowed for its cooking—two hours at least; but the necessary time could be determined, as it would be done if the flesh would give way on sticking a fork into it. Serve with parsley and butter sauce and a ham.

If a fowl be old, the toughness of its flesh may be remedied by giving the bird a teaspoonful of vinegar a few hours before killing it.

Roast Goose, No. 3.

Hang it till tender, when ready boil a couple of onions with a few sage leaves (or if they disagree substitute other herbs), chop them fine, and mix with a cupful of stale bread crumbs and a piece of apple cut up fine; mix this with a lump of butter, a little pepper and salt, also the yolk of an egg; stuff the goose with it, tying the end; dredge it with flour, bake, keeping it well basted with butter. Serve with apple sauce and gravy.

Roast Turkey and Sausages.

After having trussed, drawn the sinews, and cleaned the turkey, fill the breast with forcemeat, and if a trussing needle be used sew the neck over to the back. Run a skewer through the pinion and thigh, through the body to the pinion and thigh on the other side, and then fasten a sheet of buttered paper on to the breast of the bird, put it down to a bright fire at a little distance at first, afterwards draw it nearer. (These remarks apply to meat roasted with a spit or bottlejack[17]; being placed in an oven answers the same purpose.) Keep it well basted all the while it is cooking. About quarter of an hour before serving remove the paper, dredge the turkey lightly with flour, and baste the bird with some butter melted. When of a nice brown and well frothed, serve with a tureen of good gravy and one of bread sauce. Fried sausages are placed around the dish. About quarter of an hour to the pound is the time needed for roasting or baking.

---

[17] A wind-up mechanical spit that gradually unwound, cooking the meat evenly

Roast Pigeons, or Turtle Doves.

Wash and clean the birds well, put a lump of butter inside, and season well with pepper and salt. Baste them well whilst roasting, and serve with parsley and butter or bread sauce and gravy. The feet only should be cut off.

Stewed Pigeons.

Stuff the pigeons with the following: Bread crumbs soaked in milk, the yolk of an egg, pepper, salt, chopped parsley, shallot, and mushroom. Put the pigeons in a stew pan with a lump of butter or dripping and a slice of bacon; fry them in it a few minutes, then add some gravy and serve.

Mrs. Winslow's Family Almanac

To Skin a Hare or Rabbit.

Chop off the legs to the first joint; then start to skin it from each side of the belly. When the skin is well loosened around the back, gradually draw each of the back legs inside from the skin. Ease the part with a knife around the end of the body, and draw the tail bone gently from the skin; this can be drawn out quite entire if carefully handled. Having the hind part now free, draw out each shoulder, and lastly the head, easing the parts around the eyes with a knife, and lastly separate the skin from the hare by cutting the end off.

Hare Pie.

See MEAT PUDDINGS, PIES, ETC.

Jugged Hare.

Into the bottom of a stone jar which has a nice-fitting lid lay some slices of salt pork or bacon, and over it spread a layer of nicely cut-up hare, in not too large pieces; over this sprinkle some fine parsley, sliced onion, three or four cloves, a few drops of catchup, a slice of peeled lemon, and a very little cayenne pepper. Cover this with another layer of cut up hare and a few more slices of salt pork. Pour a large cupful of good gravy over it, cover the jar closely, and stand it in a deep pot of cold water over the fire. It must boil for nearly four hours, at the end of which time the gravy can be poured out, the fat skimmed off, and it can be thickened with a little maizena (mixed with cold water) if necessary. The gravy is then to be re-boiled a few minutes, and poured over the hare, which in the meantime has been kept hot. It is ready then to serve.

Jugged Pigeons.

Cut up four or five pigeons after they are well cleaned and washed; place them in a jar, dividing the meat with a layer of slices of hard-boiled egg, some finely chopped suet, and a similar quantity of bread crumbs, a little pepper, salt, and parsley, with a little grated nutmeg, two or three cloves, and a dessertspoonful of butter. Pour over the whole a small quantity of good gravy, close the jar, stand it in a deep saucepan of water, and boil it for three hours. A squeeze of lemon added to the gravy before serving improves the flavour.

MOWBRAY
DISPENSARY.
HENRY GODFREY,
A.P.S.,

DISPENSING CHEMIST.

Prescriptions Dispensed at all Hours.

Sea Point Hotel.

SPECIAL Arrangements for Boarders.—Good Rooms with fine Views.—Capital *Cuisine* and Home Comforts.

This very charming Hotel has recently changed hands The present Proprietors have decided to carry it on on the best principles and at the lowest charges.

Best Liquors and Wines —Billiards.

J. BOYD,
Practical Boot and Shoe Maker.

All kinds of Ladies' and Gents.' Boots and Shoes made to order in best styles.

A large and Select Stock of best English-made Ladies' and Gents.' Boots and Shoes just to hand.

39, PLEIN STREET, CAPE TOWN.

H. WATKINS,
(*16 Years Master Tailor to the Royal Engineers*)

Tailor and Habit Maker.
Military and Naval Uniforms.
First-class Work on the Modern Cash System.

16, *Adderley Street.*

IMPERIAL HOTEL, Long Street, opposite Green and Sea Point Tram Station. H. S. PARKER & SAM GOODMAN, Proprietors. First-class Accommodation; Good Table and Efficient Staff of Servants; Special Arrangements by the week or month; Private Sitting Rooms for Ladies and Families. —Billiard Table by THURSTON.—Popular Concert every Evening.   Admission Free.

O.I.C. not made his Pile yet.
Tiddy Fol Lol

MRS. JUDSON, 62, Long-street, Cape Town
Ostrich Feathers Cleaned and Dyed in all the Fashionable Colours.
Kid Gloves Cleaned.

CAFE ROYAL, next door to General Post Office.—Tiffins at the Bar; Luncheon at all hours; Private Room for Ladies; Billiard Tables; Grill Room and Restaurant.

JOHN DUNN, Proprietor,
No. 9, Church Street, Cape Town.

OR PICTURE FRAMES in all the Latest Designs go to RAPHAEL'S Picture Frame Manufactory, 3, Grave Street.
All kinds of Novels and other Books Bought and Sold.
The Latest Novels lent to read at 3d. per Book.
Novelty Book Store, 3, Grave Street.

Part VIII. Boiled Meats.

MEMO: If the soup is to be rejected, the meat should be plunged into the water when boiling; but if otherwise, the meat should be put into cold water and gently boiled.

Mutton, Boiled.

Have sufficient water, seasoned with pepper and salt, boiling ready in the pot, place in the meat, then as soon as it boils up put the pot rather aside that it may cook slowly until the meat is ready for the table. Turnips, onions, or carrots boiled in the same water give the meat an agreeable flavour, and when there are children suet dumplings cooked in the same liquor are generally liked. In boiling meat of any sort observe its weight, and allow quarter of an hour after boiling for each 1 lb. of meat, but care must be taken that it is actually boiling slowly the whole time it is on the fire. To give a delicious flavour to lamb which is to be eaten cold, put in the water in which it is boiled whole cloves and long sticks of cinnamon. To one leg of lamb allow one small handful of cloves, and two or three sticks of cinnamon.

Corned Beef, Ham, Salt Mutton, or Salt Pork:

It is a good plan if possible to find out how salt these joints actually are, as they very often require soaking in fresh water for some time previous to cooking. When the meat is not sufficiently salt, a quantity can be added to the water of the pot in which it is boiled, but no salt otherwise. The meat is better placed in cold water, for should it be too salt the gradual heat will draw it out. It may be necessary, on tasting the liquor, to change the water in which it boils once or more. Boil carrots with the beef, or turnips; it is well to put them first into a net, then they can be easily taken out when wanted.

Pease pudding often accompanies corned beef. Salt mutton or pork are boiled in the same way as the beef.

A ham is boiled at the rate of 4 lb. to the hour, when sufficiently cooked take the rind off, holding the knuckle firmly with a cloth or fork, sprinkle some bread raspings or grate the crust of a loaf over it, embellish it with cloves, and cut a frilling of paper, which needs fastening around the knuckle before sending to table. Cloves, thyme, and bay leaves boiled in the water a ham is cooked in improve its flavour. Some persons, when it is cooked enough, let it remain in its own liquor until it is cold; it preserves its flavour more then.

Spiced Ham.

Put a ham of medium size on the stove in cold water sufficient to cover it; when it begins to boil allow it to do so for half an hour, then remove from the fire; lay the ham in a pan while you turn off this first water, and replace it by hot (boiling if possible) water, into which water you stir one tablespoonful each of ground cloves and mace, one teaspoonful each of ground allspice and pepper. In this spiced water lay the ham, cover closely, and cook until the bones are loose. Then remove from the kettle, take off the skin, ornament with whole cloves, and place in the oven for a few moments to give a pretty brown and crispness to the fat side. If you fear the meat will be discoloured wrap the ham in a cloth before placing in the last water.

Brine, To Make.

Ascertain first the quantity of meat to be immersed. Get a tub or earthenware pan ready, put in enough good water to cover the whole of the meat, turn in a quantity of coarse salt, and a sound uncooked potato. The potato will rise to the top when the dissolved salt makes the liquor sufficiently strong; then to retain the fleshy colour of the meat put in a small quantity of saltpetre and a teaspoonful of coarse brown sugar.

Pork, beef, and mutton are better for being well rubbed with salt before being placed in the pickle, and if the joint be thick make holes in the meat and rub the salt well into them. On farms the whole of the mutton not consumed from the slaughtering is thus immersed; or if it be the breast or thin part left, it is sufficient to rub the same well with salt for some days. Take care the meat to be salted is kept well under the brine.

Sauer Braten (German).

Five or six pounds of rolled ribs of beef, aitch bone, fillet, or silverside, not too lean; put it in the best mild vinegar, and let it remain for three days in summer, or more than double that time in winter. Cold vinegar will do, but when boiled with the spices and poured hot over the meat it renders it much milder and more agreeable to the taste, and will be ready for use in half the time. In hot weather the meat should be kept in a very cool place, and be entirely covered with vinegar, but in winter it need be only half covered and turned daily. To every five or six pounds of beef allow four onions, three bay leaves, and six or eight cloves. When ready for cooking lard the joint, rolling the pieces of bacon first in a mixture of pepper, salt, and ground allspice, and sprinkle the whole with a little salt, remembering that sauer braten should never be very salt. Put some finely chopped kidney suet and a piece of butter into a stew pan, and keep over a clear fire until the fat is of a pale golden colour and is quite boiling; then put the meat into it (with the lid off), and turn frequently until it is a light brown. Sprinkle a tablespoonful of flour into the fat, leave until brown, and then pour quickly into the pan sufficient boiling water to half cover the meat, and cover closely that the steam may not evaporate. When it comes to the boiling point put in two small carrots, two small onions, a slice of toast, and the spiced vinegar, and let it simmer gently but uninterruptedly for two hours and a half, adding a little boiling water, if necessary, to replace the loss by evaporation. A cup of sweet cream, or some condensed milk, improves the gravy very much. Now take the meat out of the liquor, and put it into the oven on a hot dish, while the sauce is being prepared. If the gravy be too thick it must be thinned with boiling water or milk, then strained, and part poured over the braten, and the remainder put into a large sauce boat.

Sylvia's Home Journal.

Pease Pudding.

Wash and dry say 1 lb. of split peas, thoroughly tie them up into a cloth, boil them two or three hours till they are tender, turn them out, beat them up well in a dish with a little salt and a little butter, make it smooth, tie it up again in the cloth, and put back into the boiling water for a half-hour more.

Part IX. Vegetables, etc.

These are an important item on a dinner table, but too often are so badly cooked that they become indigestible and unwholesome instead of being otherwise.

To Boil Cabbage.

The best cabbages to boil are those which have a nice green, not yellow colour, as they are better when cooked. Cut the cabbage into four parts if it is large, and remove the thick part of the stumps from it. Wash it well, and let it remain in some cold water awhile, then remove it, place it into a colander to drain, otherwise it will become tough if it takes too long to boil up. It must be plunged into plenty of boiling water, which should first have a small lump of carbonate of soda the size of a pea thrown into it, or less soda should the cabbage be very young. Take care to push the whole of the cabbage well under the water. Close the lid until it boils, then remove it, and let the water continue to boil fast until the vegetable is tender. Remove at once, strain through the colander, and sprinkle with salt, turning it over the while so that both sides have a share. Cut it through once or twice, when it is well drained, and serve. The cabbage must not be sodden; it should be tender, yet firm, and of a bright green colour. Twenty minutes' boiling is generally sufficient.

To Boil Cauliflower.

Wash it well, let the leaves remain around the flower, unless very discoloured; let it stand in salt water, drain it, boil till tender, say for twenty minutes in water, with a tiny piece of soda in it; remove from saucepan, strain, and sprinkle nicely with salt. Serve with or without melted butter.

To Boil Green Peas.

Shell, and let them remain a short time in salted water, then plunge them into boiling water, containing a grain of carbonate of soda, and a sprig of clean mint. Remove the peas when tender, sprinkle with a little salt and white pepper, add a small lump of butter, stir it into them gently, and serve very hot.

To Boil French Beans.

Be careful in buying them to see they are young and tender. This can easily be done by breaking one open. If they are tough, and the beans large and hard inside, they are useless. The usual mode is to slice them (after removing the tips from each end) with a sharp knife into very thin slips lengthways, keeping each strip as long as possible; they are then left awhile in salt water; then plunged into boiling water for about twenty minutes, removed, drained, sprinkled with salt, and served nicely.

To Boil Vegetable Marrow and Squashes.

These are pared and cored, then cut into convenient-sized pieces, laid awhile in salt water, then thrown into fast-boiling water, which has some salt in it, but not too much. When tender they are removed, well drained, and usually served with melted butter.

To Boil Carrots.

If young scrape them, if old ones pare them thinly and evenly, but if too large to boil whole split them lengthways into two or more pieces, and boil in slightly salted water. They are liked when boiled with salt beef—of course then no other salt is necessary; and if the water be too salt in which the meat is boiling, replace it with a fresh quantity before putting the carrots into it. A twine net is handy for all such vegetables, as they are more readily removed from the pot. For stews of all sorts the carrots should be cut into round thin pieces.

To Boil Parsnips.

Proceed as with carrots, but they are more generally liked if boiled with salt pork instead of beef.

Pare them, boil with meat, or in salted water alone. If served whole melted butter often accompanies them, or if mashed add white pepper and butter to taste.

To Boil Turnip Tops and Spinach.

Turnip tops when young are a wholesome vegetable. Strip the leaves off the stalks, wash them thoroughly, or they will be gritty.

Warm water is the best for the purpose, then lay them in salt water awhile, after which plunge them into boiling water containing a very little soda, stir them under it, and they generally shrink to a very small quantity, therefore always have plenty of them at hand. In about a quarter of an hour they will be sufficiently cooked, then drain them well, press all the water out, sprinkle with a little salt whilst turning them over, add a little pepper and butter, cut through it several times with a knife, and serve very hot. Vinegar is generally taken at the table with them. Spinach is cooked in exactly the same way.

Broad Beans, To Boil.

These are to be seen in various parts of the colony, and are very tasty when well prepared. The beans should be young when gathered, and shelled as peas.

The best way to boil them is in water in which a piece of sweet bacon has boiled, and is nearly ready. They can then be placed in a net and thrown into the boiling water. If young they will soon be ready, remove them then, sprinkle with pepper, serve with the bacon (a fowl may also be boiled the same time in the pot). Mashed potatoes are usually sent to table with broad beans.

Pumpkins, To Boil.

There are several sorts of pumpkins[18], but the deeper the yellow of the colour inside the more they are preferred. On many farms, although many farmers have much land near water at their disposal, pumpkins for many months of the year are the only vegetables to be seen, as the growing of them requires but little attention. It is a common sight in some parts to see the whole of the farmhouse roofs covered with pumpkins; they seem to ripen and keep better when exposed to the air. They are a very wholesome, fattening vegetable, and usually liked in the country.

They are pared and cored, cut into very small pieces, and boiled in salted water until tender; then well strained, mashed, a little pepper, and sometimes butter, is added, and thus served.

Some pumpkins are baked with the meat after being cut into larger slices; they are often very nice, especially if they are well basted with the fat and gravy, and lightly sprinkled with pepper and salt. Mashed pumpkins can be reserved for making fritters, but before the seasoning is added.

Potatoes, To Boil.

Lay them in water and pare them thinly, letting the potato keep its original shape as much as possible; remove the eyes with a short firm knife, then let the potatoes remain in clean water until they are to be placed on the fire. Put them into cold water with about a teaspoonful of salt to one and a half pints of water; directly they are tender, which you can ascertain when piercing them with a fork, throw off all the water at once, fold a small clean cloth over them under the lid to absorb the steam, and let the pot stand by the side of the fire until serving. If they are to be mashed, for want of a better masher the end of

---

[18] Varieties available in British supermarkets are largely confined to butternut, pumpkin and gemsquash

the rolling pin will do, taking care to turn the potatoes well over, so that the lumps are well crushed, then add a dessertspoonful of milk, a little pepper and butter, stir up well, and cover until ready to serve.

Potatoes, To Bake.

The skins of these are not removed, but they are well washed and dried, then baked or roasted in hot ashes, until by squeezing them you can tell they are quite tender. Serve them hot with good butter and seasoning.

Onions, To Boil.

Many persons consider these a favourite dish. Select large ones, pare them, but do not cut them up; boil them in water slightly salted until they are tender. Have ready a vegetable dish of good melted butter, sprinkle the onions with pepper, and serve in the sauce,

Radishes, To Boil.

Young radishes should be pared and boiled as turnips are, then mashed. Having added a little butter and pepper, they then become an extremely palatable vegetable. Serve with melted butter.

Cucumbers, To Stew,

Pare about three or four cucumbers, cut them lengthways, and take out the seeds; put layers of cucumbers and bread crumbs, with pepper, salt, and a little grated nutmeg, breaking small bits of butter, or placing a little fresh minced meat between. Simmer the cucumber until it is quite tender, say for about an hour, and serve with or without melted butter.

Green Mealies, To Boil.

Strip them of their husks, and boil till tender in salted water. Serve hot with butter.

Green Mealies, To Roast.

Strip the cob of its husks, and put it in the hot ashes of the fire, until it is nicely done without being burnt. Colonial children like them especially cooked thus. In eating the mealie, hold it firmly with a fork at the thick end, and bite off the mealie grains after spreading butter over the cob.

Sweet Potatoes.

These can be boiled and served as other potatoes, or they can be sent to table with melted butter poured over them. Another way is to cut them when large, after paring into convenient-sized pieces, and bake them with the meat, basting them well with the fat and gravy. Sometimes they are served in small pieces instead of pudding, with a sweet sauce well flavoured with ground cinnamon poured over them. (See SWEET POTATO PIES.)

Natal Beans[19], Dried.

A great many of these dried vegetables are used in different parts where others cannot be obtained, and they are more or less cooked in the same way. Pick the beans over well, place them on the fire early to boil in two waters. When they are tender, into the second water add a little salt, pepper, butter, sugar, vinegar, and a little maizena for thickening; let it all boil up gently a few minutes, and serve.

Dried Green Peas.

The peas are better for soaking in water overnight; they are then boiled with a small lump of carbonated soda in the water. Remove the first water after a while, and place them in a second quantity, with a little more soda, and a small lump of butter, and sprig of mint. When tender remove, drain them

---

[19] Dried haricot beans—often known as 'sugar beans' in South Africa

well, sprinkle with salt and pepper, then serve. If well prepared they are often mistaken for fresh peas.

Beetroot, To Boil.

Wash well, but do not break off the skin; cut the tops off the leaves, but not too near the beet; plunge them without paring into boiling water containing a little salt. If small boil for half an hour, if larger more. Drain in a colander, and pare when cold.

Tomatoes, Fried.

Cut tomatoes in slices without skinning; pepper and salt them, then sprinkle a little flour over them, and fry in butter until brown. Put them on a hot platter, and pour milk or cream into the butter and juice. When boiling hot pour it over the tomatoes.

From the Royal Baker and Pastrycook.

Sweet Potato Pies.

Take large sweet potatoes, and steam till they are soft, slice thin; pastry is made in the usual way. Lay potatoes in a deep pie pan, sprinkle some flour over them, add 2 teaspoonfuls of vinegar, 1 teaspoonful butter, ½ teacup water, sugar, and nutmeg or allspice, to suit taste. Sweet potato pies should be eaten warm.

From the Royal Baker and Pastrycook.

Fried Potatoes and Onions.

Slice a large onion in thin rounds, and fry gently in a saucepan with butter till it begins to brown; have ready some sliced boiled potatoes, add them to the saucepan, then flavour with salt and pepper to taste, stir all gently together till it becomes a nice brown. Good dry beef dripping can be used instead of butter.

Part X. Meat Puddings, Pies, etc.

MEMO: Pudding cloths will not stick to the pudding if, before being used, they are dipped into warm water.

Before proceeding with instructions and recipes for making puddings, cakes, etc., I would strongly recommend the use of the Royal baking powder. Whenever the ingredients cream of tartar and carbonate of soda have been combined in use before, the Royal baking powder, I find from experience, answers the same purpose better, and is more wholesome; thus when the quantity used has been at the rate of 2 teaspoonfuls cream of tartar, and 1 of carbonate of soda, use 2 teaspoons of Royal baking powder instead, and the result will be highly satisfactory.

Suet Crust.

For about 3 cupfuls of flour take 1 cup of finely chopped suet, ½ teaspoonful salt, and ½ teaspoonful Royal baking powder. Mix the whole rather stiffly with lukewarm water, and roll out on a well-floured board. Sometimes a little soft beef dripping is used instead of suet, and answers well, being considered by many more digestible. In making the crust for fruit or sweet puddings add about 1 teaspoonful of sugar.

Suet Dumplings.

Take some of the suet crust, roll into small balls, and boil for about an hour.

Batter Pudding.

Take about 1½ cupfuls flour, 3 or 4 eggs well beaten up, a pinch of salt, about ½ pint milk (condensed will do, if there be none other at hand), and ½ teaspoonful Royal baking powder. Beat well up together, add a lump or two of butter, and bake under the meat (which should be raised on a wire stand) until the pudding becomes a nice light brown. Cut it then with a knife into three-cornered pieces, place them round the joint, which must be on a well-warmed dish. Do not open the oven door often whilst it is baking.

Toad-in-the-hole Batter.

Fresh steak, chops, cold fried chops, or other underdone meat can be baked in batter made as last directed, but the dish or tin must be well greased, and rather more butter used. Bake a nice brown, and send some gravy to table with it in a gravy boat.

Sea Pie, No. 1.

This is a good change from roast and boiled joints, or when dinner is likely to be kept waiting long, for the longer the time it is kept slowly boiling the better it is. Cut the mutton into rather small pieces, put some in a deep iron pot, sprinkle with pepper and salt. Have ready vegetables of as many sorts as you possess, cut up in slices with some onions, put in a layer of these with a little more seasoning; then another layer of meat, and so on until the pot is three-parts full. By the time it boils have ready some plain suet crust rolled out, to about the size of the top of the pot, half-inch thick; cut it into four pieces, and close over the inside of the top of the pot as a lid; boil very slowly for a few hours and serve.

Sea Pie, No. 2.

Take some fresh meat, cut it in slices, season, and put it into a saucepan; peel some onions and turnips, cut them into slices, and put into the meat, with sufficient water for them to stew; then place a steamer or small plate on the top. Peel some potatoes, and place them on the plate, covering them over with paste made of flour, dripping, and a little water, the steam from the meat will cook these. Boil for over two hours, turn out the whole, and eat very hot.

Beefsteak Pudding.

This requires long boiling, so it must be prepared early. One containing about 2 lb. of meat should boil over three hours.

Cut the meat into moderate-sized pieces, about the size of the palm of the hand, pepper and salt each piece separately, have the dry pudding basin well greased with fat, having no moisture in it, or the pudding will break on being turned out; roll out the suet crust about quarter inch thick, line the basin entirely inside with it, allowing the crust to fall over the edges a little way. Place in the meat, an ox kidney may be added cut up small, and if an onion be liked, slice one very finely, and mix with it; pour some water over the meat, but not enough to run over. Then place on the top crust, which should be wider than the basin; trim the two edges off neatly together, bind the remainder firmly together—taking care to prevent a leakage of the water inside. Wet the cloth well, and tie it firmly over the pudding, tie the corners of the cloth well together, put it into the boiling water, and cook as long as required. The water often steams away, in which case it must be replenished with other boiling water in a sufficient quantity to keep the pudding covered.

Pastry Crust.

To about 4 cupfuls of flour add about 1½ cupfuls of butter, which must be rubbed in, and 1 teaspoonful of Royal baking powder. When butter is scarce the quantity can be reduced to half, if some soft dripping or sheep's tail fat is used equally with it. Mix the paste with lukewarm water, not too stiff, after adding 1 saltspoonful[20] of salt. Roll out on a floured pastry board or a marble slab, two or three times, each time spreading more butter, dripping, or lard, and sprinkling with flour before rolling it up again, taking care to roll it each time

---

[20] About half a teaspoon

the same way. Bake in a brisk oven, with paper, greased, spread over the top to prevent its being scorched.

Tart Crust.

Beat an egg till quite thin, have ready 10 oz. of butter melted. The butter must not be too old. When cold, mix the egg with it and stir it into 1 lb. flour, which should be well dried.

French Puff Pastry.

One lb. flour, 1 lb. fresh butter, yolks of 2 eggs, a pinch of salt. Break 2 oz. of the butter into 1 lb. of flour, then beat the yolks of 2 eggs with a little water, and add them gradually to the flour, forming the whole into a smooth paste. Press the moisture from the remainder of the butter, and having rolled out the paste, put a third of the butter on in patches; fold over, dredge lightly, and roll out very thin, taking care that the butter does not break through the paste. Repeat this three times, and then put it in a cold place for three or four minutes. Roll it out again very thin and lightly, then set aside for a few minutes; fold over and roll out again, when it will be fit for use.

Swinborne's Pastrycook and Confectioner.

Beefsteak and Kidney Pie.

Stew the kidney, which must be cut up into small pieces, awhile by itself before adding the steak, cut into a few pieces, or roll it, add some sliced onion, and the seasoning. Skim off the fat when it is sufficiently done, and thicken (if not already so with a little fine sago when the steak was added) with a little maizena. Add a little sauce if cared for. Cover the edges of the pie dish with a crust rolled about a quarter inch thick after greasing the dish, and place the meat with the gravy in it, comfortably filling the dish. Roll out the crust for the top larger than required, and after laying it on cut the edges off level with the outside edge of the dish. A meat pie can be ornamented with leaves of pastry, or in other ways, and glazed over with an egg beaten up. Bake rather briskly, having a sheet of greased paper spread over the top.

Mutton Pie.

Cut the meat into small pieces, stew it for about half an hour with some onion and seasoning, after which proceed with the foregoing directions.

Hare Pie.

Cut the hare into joints regularly, and in pieces not too large. Stew in a saucepan with small pieces of ham, bacon, or pork, a few herbs and whole allspice tied in muslin, which can afterwards be removed. When the meat is tender, skim it, add a little sauce, thicken the gravy with a little maizena, cover with crust, and bake as any other pie.

Fowl Pie.

To be made as hare pie, only add no allspice, but a little milk.

Pigeon Pie.

Lay a border of paste round a large dish, and cover the bottom with a veal cutlet or tender rump steak free from fat. Season with salt, cayenne, and nutmeg. Prepare with great nicety as many freshly killed young pigeons as the dish will hold in one layer, put into each a lump of butter, seasoned with a little cayenne or mace, lay them into the dish with the breasts downwards, and between and over them put the yolks of 2 doz. or more hard-boiled eggs; stick plenty of butter on them, and season the whole well with salt, and spice if liked; pour in some cold water for the gravy, roll out the cover three-quarters of an inch thick, secure it well round the edge, ornament it highly, letting several cleaned feet stick out round the crust, and bake for one hour or more in a well-heated oven. Protect the crust of the pie from burning with a piece of oiled paper.

Giblet Pie.

Clean well the necks, wings, gizzards, liver and hearts, stew them well with some onion, pepper, and salt, and a little allspice; thicken with a little butter and maizena, then proceed as for any ordinary meat pie.

Sausage Rolls.

Take some light paste, which roll out to about a quarter inch thick. Cut some circular pieces, and on the half of each place some nicely seasoned sausage meat. Fold the remaining half of the paste over, bind the edges neatly together, glaze with egg, and bake for three-quarters of an hour.

Oyster Patties.

Place a layer of thin paste in some patty pans, cut covers for same size of tin for the tops, removing a paste circle from the centre of each, which is used later on. Scald some oysters in their own liquor, beard them, and cut them small. Into a stew pan put a small quantity of butter, then dredge in enough flour to absorb it. Add the oyster liquor with a little cream, lemon juice, some pounded mace, and very little cayenne. Put the oysters now into the pan, letting them heat gradually and simmer awhile. When ready, fill the lined patty tins with mixture, place on cover firmly, and centre circle lightly, egg it over and bake for half an hour. Garnish with parsley.

NOTE: the cover of a small tin will cut the circles nicely.

Mincemeat for Christmas Pies.

One lb. raisins, 1½ lb. currants, 1 lb. lean beef, 1½ lb. beef suet, ½ lb. moist sugar, 2 oz. mixed candied peel, 1 small nutmeg grated, 2 large apples, rind of large lemon and juice, and ½ pint brandy. The suet and beef must be chopped very fine, also the peel; the apples after being peeled and cored must also be cut fine; the raisins must be stoned, and cut small with a knife; the currants must be clean and dry. Brandy to be added when the other ingredients are well mixed.

To Make Mince Pies.

Mince pies are usually eaten warm. The paste is rolled out to a quarter inch thickness, the bottom crust laid in patty pans, the mincemeat in the centre, and a top rather thicker crust to cover it neatly. This crust is often glazed over with the white of an egg and sprinkled with sugar; but the pies are never ornamented.

Raised Pork Pies.

Use minced pork or sausage meat. Put ¼ lb. lard into ½ pint water; when boiling hot pour it into 1 lb. flour with a little salt. Roll it out thin, shape it round a large smooth tumbler or wooden block. Next day make paste for lids of pies, filling inside with the mince. When sufficiently baked, which should take nearly one hour, pour a little gravy to the inside through a tiny hole in the lid. Glaze with egg.

Cornish Pasties.

These are made in a variety of ways. The pasty, if to be eaten hot, has the paste often made of fine suet, but if eaten cold, dripping or butter, with a small quantity of baking powder, can be used, as the crust does not then become so dry. An ordinary pasty has a firm crust rolled out to more than a quarter inch thick; it is then cut to the size of a medium plate, and the ingredients (composed of fresh meat, onion, turnip, and potato finely cut up, nicely seasoned with the addition of a small lump of butter) are placed over one-half of the paste. The other half is then turned over it, and the edges firmly joined to each other. With a rapid movement of the finger the Cornish housewife forms the edge into a particular shape, and the pasty is then baked for an hour or more in a moderately hot oven. The paste looks more appetising if glazed with a beaten egg. Care must be taken to keep the gravy from coming through the pasty whilst baking.

Fresh pork pasties, with an egg or more broken over the meat, and nicely seasoned, are well liked, but when eggs are added it is easier after the paste is cut to lay it into a deep tin plate, to keep the eggs steady whilst forming the pasty. Apples or many other kinds of fresh fruit can be used for sweet pasties, and then the addition of a little sugar to the paste is an improvement.

Part XI. Bread.

Country brick-built ovens, whether of sun-dried bricks or ordinary kiln bricks, are all built more or less alike. There is generally a hole left in the back, which is closed up with a spare brick and moist earth when the oven is cleared of the embers of the hot wood ash, and sometimes the stone, which is used instead of an iron door, has to be secured in the same way when the bread is put in. A practised hand can tell the right heat of the oven for the bread by a white shimmering look in it, or others will thrust in a bit of dough to observe the action of the heat. If it be too hot they wait awhile after the ashes are raked out. It is then put in quickly, in tins, for sometimes not having the necessary oven appliances the bottom of it is often too dusty for use otherwise; the mouth is then closed up, and the bread remains about two hours, but the oven must not be opened whilst it is baking. Those who bake often, do well to observe the quantities of flour, yeast, water, etc., which are found to answer best.

In raking out the hot wood embers of the oven, a woman especially should take care to avoid setting her clothes on fire, especially if a wind be blowing, and she should see that the embers are quite deadened by water, or they may set other things smouldering. Large ant-heaps are often scooped out in country parts, and make good ovens, a stone daubed around with earth securing the door opening.

Bakers' Yeast.

In summer take ¼ lb. hops, in winter ½ lb., to 18 lb. flour. Let the hops boil for twenty minutes in about 3 gallons of water. Use ½ lb. salt to a bucket of water in kneading.

Home-made Yeast and Bread.

Take 5 pints of cold water, and to it add 1 small teacupful of hops, boil it half an hour, strain, then add to it the batter prepared of 2 tablespoonfuls flour, 1 tablespoonful brown sugar, and 1 dessertspoonful of salt mixed with cold water smoothly. Add it to the hop liquid whilst hot, and return it to the pot only long enough to boil up. When cool, bottle it, adding if at hand (to make it ferment quicker) 1 tablespoonful of the last yeast or a few raisins. This yeast will be ready for use the next evening, and about ¾ teacupful can be used to about 5 lb. flour. It can be kneaded up with warm water at night (salt not being omitted), re-kneaded a little in the morning, formed into two loaves, which will keep well separated if slightly greased between them, then if they stand awhile they can further be placed in the oven and usually baked before breakfast time, as the baking only requires about one hour and a half, but in winter time it will be rather later before it will be sufficiently ready to bake.

Home-made Yeast, No. 2.

Two oz. of good hops, 1 lb. flour, 4 quarts of water, 3 lb. good potatoes, ½ lb. moist sugar. On Monday morning boil 2 oz. of the best hops in 4 quarts of water for half an hour, strain it and let the liquor cool down to new milk warmth, then throw in a small handful of salt and ½ lb. moist sugar; beat up 1 lb. of good flour with some of the liquor, and then mix all well together. On Wednesday add 3 lb. potatoes boiled and then mashed, to stand till Thursday; then strain it and put it into small bottles, and it is ready for use. Cork tightly and tie the bottles up well. It must be stirred frequently whilst it is making, and kept near the fire. Before using shake the bottle well up. It will keep in a cool place for two months, and it is best at the latest part of the time. The beauty of this yeast is, that it ferments spontaneously, not requiring the aid of other yeast, and if care be taken it will ferment well in the earthenware bowl in which it is made. To make a lesser quantity use say one-half of these ingredients.

Another Recipe for Yeast.

Take the water some potatoes have boiled in, and into it put a small tablespoonful of hops, and boil for fifteen or twenty minutes, then strain, let it cool a few minutes, then add 3 tablespoonfuls each of sugar and flour, mixing the latter into a batter before adding it with some of the cooled liquid. Bottle at once, and put two or three raisins into each bottle. It will ferment quicker if put into the same bottles containing a little of the last yeast. It makes about two fruit bottles full, and if made at noon one day in warm weather it will be ready for use the following morning.

Good Yeast without Hops.

To 1½ pints of water, in which potatoes have been boiled, when lukewarm add 1½ tablespoonfuls of white sugar and 3 small tablespoonfuls of flour. Bottle and cork tightly for one night. It is then ready for use next evening, if kept in a warm place. Add to the end of the same yeast from day to day.

Remedy for Bitter Yeast.

It sometimes happens that yeast has a bitter taste; it can be detected if a piece of bread is dipped into it and tasted. If such be the case, drop a piece of red-hot wood or cinder or a hot poker into it, and strain before using.

Bread Made from Yeast.

Put the flour to be used into a large earthenware pan or bread trough. Mix the usual quantity of yeast (how much must be determined by its strength and the amount of flour to be used) with some warm water, but it must not be hot. Make a hole in the centre of the flour, pour in the yeast and water, mixing the flour gradually into it until it becomes a thick batter;

sprinkle a little flour over the top, cover with a blanket or thick cloth, and let it stand in a warm place for an hour or two until it has well risen and run over the top of the flour; then have ready more warm water, with some salt in it, and knead it well, but it must never become so moist that it will stick to the hands when handling. When the kneading is completed, cover the dough up and leave it to rise. When risen sufficiently, make it into loaves, and bake them in tins or on the bottom of an oven. Some people mash potatoes into a fine pulp and mix them well with the flour before they begin to knead; this will often improve the bread by adding to its lightness. Bakers generally use them. Should you fear that the yeast is not very good, add a teaspoonful of well crushed carbonate of soda to it.

Bread Made from Baking Powder.

For every 1 lb. of flour use a tablespoonful of baking powder and a pinch of salt. Mix with lukewarm water or milk with the hand, as lightly as possible, taking care it is not very stiff. Bake in rather small pieces in a quick oven, protected with greased paper.

Malt Yeast.

Two tablespoonfuls malt to be added to 1 lb. mashed potatoes, 1 teaspoonful of white sugar, and 2 tablespoonfuls of boiled crushed rice. This has to be well mixed with 1 quart of water and bottled.

Royal Unfermented Bread.

One quart flour, 1 teaspoonful salt, ½ teaspoonfuls sugar, 2 teaspoonfuls Royal baking powder, 1½ pints milk. Sift together thoroughly flour, salt, sugar, and powder; add the milk; mix smoothly and rapidly into a softer dough than can be handled. Turn from bowl into a greased bread pan. Bake in moderate oven forty-five minutes. Protect by placing paper on top during first fifteen minutes' baking.

Breakfast Rolls.

If good, 1 tablespoonful yeast, if not very good take 2 tablespoonfuls to 2 lb. of flour. Mix the yeast with warm milk and half the yolk of an egg. Beat yeast, milk, etc., well together, then put it into the middle of the flour and set it to rise. When ready take 1 oz. butter, melt it with a little more warm milk, and make the dough with it. Put it by covered over to rise again a little, then divide into 12 rolls, and bake for about twenty minutes.

Lunch Rolls.

One quart of flour, 1 teaspoonful of salt, 2 teaspoonfuls of baking powder, 1 tablespoonful of lard, 1 pint of milk; sift flour, salt, and powder together; rub in the lard and add the milk; mix to a smooth dough; knead the dough once or twice to give it a smoothness; roll out to one-half inch in thickness; cut with a round cutter; lay in a pan so that they will just touch each other; wash on the top with milk, and bake in a good oven thirty minutes.

Breakfast Scones.

Take 5 handfuls of flour, a tablespoonful of Royal baking powder, and a good pinch of salt. Mix together with sweet milk to the consistency of light dough, let it stand a few minutes, then roll it out about half-inch thick, cut it into half squares and put into dry frying pan over a fire not too fierce until well risen and browning slightly, turn them over, and when ready serve hot.

Part XII. Soups, Sauces, etc.

A good cook never wastes gravy, but always stands it aside in her pantry cool and ready for use. For this purpose a basin answers very well, a small cover of net can be made rather larger than the top and tied round it, to prevent flies and dust from falling in. To get some nice gravy, for a start, take some good soup, strain and put aside for the purpose, thicken it when required with a little maizena, and if it be not of a rich brown colour, mix about a teaspoonful of chicory in water, strain, and add to it. This will not at all affect the flavour, for it is tasteless, and cannot be detected. Instead of black-jack[21] or burnt sugar many cooks use this, and have a little ready bottled always near at hand. The gravy not used at the table should never be thrown away, but be placed again with the other on hand. In many kitchens a stock pot is seen; this is a good-sized round pot with a tap at its base, into which all small pieces of meat and bones are consigned; it is then stood by the side of the fire where it can slowly simmer, and good soup it will produce; many a poor sick person has with little trouble been benefited by such, for if a few vegetables are sliced up and boiled awhile with its liquor it is most strengthening and agreeable, and otherwise much that is nourishing would be wasted.

Soups are made in many ways, but some of them are not at all strengthening, for there is little real extract of the meat in them, although they may be blessed with very high-sounding names. The chief thing to remember is, that it is not hot water required, but the strength and essence of the meat, and this must be slowly and gradually extracted. If soup be liked with vegetables boiled in it, cut them into small pieces. Sometimes the flavour of onion is not approved of, in which case omit it.

---

[21] Black-jack: burnt caramel for colouring

Some like barley well boiled in it, others celery or its seed, sago, maccaroni, vermicelli, rice, or other ingredients; some like soup light, others dark. This is easily altered by the addition of a little liquid chicory. A little thickening of maizena will often improve a soup, or a little of the Liebig's Extract of Beef may be added. This extract is often given to invalids, when other soup is not at hand, but is not considered so beneficial. Skim soup well of all its fat before serving. By pouring in a cupful of cold water whilst the soup cooks, now and again, the scum will better rise to the surface for skimming off. Shells of green peas boiled in it give an agreeable flavour to soup.

Beef Tea.

Where nourishing beef tea is required, stew the most tender lean beef slowly for a few hours, seasoned delicately; or cover it over, cut up small, in an earthenware jar, and place it in the oven. The strength will then slowly and surely be extracted by the time the meat will fall to pieces with the pressure of the finger and thumb. It can be seasoned and served as required.

Pea Soup, No. 1.

Soak the peas overnight in soft water, then when required put them on the fire for some hours to boil. When getting tender and breaking, put in a sweet ham bone, and what other meat may be necessary. A stick or two of celery cut up, or a little celery seed is sometimes thrown in. If the ham bone or salt beef does not season it sufficiently, add with the pepper more salt. Skim off all the fat which rises to the surface, and let the peas remain until they are boiled to a pulp. Good pea soup should be rather thick. Symington's Pea Flour makes an excellent soup, especially if wanted quickly, or a little of the flour can be added to the ordinary soup prepared.

Pea Soup, No. 2.

Soak ¾ lb. of split peas overnight, take ¼ lb. of onions, ¼ lb. of carrots, 2 oz. of celery, cut them into small pieces, and fry for ten minutes in a little butter or dripping. Pour 4 quarts of water on these fried vegetables, and when boiling add the peas. Simmer for nearly three hours, or until the peas are thoroughly done. Add a little mint shred fine, 1 tablespoonful of coarse brown sugar, salt and pepper (not much), and boil for another quarter of an hour.

White Bean Soup, No. 1.

Wash and boil your beans with a piece of salt pork. When the beans are soft, take them out, press them through a sieve, and put them back into the water they were boiled in; quarter 4 hardboiled eggs, add them with pepper and salt, and half a lemon sliced.

White Bean Soup, No. 2.

Soak a quart of beans overnight; in the morning pour off the water, add fresh, and set over fire until skins will easily slip off; throw them into cold water, rub well, and skins will rise to top, when they may be removed. Boil beans until perfectly soft, allowing 2 quarts of water to 1 quart of beans; mash beans, add flour and butter rubbed together, also salt and pepper. Cut bread into small pieces, toast, and drop on soup when you serve.

From the Royal Baker and Pastrycook.

White Celery Soup.

Take 3 heads of celery, and having well washed and trimmed them, put them to boil with 4 onions in 2 quarts of any white broth or stock. When the celery is perfectly tender, rub it through a sieve, put it back in the broth, and thicken with a dessertspoonful of corn flour, and one of flour mixed with a pint of milk. Add two lumps of sugar and a little salt if necessary; stir the soup until perfectly thickened, and then break in 2 oz. of fresh butter. When it is melted, pour the soup in a tureen and serve.

Melted Butter.

Mix a teaspoonful of maizena, or rather more of flour, smoothly with water, put it into a small saucepan in which some small bits of butter have been dissolved; add a little salt, and boil for a few minutes, stirring the while.

Herbs.

All housekeepers are glad of fresh herbs, and those herbs not used up at once can be washed, dried, stripped of their stems, and bottled for future emergencies, or dried herbs can be procured now at most grocery stores, dried and bottled.

Parsley and Butter.

Chop up some well-washed fresh parsley very fine, and after having mixed a dessertspoonful of maizena into a smooth paste with a little cold milk or water, put in the parsley and mix the same into 2 pint of milk. Boil a few minutes, stirring the while; add a lump of butter, a little salt, and it is ready.

Caper Sauce.

This is prepared similarly to the former, only no milk is used, and capers are substituted for the parsley, and the liquor of the pot in which the meat has boiled instead of milk. This sauce is generally served with boiled mutton.

Mint Sauce.

Wash the leaves well, chop them up fine, mix and keep in a suitable bottle ready. Good vinegar must be used, and some sugar. Serve with lamb.

Tomato Sauce.

Pare and slice tomatoes, put them in a saucepan without water, add some sliced onion, with pepper, salt, and a teaspoonful of butter, and stew gently until tender. A nice relish with either cold or hot meat.

Bread Sauce.

Take an onion, cut it up and cook it gently in some milk till tender, break the crumb of some bread into small pieces, pour the milk in which the onion has been boiled over it; cover it up and let it stay awhile, then beat it up smoothly, add a little cayenne, salt, and butter just before using. A little cream added to it will improve the flavour.

Cream Gravy for Baked Fish.

Have ready in saucepan 1 cup of cream, diluted with a few spoonfuls of hot water; stir in carefully 2 tablespoonfuls of melted butter and a little chopped parsley. Heat this into a vessel filled with hot water. Pour in gravy from dripping pan of fish. Boil thick.

From the Royal Baker and Pastrycook.

Horseradish Sauce, No. 1.

Wash it, and scrape very fine, pour about ½ pint of good vinegar to it, adding a very little cayenne pepper. It is generally served with cold meat.

Horseradish Sauce, No. 2.

Scrape some horseradish finely, mix it up with cream, a-little salt, and a small quantity vinegar. Serve with cold roast beef.

Veal Stuffing.

Quarter lb. beef suet, 4 lb. bread crumbs, a little parsley, lemon peel and herbs, pepper and salt, pounded up well with 2 eggs.

Hare Stuffing.

Boil the liver, chop it up, add 2 oz. finely chopped suet, a little parsley, some sweet herbs, pepper and salt and grated lemon peel, mixed together with a beaten egg.

Seasoning for Pork, etc.

Half lb. of salt, 1 oz. white pepper, ½ oz. ground mace, 30 grains powdered cloves, a teaspoonful of cayenne, 1 nutmeg grated, and a pinch of sugar. Mix altogether for use.

Mushrooms, Baked.

Well butter a tin baking dish, lay in it large fresh mushrooms, which have been peeled and had the stalks cut off, add butter and seasoning, and let them bake for quarter of an hour or rather longer. Serve hot, with a spoonful or two of brown gravy poured over them.

Mushrooms, Dried.

Wipe them clean, removing the brown part from the inside of the large ones, lay them on paper in a cool oven to dry, and keep them ready for use hung up in paper bags in a cool place. In using them simmer them in some of the gravy into which they are to be put, and they will swell to nearly their original size; or, wipe and clean them, and simmer them in their own moisture until it is dried up in them, shaking the pan well, so that they do not burn; dry them on tin plates, at the bottom of the oven, with spice or not as you choose; they can then be powdered and tied down carefully in bottles. A teaspoonful of it gives a rich flavour to gravies, hashes, etc.

Apple Sauce.

Core and peel some apples, stew them with a few cloves in a little water till tender, drain it off, beat them up, add a small piece of butter, a little sugar, and grated nutmeg.

Plum Pudding Sauce.

Mix ½ lb. white sugar with some melted butter, and some sherry or brandy, a little nutmeg and grated lemon peel.

Brandy Sauce.

Take 2 teaspoonfuls maizena, mix with cold water and boil in ½ pint ditto, add a dessertspoonful butter, and into it also put 1 tablespoonful of sugar and a wineglassful of brandy. Bring it to a boil, and serve in tureen.

Custard Sauce.

See BOILED CUSTARD.

An Excellent Substitute for Cream.

Dissolve two small dessertspoonfuls of maizena in a little cold milk, add to it a pint of milk (if thin or skim), or, if rich, to a quart; stir till it boils a few minutes. So prepared, it greatly improves coffee, chocolate, tea, etc.

White Schaum Sauce (German).

Two large eggs well beaten, ½ pint of light white wine, or stronger wine, brandy, or whisky mixed with water, 1 teaspoonful of corn flour, 1 tablespoonful of castor sugar, half the rind of a lemon, and some cinnamon tied in a muslin bag. Put the jug or basin containing the sauce into a pan of boiling water, set it over a strong fire, and beat thoroughly with an egg whisk or large fork, until it becomes thick, taking care not to let it boil. Have another vessel ready, and pour the sauce backwards and forwards for a minute or two, when whisk for a minute (this is to prevent its curdling) and send to table very hot, either in a sauce boat, or poured over a Vanilla pudding.

Sylvia's Home Journal.

Part XIII. Dried Fruits.

Apricots and Peaches.

Sometimes it is necessary to wash these first before placing them on the fire to boil with sufficient water to cover them. Add sugar to taste. They must be cooked until tender. Allow plenty of room in the pot for them to swell. Do not give them to a child or person troubled with diarrhoea. They make a pleasant accompaniment to a blanc-mange or milk pudding.

Dried Apples or Apple Rings.

See they are nicely picked over, then place a quantity in an enamelled-lined saucepan, with sufficient water to cover them. Allow room for swelling. Add some cloves and some sugar to taste. A wineglassful of sherry improves the flavour. Stew until quite tender with the lid on the pot. Serve when cold.

Part XIV. Salads.

Tomato Salad.

Pare with sharp knife. Slice and lay in salad bowl. Make dressings as follows :

Work up a saltspoonful each of salt, pepper, and fresh-made mustard, with two tablespoonfuls of salad oil, and when thoroughly mixed, adding only a few drops at a time, whip in a beaten egg and 4 tablespoonfuls vinegar; toss up with a fork.

From the Royal Baker and Pastrycook.

Cucumber Salad.

Pare the cucumbers evenly, slice up in very thin rounds, sprinkle well with salt, and lay them on an inverted plate to drain, or shake them well between two plates, pouring off the water. When this is done sprinkle with white pepper, and pour some good vinegar over them. A white onion very thinly cut into rings is generally liked served on the top of it.

Lettuce Salad.

Wash well, cut up into small pieces, also slice some white onion thinly, and a couple of hard-boiled eggs. Pour over this a sufficient quantity of vinegar, in which has been put some pepper, sugar, and a little salt. Salad oil can also be added, if liked, or thick cream. Use one-third as much salad oil as you do vinegar. Stir up the dressing with a fork to mix all well together.

Dressing for Salad.

When vinegar and sugar are not liked, boil an egg hard, take out the yolk, beat away till it is quite smooth, add 2 tablespoonfuls of thick cream, 3 teaspoonfuls mixed mustard, 4 tablespoonfuls vinegar, and mix well together.

Mustard and Cress.

This will grow from seed procurable of any garden seedsman in a very short time. After being well washed and freed from grit it can be served alone, or for a tea table it is placed between thin slices of good bread and fresh butter, sprinkled lightly with salt. In this way it is usually relished. The edges of the bread should be neatly trimmed.

Potato Salad.

Take cold potatoes, cut them into dice-shaped pieces, put into a salad bowl with vinegar, oil, pepper, and salt; have ready a teaspoonful of finely minced parsley, and another of minced ham. Mix well, and let stand some time. Garnish with mint.

Beetroot Salad.

Slice some beetroot, and over the top spread some thin white slices of onion. Pour over it good vinegar, in which has been stirred a little sugar.

Cheese and Apple Salad.

Peel, core, and cut into dice three rather sour cooking apples of medium size; clean some celery, and cut that also in dice, making the quantity equal to that of the apples. Grate a pound of cheese of any dry white kind over the apples and celery, and mix all together, in enough mayonnaise sauce just to cover them. Pile in a glass dish, and garnish with watercress and slices of beetroot.

Part XV. Cooling Drinks.

Ginger Beer, No. 1.

One lb. bruised ginger to be boiled with 2 gallons of water for about half an hour, then strained through a sieve. Take 10 lb. sugar, dissolve in the ginger water while hot. 2 oz. tartaric acid is to be first put to the sugar. When this is done, add carefully 8 gallons more of clear cold water, after which ½ oz. oil of lemons. Then add 1 cup of yeast, stir it well, and tie the cask over with a thick flannel. When fermentation has continued for a few hours, put it into bottles, and secure the corks down.

Ginger Beer, No. 2.

Three pounds of loaf sugar, 3 oz. of whole ginger (bruised), ½ oz. of cream of tartar, 2 tablespoonfuls of brewers' yeast, 1 large lemon, 3 gallons of boiling water, and the white of 1 egg.

Method: put sugar, lemon, ginger, and cream of tartar into an earthen pan; pour the boiling water on; let it stand until nearly cold; then add the egg, well beaten, with the yeast, and mix well. A slice of toast may be added. Cover close, and let it stand in a warm place until morning. Take the yeast off, and strain the beer through a cloth. Bottle, cork, and tie down; always keep the bottles lying down.

Lemonade.

One gallon water, 1 lb. loaf sugar, 10 drops essence of lemon, 10 slices of lemon, 2 oz. cream of tartar, and 1 glass of French brandy. Put the ingredients into a vessel, and pour the (1 gallon) boiling water over them, then shut it down to keep the steam in.

When nearly cold, put in 1 cupful of good yeast; let the lemonade stand till it has a head; then bottle, corking tightly after skimming it. For a larger quantity, double or treble these ingredients given.

Lemon Syrup, No. 1.

Twenty-five lb. white sugar to 2 gallons of water. Boil together for two hours, then add 4 oz. tartaric acid and 1 oz. oil of lemons. Strain all off through a flannel, and bottle.

Lemon Syrup, No. 2.

Take 15 lb. white sugar to 3 gallons water; boil both together nearly two hours; skim well. Put in 3 oz3 tartaric acid and 2 teaspoonfuls essence of lemon. When cold bottle it.

Lemon Syrup, No. 3.

Boil 4 cups of sugar in 5 cups of water for half an hour. When cold add 4 teaspoonfuls of tartaric acid, and 10 drops lemon acid.

Hop Beer, No. 1.

To 2 gallons water add 1 teacupful hops, 3 lb. brown sugar, 2 oz. bruised ginger, and boil the same for two hours. Strain, and when lukewarm add 2 cupfuls of good yeast. Next morning bottle it, and the following morning cork and tie it up, and it is ready for use in a few hours.

Hop Beer, No. 2.

Half-pound hops, 2 lb. bran or 2 lb. Kafir corn[22]. Boil in 4 gallons water for one hour. When ready strain carefully into a cask, then add 6 gallons more of clear cold water. Then dissolve 10 lb. of sugar in warm water, add to it 1 pint of yeast, and mix

---

[22] Sorghum

all well together into the hot water. This done, cover it with a cloth, and tie down close the first day. Skim off next day, and tie down again; then it is ready to bottle. All beer is better lying when it is bottled.

Hop Beer, No. 3.

Two ounces hops to 2 gallons water, boil for half an hour. Strain carefully into a vessel, then add 2 lb. light sugar into the same water, and 2 tablespoonfuls of yeast. Stir well all together, and it is ready to bottle next day.

Boston Cream.

Three quarts of water; 1½ lbs. of sugar; put into a pan and boil for a few minutes. Pour out into a mug, and when quite cold add 1 teaspoonful of essence of lemon, 2 oz. of tartaric acid, 2 oz. of cream of tartar, and the whites of 2 eggs beaten stiff. Then bottle it. A wineglassful of Boston cream to a glass of water. In each glass put a pinch of carbonate of soda.

Sherbet.

Take of pounded tartaric acid one part, of carbonate of soda one part, and of castor sugar two parts; add as many drops of essence of lemon as may be liked. Mix all the powders thoroughly together, and keep corked up for use.

Strawberry Acid Drink.

Three pounds strawberries are to be put into an earthen pan, over them pour 1 pint of cold water, mixed with 1 oz. tartaric acid. The next day the clear liquid is to be strained through a hair sieve, sweetened with rather more than 1 lb. of sugar to 1 pint of the juice. It is then to be put by in small bottles for use, and only requires the addition of cold water to suit the palate. It is a pleasant old-fashioned drink.

Part XVI. Sweet Puddings, Pies, Tarts, etc.

Boiled Batter.

Beat up 3 eggs, mix well with milk 1 tablespoonful sugar and 6 oz. of flour till it is of the thickness of cream. Butter a basin, tie the mixture well into it, and boil for about one hour and a half, without letting it stop. It can be served with stewed fruit, pudding sauce, jam, or in other ways. If to be served with meat, omit the sugar.

Yeast Dumplings.

Take some dough, roll in floured hand into balls, plunge them into plenty of boiling water, and let them remain twenty minutes without removing the cover. Serve hot and quickly, parting each one open with two forks. Butter, sugar, golden syrup, or jam is eaten with them. Instead of using dough they can be made of flour and Yeatman's yeast powder. Use a heaped teaspoonful to 1 lb. flour, and a little salt; then boil and serve in the same way.

If well made they are often mistaken for those made of bread dough.

Apple Dumplings, Boiled.

Make ordinary suet crust, roll out rather thin, pare and core, place 2 cloves in centre of each with a little sugar; stand each apple into its shape; cut crust round with a plate or saucer the size you require; stand apple on each round of crust, and bring with the hand the same all round the apple, pressing it well together at top. Tie each dumpling into a small cloth, put them into a saucepan of boiling water, having a plate at the bottom of it, to prevent their sticking and burning. Cook for an hour; serve with cream or butter and sugar.

Apple Dumplings, Baked.

Have ready some ordinary pie paste, roll out rather thin, pare and cut some apples into quarters (good baking ones), remove the cores, add a little sugar and a clove or two to each, then proceed as above. Lay the dumplings in a tin, glaze with the white of an egg, and bake for nearly an hour in a gentle oven. Sprinkle with white sugar.

Apple Dumplings, Baked, from Bottled Apples.

Pour all the water from the apples, then proceed as before, only a little sherry wine over the apple improves the flavour, with a clove or two. The dumplings will not take more than half an hour to bake.

Apple Pie.

The usual pie paste. Have some apples pared, cored, and cut into rather thin slices, then put them into a stew pan with about 4 lb. sugar to each 1 lb, apples (some apples may require rather more), a little water, a few cloves, and a glass of sherry. Let them remain a few minutes until they begin to get tender. Lay a strip of paste round a pie dish, pour in the apples, and place a small cup or little stand to keep the crust from sinking into the syrup. Pie crust raisers of porcelain are sold for the purpose. Cover with crust, neatly glaze with the white of an egg, bake in a quick oven for about three-quarters of an hour, sprinkle with white sugar before serving.

Apple Pudding.

Pare and cut the apples into quarters, remove the cores, lay the apples in a basin lined with thin pudding crust, add some sugar, a few cloves, a glass of sherry, and s tablespoonful of water. Cover with crust, tie over with cloth, place into boiling water, and cook for about one and a half hours, perhaps longer if the apples do not cook well. Fruit puddings are all made more or less in the same way, only no wine or spice is usually added.

Open Jam Tart.

This tart is better baked on a tin plate, as the underpart of the crust becomes better baked, especially if the jam be placed in it, in the oven. Line a plate with paste, trim the edges off neatly, form edge of tart into any fancy pattern, and place the jam in the centre. Roll a small piece of paste out very thin, cut it into very narrow strips, twist as you hold, draw out each strip in the hand, and form a lattice pattern over the jam. Glaze, and bake in a moderately hot oven. Sometimes the crust is preferred baked without the jam; if so, when it is removed from the oven, place the jam in it, and ornament the top with stars, leaves, or other small paste ornaments, already baked. Sift white sugar over the tart before sending to table.

Green Apricot Pudding and Pie.

When sufficiently large, green apricots make better pies and puddings than ripe ones, nor do they require so much sugar then. To make the pudding see instructions for apple pudding. For the pie stew the fruit a little before using.

Child's Delight.

To use up the remainder of any paste, roll it out thin, and spread upon it a mixture of raisins, currants, suet, and apple, or the two former alone, minced finely by passing it through a sausage machine. Form into half-squares, cover and bake.

Plum Pudding, No. 1.

Two cups flour mixed dry with a heaped teaspoonful of Royal baking powder, a cupful of light yellow sugar, 1 small cupful raisins chopped, 1 cupful currants, ½ lb. finely chopped beef suet, 3 beaten eggs, ½ pint of milk, a little ground spice, 1 saltspoonful salt, and a little mixed peel cut small. Mix well together, tie in a cloth, and boil three hours.

Plum Pudding, No. 2.

One lb. raisins stoned and cut, 1 lb. nicely washed currants, well dried, 1 lb. suet chopped fine, 1 lb. coarse sugar, 1 lb flour, 12 eggs or 1 ostrich egg, ½ tumbler of French brandy, 2 oz. candied peel cut small, a little ground allspice, and a little salt. Beat up the eggs, and mix the other ingredients into it alternately and by degrees. Stir all well together, and boil eight hours at least.

Plum Pudding, No. 3.

The grated crumbs of 6 small breakfast rolls, 3 cups flour, 1 lb. stoned raisins, 1 lb. currants, 1 lb. fine beef suet, ½ grated nutmeg, 1 cup of milk, a little ground cinnamon, 1 teacupful sugar, some pounded naartje[23] peel, 1 saltspoonful salt, 1 wineglass French brandy, some mixed candied peel, the juice of 2 or 3 lemons, 6, 8, or 10 eggs, or an ostrich egg. Boil six hours in a mould.

Rice Black-cap Pudding.

Butter a pudding basin, and stick raisins or prunes all over the bottom, and pour into the centre a cupful of previously cleaned and dried rice, this quantity being sufficient for a basin that will hold 1 pint of water. Tie a cloth tightly over the basin and plunge it into boiling water. Boil for one hour, when it will turn out a nice shape, with the raisins or prunes covering the top of the rice. Serve with butter and sugar, golden syrup, or plain pudding sauce.

Mrs. Winslow's Family Almanac.

---

[23] Naartje: clementine or small orange

Rice Mould.

Boil a teacupful of rice in 1½ pints of milk until perfectly tender, add 2 oz, white sugar, 1 egg, and a little grated lemon rind; beat all together for a few minutes, turn into a mould, previously wetted with cold water, but before doing so add the water in which a good pinch of isinglass[24] has been dissolved. Let it stand an hour or two, turn it out into a glass dish, and apricot jam around it.

Rice Pudding, Baked.

Rice on hand previously boiled will save time in preparing the pudding. Place the rice in a dish, making it rather more than half full, add sugar, essence, and pour a rich custard over it, a tiny lump or two of butter, and a couple of bay leaves. Bake until it is a light golden brown. Jam, or preserves, are often served at table with such puddings.

Ground Rice Pudding.

Quarter lb. ground rice, 2 pints of milk, ½ teacupful white sugar, and 3 eggs. Have the milk nearly boiling, put in the sugar, the ground rice, with a little cold milk; add the beaten eggs, pour gently into the hot milk, continue to stir well until it boils. Put it into a buttered pie-dish, grate a little lemon peel and nutmeg over the top, and bake for half-hour in a quick oven.

Potato Pudding.

Pare six medium-sized potatoes, wash, and chop them fine, and to it add nearly ½ lb. of chopped suet; sprinkle well with flour, and work well with the hands into a stiff mixture. Add a little salt, and the preparation can be either baked in a

---

[24] Gelatine may be substituted for isinglass in all Mrs Barnes' recipes

greased tin, or boiled as a pudding in a cloth for two hours. To be eaten hot.

Baked Plum Pudding.

One lb. flour, 6 oz. fine suet or rather less dripping, 1 lb. raisins, ½ teacupful sugar, ½ teaspoonful Royal baking powder, a little salt, 2 eggs, and spice if liked. Mix the ingredients with milk or water, and bake slowly in a well-greased tin.

Golden Syrup Pudding.

Mix some flour with suet or dripping, salt, and a little baking powder in the usual way, letting it be rather stiff, line a greased mould, with some of it rolled out, let it overlap the edge; pour in the bottom of the mould some syrup; above this place a layer of thin crust, then another quantity of syrup, and continue it until the mould is full, leaving a crust on the top; then turn over the overlapping paste, and secure the edge firmly to prevent the syrup boiling out. Tie it over with a wet cloth and boil for two hours. This is a favourite pudding for children.

A Minute Pudding.

Place over the fire 1 teacupful sweet milk, let it come to a boil, and stir in an egg well beaten, 1 tablespoonful of flour, mixed smoothly with milk, and a dessertspoonful of sugar. Stir it well whilst cooking for five minutes. Oil a dish, put the pudding in it, and when cold turn it out. Serve with sweet sauce or cream.

Baked Roly Pudding.

Two cups flour, 1 cup of white sugar, 2 eggs, 2 teaspoonfuls cream of tartar mixed in the dry flour, 1 teaspoonful carbonate of soda, 2 cups sweet milk, and the rind and juice of 1 lemon. Bake in flat tin, lined with buttered paper.

When done, spread the underside with apricot or other light jam, roll up, or cut into fancy sandwiches. Serve hot.

Nelly's Pudding.

Two eggs and their weight in butter and flour, with the weight of one in light sugar. Beat the butter to a cream, add the butter and flour with 1 tablespoonful jam to it, and beat up well. Now beat a teaspoonful of carbonate of soda to the eggs, and add this to the other mixture, which has then to be put into a buttered basin, tied up, and steamed for two hours. Serve hot, with sweet sauce.

Universal Pudding.

Four oz. each of flour, suet, currants, raisins, and bread crumbs, 2 tablespoonfuls of treacle, and ½ pint of milk. Mix thoroughly, and boil in a mould three hours.

Batter Pudding, Baked.

One lb. flour, 1 teaspoonful Royal baking powder, 3 eggs well beaten. Mix with milk into a batter the thickness of cream. Bake in a well-greased tin. For a sweet batter add sugar and currants, if desired.

French Pudding.

One quart milk, 1 cupful flour, 8 eggs, 1 cupful white sugar. Beat the eggs, add them to the milk, butter a dish, and bake nicely. Serve with sweet sauce.

Sultan's Pudding.

Put into a bowl 12 tablespoonfuls of flour, 4 tablespoonfuls of bread crumbs, 1 tablespoonful of moist sugar, 1 teaspoonful of baking powder, and a pinch of salt. Chop very fine ¼ lb. of beef suet, and add it to 4 tablespoonfuls of sultana raisins. Mix all well. Pour 2 teacupfuls of warm milk on to 1 teacupful of treacle, and then add it slowly to the dry ingredients, and mix thoroughly. Boil for three hours in a well-buttered basin or mould tied firmly with a floured cloth.

Dainty Roll Pudding.

Take a pint of hot mashed potato, a pint of flour, ¼ lb. of butter, a pinch of salt, and moisten with milk or water into a dough "just in the old sweet way". Roll the paste out, spread it with any jam that has no stones, roll and tie up, and steam for an hour and a quarter. A very nice sauce to eat with this dainty pudding is 2 oz. of butter and 2 tablespoonfuls of sugar beaten together, and added to 1 well-beaten egg. Go on beating, pouring in by degrees a little boiling water, till the sauce looks like cream, and for many digestions it is far more wholesome.

Baked Marmalade, or Apricot Jam Pudding.

Cut slices of bread without crusts, butter them, spread with marmalade or jam, and sprinkle over with sugar. Pour a small quantity of boiling water over them, and cover awhile, so that they are quite softened; add 2 or 3 eggs beaten up into some milk, enough to cover the bread. Bake for about half an hour.

Orange, or Lemon Pudding.

Take ½ lb. fresh butter, mix it with the same quantity of powdered sugar and a wineglassful of brandy. Grate the rind of 3 large oranges, squeeze out their juice; beat 6 eggs well, and stir them into the sugar, mix together, and place it in a pie dish lined with good paste. Bake for half an hour, and eat cold with sugar. Lemons can be used in the same way.

College Pudding.

A few sponge cakes, a few stoned or sultana raisins. Cover this with custard. Boil it in a well-buttered basin or mould for half an hour, taking care to keep it well upright.

Early Pudding.

Two eggs, their weight in butter and flour, the weight of 1 in sugar, 1 tablespoonful of raspberry jam, and 1 teaspoonful of carbonate of soda. Melt the butter, stir in the flour, add eggs and soda, well crushed. Mix well. Steam for one hour in a floured cloth.

Lemon Custard, Boiled.

Beat the yolk of 8 eggs, with ½ lb. sugar, add 1 pint of boiling water, the rinds of 2 lemons grated, and the juice of the same; boil until it thickens, and then add 1 glass of light wine, ½ glass of brandy; boil a few minutes, strain into glasses, and eat when cold. A little nutmeg to be grated on top of each glass.

Lemon Custard, Baked.

Two white potatoes grated, the rind and juice of 2 lemons, 2 eggs, 1 cup of sugar. Line the pie plate with good crust, pour in the custard, and bake till done.

Maizena Lemon Pudding (Duryea).

Grate the rind of 2 lemons, add the juice and rind to 6 oz. of sugar, and 3 oz, of maizena; stir this well into some cold water sufficient to make it smooth, place 3 pints of milk on the fire; when boiling add the above, stirring all the time until it thickens. Remove it from the fire, and add 1 oz. butter and 4 eggs; stir again while on the fire, taking care not to allow it to burn; as soon as it becomes thick remove it, and fill out some small cups or forms previously dipped in cold water; place them aside; in one hour they will be fit to turn out. Cream and sugar, or any sauce preferred.

Crystal Palace Pudding.

Soak 1 packet of Swinborne's isinglass or gelatine in 1 pint of cold new milk for twenty minutes, then put it into a saucepan, and stir over the fire till dissolved, add the yolks of 4 eggs well beaten, and 1½ ozs. of powdered loaf sugar to form a custard.

Well wet a mould, and then fill up with alternate layers of sponge cakes and ratafias soaked in the wine, with jam between them.

When the custard is nearly cold, pour it into the mould, and set aside in a cold place till wanted.

Swinborne's Pastrycook and Confectioner.

Gelatine Fruit Pudding.

Soak ½ pint of Swinborne's gelatine in ¼ pint of cold water, and boil either 1½ pints of Cape gooseberries, sliced apple or other fruit with 1½ lbs. white sugar, in another ¼ pint water. As soon as the fruit is tender add the soaked gelatine and stir till it is dissolved; pour into a basin, and when nearly cold, turn it into a porcelain mould, cups, or a pudding basin.

Swinborne's Pastrycook and Confectioner.

Carrot Pudding, No. 1.

Quarter lb. mashed carrot, 1 lb. bread crumbs, 3 oz. suet, ½ lb stoned raisins, 2 oz. sugar, 2 eggs. Mix rather stiffly with milk. Boil two and a half hours.

Carrot Pudding, No. 2.

One lb. nicely mashed carrot, 2 lb. fine suet, ½ lb. sugar, 3 eggs, citron peel, a few bitter almonds[25], or the kernels of a few bitter apricots will do. Mix well, and boil in a mould for two hours.

Easy Pudding.

Three quarters lb. flour, 6 oz. butter, ¼ lb. sugar, 4 eggs, and a few currants. Boil in a mould three hours.

Lemon Pudding, Baked.

One lb. bread crumbs, the yolks of 4 eggs, ¼ lb. sugar, the grated rind and juice of 1 lemon, 2 oz, butter. Bake in well-greased pie dish.

Currant Dumplings.

Take about 1 lb. flour, 3 lb. currants, ¼ lb. sugar, ¼ lb. suet, and mix with teaspoonful of baking powder, not too stiffly. This will make 6 or 8 dumplings. Put a plate in the bottom of the saucepan of boiling water, and boil the puddings in small cloths for about an hour.

---

[25] Bitter almonds are difficult to find nowadays—they are illegal in the United States!—so almond essence may be substituted

Pyramid Pudding.

Soak a few small sponge cakes in milk, say 6, and pile them up carefully in a glass dish, putting first 3, then a layer of jam, then 2 with some more jam, and the remaining 1 on the top. Just before serving pour some cream or custard over the whole.

Swinborne's Pastrycook and Confectioner.

Queen Pudding.

One lb. bread crumbs to be mixed with the yolks of 3 or 4 eggs, tablespoonful of white sugar, a little essence of lemon, and a little milk. This is to be baked until it is a light golden brown. Spread over it some apricot or other light-coloured jam (English apricot is the best); over this jam spread the whites of the eggs which have been beaten to a stiff froth. It can be made to look still prettier if a little of the white froth of the egg be mixed with one drop of prepared cochineal, and dotted over the jugged tops of the snow. Return the pudding to the oven, and watch it with door open a few moments, until the snow is set, but do not leave it long enough to get brown. It is well, if the pudding be wanted the following day, to leave adding the snow until just before using.

Sweet Potato Pudding, Baked.

Six good-sized potatoes grated raw, 1 tablespoonful of butter, 1 tablespoonful of lard, 1 pint molasses or golden syrup, 3 tablespoonfuls brown sugar, 3 pints of milk, 1 egg, 1 teaspoonful each of cloves, allspice, and ginger, 2 teaspoonfuls of salt; water to make a soft batter; stir two or three times while baking. Bake slowly for two hours.

Royal Baker and Pastrycook.

Fairy Pudding.

Soak 1 oz. packet of Swinborne's isinglass or gelatine in 1½ pints of milk, then dissolve it over the fire, adding 3 oz.

sugar, the peel of a lemon, and the well-beaten yolks of 5 eggs. Stir till the whole becomes the thickness of a custard, strain it through muslin into a basin, and stir occasionally till nearly cold. Place some crystallized fruits at the bottom of a mould previously wetted with cold water; pour in the pudding, and fill the centre with a few Savoy biscuits. Serve with some fruit syrup in the dish, or make a sauce in the following manner: put a tablespoonful of jam, a glass of wine, and 1 oz. of castor sugar, in a saucepan with a little water, and melt it over the fire, strain through a sieve, and when cold pour it around the pudding.

Swinborne's Pastrycook and Confectioner.

Favourite Pudding.

A few sponge cakes sliced, apricot jam or orange marmalade, 2 tablespoonfuls white sugar, and the whites of 4 eggs. Place in layers in a mould and boil or bake in a buttered pie dish. Dip the sponge cake slices into milk first.

Black-cap Pudding.

One lb. bread crumbs, 3 eggs, 2 oz. butter, mix with milk or cream to a stiff batter. Throw a few currants into the bottom of the mould after greasing before the mixture is poured in. Boil two hours.

Date Pudding.

One lb. dates well chopped up to be added to 1 lb. bread crumbs, ½ lb. suet, ¼ lb. sugar, salt, 3 eggs, and a little spice. Beat all together with a little milk, and boil for three hours.

Vanilla Pudding (German).

Three-quarters of a pound of stale bread crumbs, 1 pint of fresh milk or cream, 2 oz. butter, ¼ lb. almonds finely minced, 4 oz. castor sugar, 10 eggs, and some essence of vanilla. Put the bread crumbs into the milk to soak for two or three hours, beat them and the butter with a fork, then add the yolks of the eggs, almonds, sugar, and vanilla, and beat thoroughly for fifteen minutes, always in the same direction; whisk the whites of the eggs into a stiff froth, and mix thoroughly with the other ingredients, and pour all into an oiled shape, plunge into boiling water, and let it boil uninterruptedly for two and a half hours. Serve this pudding with schaum sauce.

Sylvia's Home Journal.

Yorkshire Pudding.

Mix 3 tablespoonfuls of flour smoothly with 1 pint of milk, ½ teaspoonful salt, and 1 egg beaten to a froth. 1 egg beaten in this manner will go as far as 2 lightly done. Put a few spoonfuls of the gravy from under the roasting meat into a dripping tin, pour in the pudding, put a few more spoonfuls of gravy over it, and bake in a moderately hot oven. Serve, cut up into three-cornered pieces.

Potato Pudding, No. 1.

Take 1 lb. mashed potatoes, with it add about 100 sweet or 20 bitter almonds finely stamped, ½ lb. sugar, and 8 eggs. Mix well together and bake in a well-greased mould.

Potato Pudding, No. 2.

Some mashed potatoes, 3 eggs, 1 tablespoonful butter, ½ cup of sugar, 1 glass of light wine, a little salt, and ground nutmeg. Mix with about ½ pint of milk, and bake. If it be preferred richer, add more butter, some almonds, and more eggs.

Bachelor's Pudding.

Half a pound of bread, 1½ cups of flour, 1 cup of currants, ½ cup of butter or dripping, mix with 1½ cups of milk, 1 teaspoonful carbonate of soda, some lemon juice, a little ground ginger, and one wineglassful of brandy. Boil for two hours.

Flour Pudding.

Take 1 pint of milk, 9 eggs, beat well together; take 9 spoonfuls of flour, mix it smoothly with cold milk, and add to the former. Grease a basin well with butter, and pour it in. Tie a floured pudding cloth over the top, see the water in the pot is boiling, and let it remain one and a half hours. Serve with a sweet wine sauce.

Hasty Pudding.

Two tablespoonfuls of flour, 4 eggs, ½ teaspoonful soda, rather less of salt; ½ pint of milk, and a little ground cinnamon. Bake in a greased dish one hour.

Bread-and-rice Dumplings.

Soak some white bread in water, drain it, and mix with an equal quantity of boiled rice. Take 8 beaten eggs, and 1 tablespoonful of butter melted, and stir all together with a little flour.

Add raisins or currants, form into dumplings, placing each in a small cloth, and plunge them into boiling water for about three quarters of an hour.

Custard Pudding, Boiled.

Quarter lb. flour, 6 oz. sugar, 1 quart of milk, and 6 eggs. Mix the flour with a portion of the milk, and boil the rest with the sugar, some ground cinnamon, or ginger if liked; then add the flour, and when sufficiently thick, the yolks of the eggs, and lastly the whites beaten to a froth. Stir very quickly, pour into a mould flavoured with almond essence. Tie securely with a cloth, plunge into boiling water, and cook one hour. Sprinkle with white sugar before serving.

Soda Pudding, Boiled.

Three cups flour, 1 cup sugar, 1 cup raisins, 1 tablespoonful ginger, 1 teaspoonful carbonate of soda, ½ cup of butter, ½ cup of dripping, and 2 cups of lukewarm water. Melt the butter and dripping in the water, mix all together, and boil for about two hours.

Chiswick Pudding.

Take 6 oz. of crushed white sugar and dissolve it in 1 pint of milk, put it into an enamelled or well-tinned bright saucepan, and place over a slow fire. Add ¼ lb. good butter, and stir until it shows no sign of clinging to the saucepan. On removing it from the fire, add 4 eggs, previously well beaten, and 1 teaspoonful essence of vanilla. Have ready a mould well greased with butter, and pour in the mixture. Set the mould in a saucepan of boiling water over the fire for an hour. When the mould is removed place it a minute into cold water, remove and lay a plate over the top, turn it over, and the pudding will turn out well. Stick it then all over with blanched almonds.

Bread Pudding, Baked, No. 1.

Put 1 pint of stale bread into a pudding pan; cover it with 1 quart of milk, and soak thirty minutes; the bread should absorb all the milk; beat the yolks of 4 eggs, 1 cupful of sugar, and 1 oz. butter together until light; add them to the bread and milk, with the grated rind of a lemon, and bake in a moderate oven half an hour; beat the whites of the eggs until light, and add 4 tablespoonfuls of powdered sugar; beat until stiff; put a thin layer of jelly on the top of the pudding, then a layer of the white of the eggs, then another layer of jelly and another of the beaten whites; put into the oven to brown slightly. This pudding is good served either hot or cold; if served cold, use simple cream as an accompaniment; if hot, a lemon or creamy sauce.

Light Bread Pudding.

Beat up 2 eggs with ½ pint of milk, sweeten and flavour with nutmeg or vanilla; then grate into it as much stale bread as will make a very light consistency, put it in a basin, and boil for one hour; serve with a sweet or wine sauce, if liked.

Bread Pudding, Baked, No. 2.

Two oz. stale bread crumbs, 1 egg, ½ pint of milk, one pinch of nutmeg, 2 oz. sugar; put the bread crumbs, milk, sugar, and flavouring into a stew pan, let it simmer for five minutes, then draw the stew pan to the side and let the mixture cool; beat the egg well, pour the milk and bread into a small pie dish, mixing well with the egg, put into an oven and bake a golden brown. It should be cut into thin slices.

Ginger Pudding.

Half pound flour, ¼ lb. suet, ¼ lb. moist sugar, 2 large teaspoonfuls of grated ginger. Shred the suet very finely, mix it with the flour, sugar, and ginger; stir all well together; butter a basin and put the mixture in dry; tie a cloth over, and boil for three hours.

Apricot Pudding.

Beat to a cream 3 oz. butter with 3 oz. sugar, and the yolks of 3 eggs; then add the whites beaten to a stiff froth, and ½ lb. bread crumbs. Mix all well together. Take a buttered mould, put a layer of the mixture, then one of apricot jam, and so on, till the mould is full. Cover with buttered paper and boil two hours. Melt a little apricot jelly and pour over the pudding before serving.

Sylvia's Home Journal.

Welsh Pudding.

Take some small slices of buttered bread, spread jam over them, place in a pie dish, leave to soak awhile with hot milk or water, then fill up the dish with a custard of eggs and milk, and bake for about an hour.

Mariette Pudding.

Half a pound bread crumbs,½ lb. beef suet, ½ lb. brown sugar, 3 lemons, 3 eggs. Mix well, using grated rind and juice of the lemons. Boil in a basin for 2 hours. Serve hot with sweet sauce.

German Dumplings, No. 1.

Boil together 2 cups of milk, and 2 tablespoonfuls butter, stir in gradually 1 cupful of flour, continue to stir till it does not cling to the spoon any more, then turn it out to cool. When cold enough, mix in first the yolks and then the whites of 3 eggs whisked separately; then make into dumplings, and boil for half an hour in milk and water.

German Dumplings, No. 2.

One cup of flour, 1½ cups of milk, 3 eggs and 1 tablespoonful of butter. Mix and proceed as before.

Velvet Pudding.

Mix 2 tablespoonfuls maizena with a little cold milk, then add with it ½ cup white sugar, the yolks of 5 eggs, and some essence of lemon to 1 pint of hot milk. As soon as it thickens spread a layer of jam over it, above this the whites of the eggs previously beaten to a stiff froth. Place the pudding in the hot oven a few moments until the snow sets.

Adelaide's Pudding.

Mix 9 tablespoonfuls of flour with 2 pints of milk, 9 eggs, 1 cup of sugar, 1 teaspoonful of baking powder, essence to flavour. Bake, and serve with sweet sauce or stewed fruit.

Thick Milk Pudding, Baked.

Three tablespoonfuls of flour, 8 eggs, 1 cup of thick milk, 1 cup of butter melted. Mix and bake in a moderately hot oven. Add sugar if liked.

Citron Pudding.

One oz. packet gelatine to be soaked in cold water for an hour, then add 1 cup of boiling water, a large cupful of sherry wine, ½ lb. white sugar, juice of 3 citrons or lemons, and the yolks of 6 eggs; stir all together on the fire till it slightly thickens. Before putting into the mould the whites of 2 eggs must be added well beaten. Stir the whole well together, and bake in a buttered pie dish.

Templar's Pudding.

Beat ¼ lb. butter to a cream, and stir into it 4 eggs and ¼ lb. sugar. Cover the bottom of a pie dish with bread crumbs, spread with apricot jam, and pour the mixture over it; then bake.

Apple Fool.

This is a cheap, good, and wholesome treat for children. Soak a little white bread in milk, and beat it up with the apples, after they are slowly baked, and the peel and pulp taken away. Add a little sugar and a teaspoonful or two of fresh milk, or condensed milk will answer the same purpose.

Baked Pudding without Eggs.

At breakfast time put 1 tablespoonful of rice, 1 tablespoonful of tapioca, and a little essence, into a 3-pint pie dish with 2 cupfuls of water, and 1 cup of sweet milk. Let it soak for two hours, stirring constantly. Put 1 tablespoonful of brown sugar and a little salt to it, and some very little bits of butter on the top, and put it into an oven moderately warm. For the first half-hour stir it constantly; at dinner time you will have a pudding far exceeding in richness one made with eggs, and it has a nice flavour. Sago, tapioca, or rice alone is equally good.

Saffron Pudding, Cornish.

Tapioca, rice, and maccaroni puddings are prepared in the usual way, with a few saffron threads, placed awhile in a little hot water, which is strained then added to the pudding.

Friar's Omelet.

Stew 6 or 7 good-sized apples, as for apple sauce, stir in when cooked and still warm butter of the size of a nutmeg and 1 cupful of sugar; when cold stir in 3 well-beaten eggs and a little lemon juice. Now put a small piece of butter into a pan, and when hot throw in a cupful of bread crumbs; stir them over the fire until they are of a light brown colour. Butter a mould, and sprinkle crumbs on the bottom and sides, then fill in with apple preparation; sprinkle top with bread crumbs; bake for fifteen or twenty minutes, and turn out on a large flat dish. It can be eaten with or without sweet sauce.

Rhubarb and Bread-and-butter Pudding.

Prepare some rhubarb stalks, as for a pie, cover the bottom of a buttered pudding dish with slices of bread and butter; cover with the rhubarb sliced rather thinly; sprinkle well with sugar, then place another layer of bread and butter, and so on until the dish is full. Cover and steam whilst baking for an hour; then remove the lid and bake for ten minutes while browning.

Roly-poly Jam Pudding.

Form a crust of flour, suet or dripping, a little salt, and ½ teaspoonful baking powder. Roll it out thinly, spread well over with jam, roll it up, place in a wet pudding cloth, keeping its long form, pin the cloth in the centre, tie each end, and boil in a saucepan (having a small plate at the bottom) for two hours.

Castle Puddings.

Two eggs, ¼ lb. sugar, ¼ lb. butter, ¼ lb. flour; beat the butter to a cream, and add to it the sugar finely pounded, the eggs and flour; mix well; bake for three-quarters of an hour in a moderate oven in small cups. When done, turn on to a dish, and cover with thick sauce, flavoured with wine or essence of vanilla.

Bread-and-butter Pudding.

Butter some nicely shaped pieces of bread, cut off the crust, lay them in a pie dish, sprinkle a few currants between the slices, and a little white sugar. Pour a little boiling water over the bread to swell it, cover over with a flat dish. Have a custard ready of 3 or 4 eggs and some milk; fill the dish with it, and bake in a sharp oven till the top crust is dry and crisp.

Rhubarb Pie.

Pare the rhubarb, cut it up into short pieces. If it be very tender it will cook sufficiently in the pie, which must not be too hurriedly baked, but if the rhubarb be rather stringy it is well to boil it awhile with sugar before placing in the pie dish. Sprinkle the pie before serving with white sugar. Milk or cream is generally liked with it.

Rhubarb Pudding.

Prepare the rhubarb as for the pie, line the basin with crust, place the rhubarb in it, sweeten to taste, and boil from one and a half to two hours.

Rhubarb, Stewed.

Pare it, cut it up into pieces, about ½ inch in length, put it over a gentle fire, with sugar to taste, and a very little water. When tender it is ready. Serve with milk or cream, or spread on slices of bread for children, as it is very wholesome.

Swiss Pudding.

Quarter lb. grated cheese, 2 eggs, butter, and milk. Mix into a stiff batter, and boil for one and a half hours.

Tapioca Puddings.

Soak the tapioca in water until it swells and is quite tender, then add some white sugar and essence. Make a custard of eggs and milk, in a sufficient quantity that the tapioca will not bake dry, pour it over when it is rather cooled, and grate nutmeg or sprinkle a little spice lightly over the top. Remove from the oven as it becomes a light brown. Its richness, as of other suchlike puddings, is improved if a tiny lump or two of butter be placed on the top of it.

Sweet Maccaroni and Vermicelli Puddings.

Boil a sufficient quantity in milk and water, placing it into it when boiling with a pinch of salt, stirring it often to prevent its burning. When it is swollen well, place it in a pie dish, making it rather more than half full, and proceed as with the tapioca pudding.

Sago Pudding.

Prepare in the same way as the maccaroni.

Pumpkin Fritters.

Take some mashed pumpkin, the brighter the yellow the better, add to it a little flour, sugar, beaten egg, and ½ teaspoonful baking powder. Mix well together with a little milk until it is of the consistency of thick batter. Place in the frying pan some dry dripping or butter, and when it is well melted, pour in a little of the batter, say about 2 tablespoonfuls for each fritter. After a minute, turn them over, and fry till a light brown. Serve with white sugar sprinkled over them.

Apricot Fritters.

Make a batter as above, then proceed as with the pumpkin fritters, only throw in a few sliced apricots into the batter, and take care each fritter gets a portion of the fruit. Canned or tinned apricots answer the purpose well, but do not use the syrup of them. Other tinned fruits, apples, etc., can also be used. Serve sprinkled with sugar.

Orange Fritters.

Make a batter as before, pare and slice the oranges, drop them into the batter, and proceed as in apricot fritters.

Banana Fritters.

Prepare the batter as in the apricot fritters, pare the bananas, slice them thinly in half the length of each, and proceed as before.

Orange Tart.

Pare 4 oranges, and press out the juice from them. Boil their peel until quite soft, then pass it through a coarse sieve or colander, add to it 2 eggs, well beaten, the juice of 2 oranges, and 2 tablespoonfuls of white sugar. Mix it well together. Roll out the paste, spread it with this mixture, and bake.

Orange Float.

Ingredients: Four tablespoonfuls of "Maizena", juice and pulp of 2 lemons, 1 coffee-cup of sugar, 1 quart of water, the whites of 3 eggs, 4 or 5 sliced oranges, vanilla.

Directions: mix in the water the juice and pulp of the lemons and the sugar. Boil sufficiently to dissolve the sugar, and then strain, and again bring to near boiling; now add the "Maizena", previously dissolved in a little cold water; stir till it boils; boil for five minutes; when cool, pour it over the sliced oranges; over the top spread the beaten whites of the eggs, sweetened and flavoured with a few drops of vanilla.

Duryea.

Lemon Meringue.

Ingredients: Four tablespoonfuls of "Maizena", 1 tablespoonful and 1 teacup of white sugar, juice and grated rind of 1 lemon, 3 eggs, and 1 quart of milk.

Directions: dissolve the "Maizena" in a little cold milk, add the tablespoonful of white sugar, the grated rind of the lemon, and the yolks of the eggs; beat well together, add the quart of nearly boiling milk, stir and boil for five minutes, then pour it on a platter so it will be nearly one inch in thickness; beat up the whites of the eggs with the juice of the lemon and the teacup of white sugar to a stiff froth, then spread over the pudding and brown in the oven.

Duryea.

Part XVII. Cakes, Buns, etc.

Effectual Icing for Cakes.

Beat up the whites of 4 new-laid eggs, adding a sufficient quantity of finely sifted white sugar to make the mixture of the consistency of thick cream, continue to beat it, mixing in little by little the juice of 1 lemon; still beat it until it hangs from the fork; it is then ready for use. Smooth it well over the cakes with a soft brush, then place them (door open) in a cool oven for a few minutes, watching them the while, then put them in a dry room until next day. To colour the icing add a drop of prepared cochineal to a little of it, and dot with it over the cake, or to form a threaded pattern, gum a piece of paper into a cone shape, and inject the icing through the end on to the cake as desired.

Gingerbread, No. 1.

Two and a half lb. of flour, ¾ lb. treacle or golden syrup, 4 oz. ground ginger, a dessertspoonful of caraway seeds, 2 oz. fine orange peel, ¼ lb. butter melted, a few blanched almonds cut up, ½ lb. honey or ½ lb. sugar, and 4 oz. carbonate of soda. Mix all into the dough, making it moderately stiff, working it well. When this is done put in rather more than 4 oz. tartaric acid. Place the dough into a greased shallow tin, and bake slowly for two hours.

Gingerbread, No. 2.

One and a half lb. treacle, 1½ lb. flour, ½ lb. butter well beaten, ½ lb. coarse sugar, ¼ lb. candied peel cut finely, ½ oz. ground ginger, 6 eggs, the yolks and whites beaten separately, and a teaspoonful of carbonate of soda. Mix well together, and roll out to 4 inch thick, bake for two hours in a slow oven.

Ginger Cakes.

One lb. flour, 1 teaspoonful of baking powder, ¼ lb. sugar, 6 oz. butter, 1 oz. ground ginger, and 2 eggs. Mix flour, baking powder, and ginger together. In another basin beat the butter to a cream, add the beaten eggs, and strew the sugar on to it; then, lastly, mix in the flour, etc., gradually. Roll out and cut into small cakes with a wineglass or tumbler, and bake.

Almond Cake.

Two pints of flour, 1 pinch of salt, 4 eggs, 5 oz, castor sugar or ordinary white sugar, 7 oz. of thoroughly pounded almonds, and a lump of butter the size of an egg. Mix all thoroughly together, and bake.

Mrs Winslow's Family Almanac.

Plain Plum Cake.

Eight oz. flour, 5 oz. butter (or 2 quantity each of dripping and butter), 5 oz. currants, 5 oz. sultana or stoned raisins, 1 oz. candied peel, 1 oz. sweet almonds cut up very small, 1½ teaspoonfuls baking powder, 1 lb. brown sugar, and 3 eggs. Mix this all well together, and bake for two hours in a slow oven.

Mrs. Winslow's Family Almanac.

Bath Buns.

Mix well together with the hand 2 lb. flour with ½ lb. fresh butter, which has been made liquid by a gentle heat, add to this mixture the yolks of 2, and the white of 1 egg, 3 tablespoonfuls of cream, and the same quantity of good yeast, all well beaten together. If the mixture be rather stiff add a little milk. When all is thoroughly mixed set it in a warm place, where it may rise for about half an hour; mix in some sweets called caraway comfits, and keep some to sprinkle over top of buns. Mould into shape and bake on buttered tins. They will bake quickly.

Ordinary Plain Buns, No. 1.

One lb. flour, mixed with 2 oz, good butter, 2 oz. sugar, and a little grated nutmeg, some powdered ginger or any other spice, add a spoonful of cream to 2 oz. of yeast, make the whole into a light paste, with as much milk as may be required. Place it near the fire till it rises, divide it into suitable-sized buns, and bake in a quick oven.

Buns, No. 2.

To 1 quartern ordinary dough add 1 lb. of well washed and dried currants, ¼ lb. loaf sugar, and 6 oz of lard. Shape into buns, and bake. A second recipe is as follows: rub 2 oz. of butter or good lard into 1 lb, flour, 2 oz. sugar, a grate of nutmeg, and a few caraway seeds or currants, well washed and dried. Mix a teaspoonful of baking powder with as much milk as will make it all to a light paste; set it by the fire to rise, then bake on buttered tins. Just before they are done brush each bun lightly over with a little milk, and, if you like, a little pounded sugar, and return them to the oven to glaze.

Scottish Shortbread, Good.

With 1 lb. flour mix well 2 oz. sifted sugar, 1 oz. candied peel sliced small, make this into a paste with from 8 to 9 oz. good butter, made sufficiently warm to be liquid; press the paste together with the hands, and mould it upon tins into large cakes nearly one inch thick, pinch the edges, and bake the shortbread in a moderately warm oven for twenty minutes or longer should it not be crisp, but do not allow it to become deeply coloured.

Mrs. Winslow's Family Almanac.

Jam Rolls.

Well butter a paper, and put it on a flat baking tin. Pour the cake mixture on to the paper very thinly, and bake in a hot oven for seven minutes. Turn out quickly on to a well loaf-

sugared paper, spread with jam at once and roll. For the mixture take 1 cup of flour, ½ cup white sugar, 1 heaped teaspoonful of Royal baking powder, with 1 small cup of milk, and 1 beaten egg. Mix it well together.

Pound Cake, No. 1.

Beat to a cream 1 lb. butter, and work it smoothly with 1 lb. sifted loaf sugar, and 9 well-beaten eggs. Mix in lightly 1 lb. flour, ½ a nutmeg grated, and a little cinnamon. Beat all together half an hour, and bake for one hour. A little candied peel chopped with some sweet almonds, and ½ lb. currants, will make the cake rich.

Pound Cake, No. 2.

One lb. flour, 14 oz. butter, 10 eggs, 1 lb. sugar, 1 lb. currants, and ¾ lb. of raisins chopped fine, 1 oz. peel, 1 wineglass French brandy, 1 teaspoonful soda, 1 ditto cream of tartar. In mixing put the brandy, sugar, and butter together, to this add the flour, then the fruit, and soda, etc., lastly the eggs well beaten. Beat well together, and bake rather slowly.

Pound Cake, No. 3.

Half lb. butter, 1 lb. flour, ½ lb. currants, ½ lb. moist sugar, 1 teaspoonful of milk, 3 eggs, and 1½ teaspoonfuls Royal baking powder. Melt the butter before using. Mix well and bake in a moderate oven.

Honey Cake.

Three and a half lb. flour, 1½ lb. honey, ½ lb. sugar, ½ lb. butter, ½ grated nutmeg, 1 tablespoonful ground ginger, 1 teaspoonful of soda, 1 ditto cream of tartar. Mix together with milk rather stiffly, and bake.

Buns, No. 3.

Half a cup of butter, ½ cup of yeast, ½ cup of sugar, 1 cup of milk, flour enough to make a batter like griddle cakes. Let this rise till light, then add 1 cup of currants, cinnamon or nutmeg to taste, a little more flour, let it rise again, put in 2 teaspoonful of soda, cut in cakes, let them rise a third time, and bake.

Lemon Cake.

Three cups of sugar, 6 cups of flour, 1 cup of butter, 2 cups of sweet milk, 8 eggs, 2 tablespoonfuls soda, 4 tablespoonfuls cream of tartar, and 6 drops of lemon oil. Melt the butter, beat whites and yolks of the egg separately, mix all well together, adding last the milk with soda and cream of tartar dissolved in it. Add a little more milk if necessary.

Potato Cakes.

Take 6 cups of warm mashed potatoes, 1 cupful flour, 2 tablespoonfuls good dripping, and ½ cupful currants, a little finely chopped lemon peel, ½ teaspoonful baking powder, and pinch of salt, mix well together, roll out, score, and bake on a flat tin.

Tea Cake, No. 1.

One cup of sour milk, 1 cup of raisins, 1 cup of sugar, 1 egg, ½ cup of butter, 1 teaspoonful of soda, 2½ cups of flour, and some dark spice. Mix together and bake.

Tea Cake, No. 2.

Six lb. flour, 4 lb. sugar, 2 lb. butter or fat, 1 tablespoonful mixed spice, 1 tablespoonful of soda, and a pinch of tartaric acid. Melt the butter, mix, and bake.

American Tea Cakes.

One cup of butter, 2 cups of sugar, 1 cup of milk, 4 eggs, 6 cups of flour, 1 teaspoonful of soda, 2 of cream of tartar, or 2 teaspoonfuls Royal baking powder, and a little nutmeg ground. Roll out the paste, and cut it with a tumbler into cakes. Brush them with the white of an egg, and sprinkle on a little white sugar before baking.

French Cakes.

Half cup of butter, 2 teaspoonfuls of cream of tartar, 1 teaspoonful of soda, ½ cup of milk, 3 eggs, 3 cups of flour. Beat the eggs, add the milk, then the butter and sugar beaten together, then the flour with the cream of tartar rubbed in, then the milk and soda, lastly spice to taste, and ½ cup of currants if desired.

Bake rather slowly.

Bachelor Cake.

One lb. flour, ¾ lb. sugar, ½ lb. butter, ½ lb. currants, a wineglassful of brandy, ½ teaspoonful of soda, 1½ teaspoonfuls cream of tartar, 6 eggs, and a few stamped almonds. Melt the butter before using.

Excelsior Cake.

Three cups of sugar, 2 cups of flour, ½ cup of milk, 5 eggs, and 1 teaspoonful of soda. Mix as sponge cakes, No. 1.

Welcome Cake.

One and a half cups of sugar, ½ cup of butter, 3 cups of flour, 3 eggs, 1 teaspoonful of soda, 2 teaspoonfuls cream of tartar, 1 lb. stoned raisins, a little mixed peel, and ½ teaspoonful mixed spice.

Luncheon Cake.

Two lb. flour, 1 lb. sugar, ½ lb. currants, ½ lb. butter, a few caraway seeds, some grated nutmeg, ½ pint of milk, ½ teaspoonful of soda, and 4 eggs; stir all together, beat mixture for ten minutes, and bake in a quick oven, protected by oiled paper.

Queen Cake, No. 1.

Two cups of sugar, 1 cup of butter, 1 cup of sweet milk, 4 cups of flour, and 6 eggs.

Queen Cake, No. 2.

One lb. flour, ½ lb. butter, ½ lb. pounded loaf sugar, 3 eggs, 1 teaspoonful cream of tartar, 1 teaspoonful of soda, ½ lb. currants or muscatel raisins, essence of lemon or almond to taste. Mix, and bake slowly.

Good Christmas Cake.

One lb. butter, 1 lb. sugar, 9 eggs, 1 lb. flour, 3 lb. currants, 2 lb. stoned raisins, ½ a teacupful of brandy, ¾ lb, citron peel, 1 grated nutmeg, some pounded mace and cinnamon. Rub the butter and sugar together. Beat the yolks and whites of the eggs separately, then add first the yolks, then the whites to the mixture. Cut the citron into such slices as you like, and add it just before putting the mixture into the pan with the other fruit. Butter the cake tin carefully, and line it with thin paper, putting also a little butter on it too. Do not bake the cake in too quick an oven. After it is baked take it out of the paper, let it cool, resting it on the bottom of a hair sieve.

Matrimony Tart.

Pare and core 1 dozen nice-sized apples, put them into a saucepan with a little water to keep them from burning; boil until you can pulp them; do not forget to frequently stir them; then add ¼ lb. currants, 2 oz. candied peel, and enough sugar to season it nicely; if liked, also add a little grated nutmeg. Pour the mixture into a large tart dish, which has been lined with a thin paste, then place another layer over the top, and press the edges together all round. Bake awhile, and sprinkle with white sugar before serving.

Home Cake.

Six lb. flour, 1 lb. fat, 1 lb. sugar, 3 eggs, and 1 cup of yeast. Knead the cake overnight and in the morning again, then put it into pans. Let it rise again before baking.

Cream Cake.

One cup of cream, 1 cup of sugar, 2½ cups of flour, 2 eggs, and 2 teaspoonfuls Royal baking powder.

Puff Cake.

Three cups of flour, 2 cups of sugar, 1 cup of butter, 3 eggs, 1 cup of milk, and 2 teaspoonfuls Royal taking powder.

Potato Puff.

Two cups of cold mashed potatoes, 1 cup of milk, 2 tablespoonfuls of butter melted, 2 eggs beaten very lightly; stir in the butter first, then the eggs; when smooth add milk and a little salt; beat thoroughly, put into a buttered dish, and bake in a quick oven until it is a nice brown.

Jenny Lind Cake.

Two cups of flour, 1 cup of milk, 1 cup of sugar, 1 egg, a piece of butter the size of an egg, 1 teaspoonful cream of tartar, and ½ teaspoonful carbonate of soda. To mix: the butter, sugar, and egg is to be thoroughly well mixed together with the hand; then in a separate basin mix the cream of tartar, soda, and milk together; add the former first to the flour, then the latter mixture, and beat up well with the hand. Line a cake tin with buttered paper and bake in a moderately hot oven for one hour. To make a richer cake add more eggs and butter.

Rock Cake, No. 1.

Take as much flour as necessary, also baking powder, 2 eggs, milk, sugar, currants, and dripping or butter. Mix it stiffly, and drop on the floured hot oven. Glaze with a little moistened dark sugar.

Rock Cake, No. 2.

One lb. flour, ½ lb. butter, ½ lb. sugar, one-third of a lb. currants, ¼ lb. shred candied peel, pinch of salt, and five eggs. Beat the yolks and whites separately, add the former first, then the latter. Mix well rather stiffly, and drop in lumps about the size of a walnut on to a well-heated greased tin, and bake in a quick oven.

German Cakes.

Five eggs are to be mixed separately, one after another, with ½ lb. butter, slightly melted, and ½ lb. sugar. Flour is then to be dredged to it till it becomes a nice thick batter; the mixture is then to be laid thinly on small tin plates, and jam to be spread thinly over when baked. The cakes are then to be laid one over the other, and cut to any desired shape.

Scotch Scones, No. 1.

One lb. flour, 2 oz. butter, 1 tablespoonful of good baking powder, a little salt, and sufficient milk to roll out to a thick paste. Roll it out to about 1 inch thick, score with a knife into three-cornered parts, so as to divide easily when baked. A quick oven. The scones look nice if just before they are done they are brushed over with the white of an egg, sprinkled with powdered sugar, and left in the oven awhile to colour. Buttermilk is sometimes used to mix them with, but if so, the baking powder will not be necessary.

White Mountain Cake.

Two cups of sugar, two-thirds of a cup of butter, the whites of 7 eggs well beaten, two-thirds of a cup of sweet milk, 2 cups of flour, 1 cup of maizena, and 2 teaspoonfuls baking powder. Bake in jelly cake tins. Frosting: whites of three eggs, and some sugar beaten together, not so stiff as usual for frosting; spread over the cake, add some grated cocoanut; then put your cakes together; put cocoanut or frosting on top.

Duryea's Recipes.

Sponge Cake, No. 1.

Two oz. flour, 3 oz. sugar, a little salt, 2 eggs. The eggs must be broken on to the sugar in a basin which should stand in a larger one of hot water till they get warm whilst beating, which operation should take from five to ten minutes. Now take a teaspoonful of baking powder, and mix it with a tablespoonful of milk; add it to the flour, also the eggs gradually, and beat all together a minute. Line the cake tin with greased paper, and bake in a hot oven for ten minutes.

Sponge Cake, No. 2.

Take 7 eggs, break into a basin, leaving out 2 of the whites, and beat thoroughly; put 1 lb. loaf sugar into a pan, add a wineglassful of cold water, and heat over the fire till nearly boiling; pour this to the eggs, and whisk 30 minutes till cool; add the grated rind of a lemon, and ¾ lb. flour well dried. Pour the mixture into moulds, and bake in a moderate oven.

Sylvia's Home Journal.

Sponge Isabel Cake.

Into 1 breakfastcupful of flour mix well ¾ cupful of white sugar, and ½ teaspoonful of baking powder. Whisk well 4 large eggs, and to them gradually add the other ingredients, then beat the whole well, and bake slowly for half an hour in paper-lined cake tin. This is an easily made tea cake.

Currant Loaves.

For 2 loaves: 3¼ lb. flour, 1 lb. butter, 1 lb. sugar, 1 ¼ lb. currants, 3 oz. candied peel cut fine, 4 eggs, 1½ pints of milk, 1 oz. baking powder, and a little salt. Mix, divide into two parts, and bake in square cake tins.

Sweet Potato Buns.

Three large sweet potatoes, 1½ pints flour, pinch of salt, 1½ teaspoonfuls Royal baking powder, 1 pint of cream. Boil potatoes tender, rub them very fine with cream. Sift together flour, salt, and powder; add to potato preparation; mix into rather firm smooth dough; form into round pieces size of small egg; lay on greased tin; bake in hot oven twenty minutes.

Royal Baker and Pastrycook.

American Cake.

Two cups of flour, 1 cup of sugar, 1 cup of milk, 1 tablespoonful of butter, 1 teaspoonful of soda, some lemon juice or essence, 1 dessertspoonful of rose water, and a few caraway seeds.

N.B. The "Royal" flavouring extracts of rose, lemon, vanilla, almond, nutmeg, cinnamon, etc., are most useful, and highly recommended.

Jessie's Cake.

Three eggs, 2 tablespoonfuls of butter, 1 cup of sugar, 3 cups of flour, 1 cup of milk, 1 teaspoonful of soda, and 2 teaspoonfuls of caraway seeds. Beat the butter to a cream, add the sugar and yolks of the eggs, lastly the whites well beaten to a froth. Mix well, and bake in a moderately quick oven.

Aniseed Cake.

Four cups of flour, 1½ cups of half butter and half fat, 1 teaspoonful of aniseed, 1 teaspoonful of soda, and a little lemon juice or essence. Mix all to a thick batter, with either milk and water, or water alone.

Savoy Cake.

Take the weight of 4 eggs in pounded loaf sugar, the weight of 7 eggs in flour, and a little grated lemon peel, essence of almonds or orange flower water for flavouring. Beat the yolks of 7 eggs separately from the whites, add to the yolks the sugar and flavouring. When the whites of the eggs are beaten to a froth, add it to the yolks and continue beating. Put the flour to it by degrees, and continue to beat for about a quarter of an hour. Butter a mould, and bake the cake slowly in it.

To ice the cake: beat the whites of 4 eggs to a strong froth, and gradually sift in 1 lb. loaf sugar, which has been reduced to an extremely fine powder; beat the mixture well, and with a spoon or broad knife lay the icing equally over the cake; place in a very cool oven to dry and harden. Do not allow it to colour. If the icing is put on the cake as soon as it comes out of the oven, it then becomes firm and hard by the time the cake is cool.

Earnest Cake.

Take 1 cup of sugar, 3 eggs, ½ cup of butter, and enough milk and flour to make a soft batter. Bake rather quickly in paper-lined tin.

Plain Sweet Biscuits.

One lb. flour, 8 oz. white sugar, 3 oz. butter. Wet the butter with 3 well-beaten eggs, add 2 oz. caraway seeds, mix into a stiff paste, roll out, cut into rounds with a tumbler or other cutter, and bake three-quarters of an hour.

Mary's Tea Rusks.

Six cups of flour, 1 cup of sugar, 2 eggs, 2 teaspoonfuls soda, 3 teaspoonfuls cream of tartar, and 2 cups of milk, to be mixed together with a piece of butter the size of an egg. Roll out, cut into lengths, and bake.

Cocoanut Macaroons.

One lb. of grated cocoanut, ½ lb. sifted white sugar, whites of 2 eggs well beaten. Mix all well together, bake on thin paper in pieces about the size of a walnut in a rather slow oven.

Scotch Scones, No. 2.

One quart of flour, ½ teaspoonful of sugar, ½ teaspoonful of salt, 2 teaspoonfuls of Royal baking powder, 1 large tablespoonful of lard, 2 eggs, nearly 1 pint of milk. Sift together flour, sugar, salt, and powder; rub in lard, cold; add beaten eggs and milk; mix into dough smooth and just consistent enough to handle. Flour the board, turn out dough, give it one or two quick kneadings to complete its smoothness; roll it out with rolling pin to 3 inch in thickness, cut with sharp knife into squares, fold each in half to form three cornered pieces. Bake on hot griddle eight or ten minutes; brown on both sides.

Royal Baker and Pastrycook.

Minna's Biscuits.

One lb. flour, 4 eggs, ¾ lb. light sugar, a few caraway seeds. Beat the eggs and sugar first, then add the flour mixed dry with a teaspoonful of powdered ammonia, roll out in paste, then cut in biscuits with a wine glass or cutter.

Almond Macaroons.

One and a half lb. white loaf sugar, pounded very fine; 400 sweet and 100 bitter almonds, also pounded; the whites of 2 eggs beaten to a froth. To be baked in small lumps on greased paper in a slow oven. Use 1½ lb. flour.

Katrina's Biscuits.

One and a half lb. flour, 1 lb. sugar, 1 tablespoonful of butter, 2 or 3 eggs, 1 teaspoonful of soda, 1 teaspoonful of ground cinnamon, and 1 teaspoonful of ground ginger. Mix and roll out into a thin paste, cut into biscuits, and bake in a slow oven.

Anna's Biscuits.

Three lb. flour, 1½ lb. sugar, 2 teaspoonfuls soda, ½ pint of milk, 3 eggs, and some caraway seeds. Proceed as above.

Mamma's Biscuits.

One lb. white fine sugar, 1½ lb. flour, ½ teaspoonful of caraway seeds, 6 eggs well beaten; mix all well into the flour, knead with milk to the consistency of dough. Roll it out thin, and cut into small pieces. Bake on an oven tin in rather a slow oven.

Lena's Biscuits.

One lb. flour, ½ lb. sugar, 2 eggs beaten up, 1 teaspoonful of caraway seeds, and ¼ lb. butter. Mix all well together, roll out thinly, and cut into round biscuits, prick them, and bake them upon tins.

Sponge Biscuits.

Six eggs, 2 lb. flour, 2 lb. yellow sugar, 1 teaspoonful of soda, 1 teaspoonful of cream of tartar, and 1 tablespoonful of ground cinnamon. Whisk the whites of the eggs, and stir it into the sugar the evening before using. Next day to the other ingredients add the well-beaten yolks, 100 stamped sweet almonds and 25 bitter ones, or a little essence of almonds. Roll out, shape into biscuits, and bake quickly.

Soet Koek (Dutch).

Three lb. flour, 1½ lb. sugar, ground cinnamon, cloves, nutmeg, and ginger, about 1 tablespoonful; 2 eggs, a little potash, 1 teaspoonful of soda, 1 teaspoonful of cream of tartar, butter about the size of an egg. Mix stiffly either with water or milk. Roll out very thin, and after having cut it out into shape, glaze with a beaten egg. Bake until it looks hard and well cooked.

Rice Cake.

Quarter lb. ground rice, ¼ lb. flour, 4 eggs, ½ lb. white sugar, and flavouring. Mix well, bake in paper-lined tin in a moderately hot oven.

Scotch Oat Cakes.

Take ¾ lb. fine oatmeal, 2 teaspoonfuls bacon fat, ½ teacupful of cold water, ½ teaspoonful of carbonate of soda, 1 pinch of salt. Add 2 good handfuls of meal, put them into a bowl, with the water, soda, salt, and bacon fat; stir this mixture quickly with the hand, turn out cleanly on the board, on which you should have 2 or 3 handfuls of meal; knead more meal into it till it is of a proper consistency, but do not make it too stiff, as it will not work well; work it between the palms of the hands to make it flat; lay it on the board, flattening it and keeping it round; roll lightly with the roller, cut into four, and rub each piece with meal on both sides; put these pieces on the griddle, and when cooked on one side put them on a toaster before the fire, to dry the other side.

Sponge Rolls.

Three eggs, their weight in sifted loaf sugar, the weight of 1 egg in flour, and 1 teaspoonful of baking powder. This quantity will make 2 rolls.

Lemon Cakes.

Ten eggs, 3 tablespoonfuls orange flower water, ¾ lb. pounded loaf sugar, 1 lemon grated and its juice, ¾ 1b. flour, 1 dessertspoonful butter. Bake in tin lined with paper.

Silver Cake.

Two cups of flour, 1 cup of white sugar, ½ cup of milk, ½ cup of butter, the whites of 4 eggs, ½ teaspoonful of soda, ½ teaspoonful of cream of tartar.

Golden Cake.

One cup of butter, 2 cups of sugar, 3 cups of flour, ½ cup of milk, yolks of 6 eggs and 1 whole egg, 1 teaspoonful of cream of tartar, 1 teaspoonful of soda.

Wine Cake.

One and a half lb. flour, 1 lb. brown sugar, ½ lb. butter, 1 cup of currants, 1 cup of wine, 1 nutmeg ground, 1 teaspoonful of soda, 3 eggs, some comfits. Mix, and bake rather slowly. Sprinkle some comfits over the top of the cake.

Buttermilk Cake.

Three cups of flour, 2 cups of sugar, ¾ cup of buttermilk, some finely cut up naartje peel, and 5 eggs.

Short Cake.

Three lb flour, 1 lb sugar, ½ lb butter, ½ lard, and 2 teaspoonfuls cream of tartar. Mix with cold milk rather stiffly.

Birthday Cake.

Two cups of flour, 1 of sugar, 1 of milk, 4 eggs, 2 tablespoonfuls butter, 1 teaspoonful of soda, 2 teaspoonfuls cream of tartar, ½ lemon grated, juice of 1, a few currants, some citron cut fine, and a teaspoonful caraway seeds. Beat the whites of the eggs to a froth, beat butter with sugar, then add the well-beaten yolks. Stir the flour into the whole gradually, stick a few almonds, comfits, or hundreds and thousands sweets over the top, and bake slowly in a cake tin lined with buttered paper.

Almond Cake.

One lb. pounded almonds, 1 lb. white sugar, 1 tablespoonful of fine flour, 8 or 12 eggs beaten separately, the whites and yolks. For each egg beat the cake four minutes, and lastly stir in the almonds very gradually, and bake in a quick oven in tin lined with buttered paper.

Galette Cake.

Sift 1 lb. of the best flour, put it in a heap on the pastry board, make a hole in the middle, put into it a pinch of salt and ½ cup of sifted sugar, ¾ lb. butter, and ½ pint of water. Knead the ingredients together, and when they begin to mix sprinkle over by degrees ¼ pint of water, continuing to knead with the palm of the hand, and when the paste is perfectly smooth make it into a ball and let it lie for an hour. At the end of this time roll out the paste to the thickness of ½ inch. Mark the edges as for Scotch shortbread, put the cake on a baking sheet, brush over the top with yolk of egg, and score it in the form of diamonds. Bake in a quick oven for half an hour, or until the cake is elastic on the pressure of the finger.

Family Herald.

Plain Cake.

To 2 lb. flour add ½ lb. beef dripping or bacon fat, 2 lb, sultana or stoned raisins, ¼ lb. sugar, 1 oz. lemon peel, and a little salt. See the flour is dry, rub into it the dripping, taking care that both are well mixed and free from lumps; shred the lemon peel finely, and add with the salt sugar and sultanas. Take care the latter are well cleaned. Rub altogether, make a hole in the centre of the mass, and pour into it a tablespoonful of good yeast; then mix with warm water till the whole is of the consistency of moist dough, cover well, and stand in a warm place to rise. Make into two cakes, and bake in tins. Each cake will take about one hour and a half to bake in a moderate oven.

Heavy Cake, Cornish.

Take 6 cups of flour, 4 cup of dripping, 4 cup of sugar, 2 cupfuls of raisins, and a little salt. Rub the dripping first well into the flour, then add the other ingredients, mix with milk or water to a stiff paste, roll out to one and a half inches thick, and bake until nicely browned in a rather quick oven.

Saffron Cakes, Cornish, No. 1.

Cornish cakes are usually made of dough, instead of using baking powder, or other similar preparations, to lighten the mixture. The water which has stood on a pinch of saffron is often added to the mixture, and approved of, if the flavour be not too strong. It is considered wholesome, as it acts as a stimulant in cold weather. The plain cake above will make a good saffron one.

Saffron Cakes, No. 2.

Dry well a good pinch of saffron in the oven or elsewhere, rub it into fine powder, pour ½ cupful of hot water upon it, leaving it to soak for one day. Overnight take 4 lb. flour, and rub into it ½ lb. butter, and 1 lb. good dripping, then add ½ lb. white sugar, 1½ lb. currants, and ½ lb. sultana raisins, a little grated nutmeg, 1 teaspoonful salt, and mix well together. Make a hole in this mixture, and pour in 1 teacupful of warm water, and 1 teacupful of yeast. Mix yeast and water lightly together, sprinkle and cover over to rise until morning. Next morning add the water from the saffron to a sufficient quantity to knead up the cake. After kneading, cover until well risen. Make up into 4 cakes, and bake one and a half hours. These cakes will keep two or three weeks.

Arrowroot Cakes.

Mix 1 cup of arrowroot with 1 cup of butter well, then add 1 cup of sugar, pinch of salt, and 1 teaspoonful of carbonate of soda. Beat 3 eggs well, and add them to it. Mix well together, and bake in patty pans.

Surprise Cakes.

Into 1 lb. of flour mix ¼ lb. butter; melt another ¼ lb. butter, and to it give ¼ lb. white sugar, 2 well-beaten eggs, a few drops of essence of lemon, pinch of ground cinnamon, a little milk, and a teaspoonful of well-crushed carbonate of soda. Beat all together, and bake in patty pans.

Brighton Cakes.

Take 1 lb. sugar and 4 oz. butter, mix them together till quite smooth; then take 6 eggs, and mix them with the sugar and butter till the yolks are broken, then stir in ½ pint of milk, 1 lb. sifted flour, two heaped spoonfuls of baking powder, and pinch of salt. Mix them together, stir as little as possible, and bake in two buttered cake tins in a hot oven.

Raised Cake.

Six cups of raised dough, 2 cups of sugar, 4 eggs, 2 cups of butter, 1 lb. currants, and spice as liked. Knead together, let stand to rise again in a warm place, and bake.

Delicate Cake.

One cup of maizena, 1 of butter, 2 of sugar, 1 of sweet milk, 2 of flour, the whites of 7 eggs. Rub butter and sugar to a cream; mix 1 spoonful cream of tartar with the flour and maizena, ½ teaspoonful of soda with the sweet milk; add the milk and soda to the sugar and butter, then add flour, then the whites of the eggs, and flavour to taste. Never fails to be good.

Duryea's Maizena Recipes.

Sponge Cakes, No. 1.

Any of these recipes will make excellent sponge cakes. Break 5 eggs over ½ lb. powdered sugar, and beat altogether for fully half an hour. Take the weight of 2½ eggs in flour, grate the peel of a lemon into the flour. Add the beaten eggs to the flour. Beat it all up thoroughly, pour into a buttered tin, and put instantly into a slow oven.

Sponge Cakes, No. 2.

Break 7 eggs, and put the whites and the yolks into separate bowls. Take out the specks, and beat the yolks of the eggs, add ½ lb. of sifted sugar, the grated rind and strained juice of ½ lemon, 6 oz. of dried flour, and, lastly, the whites of the eggs whisked to a firm froth. Grease a hot tin with butter free from moisture. While still warm sift sugar upon it, pour in the butter, and bake the cake in a moderate oven. Time to bake, from three-quarters to one hour.

Almond Sponge Cakes, Very Superior.

Blanch 1 lb. of sweet almonds, throw them into cold water as they are done, dry them well, and pound smoothly, sprinkling the whole of 3 eggs on them during the process. Work thoroughly with them 1 spoonful of grated lemon rind, 1 lb. of powdered sugar, and the well-beaten yolks of 15 eggs. Take the remaining whites of the eggs (making altogether 15, inclusive of those which were mixed with the almond paste), whisk these to a firm froth, and stir them into the cake. Dredge into it ¼ 1b. of dried flour, and beat it briskly for a few minutes. Butter a mould, sift powdered sugar into it, pour the batter in till it is half full, and bake immediately. Let the cake stand a few minutes, turn it out carefully, and put it on a sieve. Time to bake, about one hour.

Wedding Cake.

Beat ½ lb. butter to cream; add the same weight of sugar, currants, sultana raisins, candied peel, cut small, and flour, 4 eggs, ½ nutmeg, grated, and a glass of brandy. Bake in a tin, lined with greased paper, for two or three hours in a steady oven. Buy of a confectioner 1 lb. almond paste; lay this on the top of the cake as soon as baked; then make the icing by mixing 1 lb icing sugar with the whites of 2 large and 3 small eggs, and a little lemon juice. It must be beaten until quite smooth; spread it roughly all over, and let it dry; then spread the second coating quite evenly with abroad paper knife. Ornament the cake by means of small white flowers, or silver sweetmeats, together with a little of the icing passed through a paper cone. This will weigh about 5½ lb. For a richer cake add 4 oz. each of dried cherries and sweet almonds to the mixture.

Strawberry Sweet Cake.

Take any kind of good cake batter you prefer, either sponge cake, cup or pound cake batter; use small patty pans; place in each enough of the batter to cover the bottom; set in the batter, points down, as many small-sized berries as can be thus placed without touching each other; drop a pinch of powdered sugar on each berry, and put over them a spoonful of batter. While the cakes are baking in a moderate oven, make a stiff frosting of the whites of eggs and sugar. When the cakes are done, spread the tops thickly with the frosting, and set it in large strawberries; remove the cap from each berry just as you place it on the cakes, and set them large end down; return to the oven for five minutes. These are delicious little cakes.

Rich Plum Cake.

Put 1½ lb. butter into a good-sized bowl, and with the hand beat it to a cream. Mix with it the whites of 8 fresh eggs whisked to a froth, and afterwards the yolks well beaten, and add a dessertspoonful of salt, 1 lb. powdered sugar, 1½ lb. flour,

2 lb. currants well washed, picked, and dried, 8 oz. each of candied lemon and citron cut into narrow strips, ½ oz. of mixed spice, 2 lb. almonds, blanched and pounded, the rind of 4 oranges rubbed upon 3 or 4 lumps of sugar, and then powdered. Add each ingredient separately, and beat it well in before adding another. A glassful of brandy may be stirred in if liked. If this cake is to be light, it should be beaten fully three-quarters of an hour. Line a tin with double folds of buttered paper, pour in the mixture, and bake the cake in a moderate oven. Put twelve folds of paper under the cake, and four or five on the top of it, to prevent it burning. Time to bake, three hours if made in one cake, one and a half hours each if made in two.

TRANSVAAL TOBACCO

(HOLLINS & ROCHER'S),

Old Judge and Progress Cigarettes

THE FAMOUS BULL DOG PIPE

And other Smokers' Requisites, at

A. H, McCAUSLAND

No. 1, GRAVE STREET,

2 DOORS FROM DARLING STREET.

THE PLACE

For a Choice Variety of Articles.

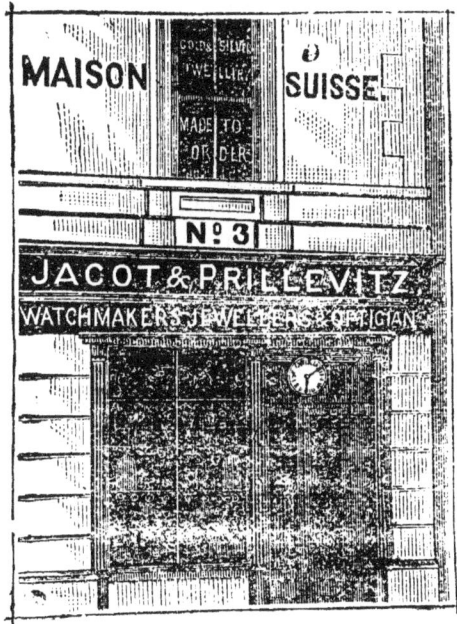

Church Street, Cape Town.

Part XVIII. Jellies, Sweetmeats, etc

The following eleven recipes of Swinborne's give some of the best ways of using isinglass. The quantity given in each recipe being calculated for ordinary temperature, a little more may be required in hot or wet weather where ice is not used.

Clear Wine Jelly.

One oz. packet of Swinborne's isinglass, 2 lemons, 5 oz. loaf sugar, ½ pint sherry, white and shells of 2 eggs, 1½ pints of water. Soak the isinglass for five minutes or longer in ½ pint water, then add 1 pint of boiling water, and stir till quite dissolved; add the rind and juice of 2 lemons (squeeze through muslin to keep out the pips, which give a bitter taste), with 5 oz. of loaf sugar, and ½ pint of sherry or other good white wine. Whisk the whites and shells of 2 eggs with a wineglassful of cold water, and stir them well into the whole; then boil five minutes without stirring; let it stand ten minutes near the fire, and then pass through a jelly bag till quite clear. This will produce a delicious jelly; more wine and less water, with brandy or any liquor to taste, will make it richer.

NOTE: See that the jelly bags, etc., are scrupulously clean. Stand in a warm place whilst the jelly is being strained; if placed in a draught or allowed to cool, the jelly will set before it is all passed through the bag; and, lastly, wet the moulds with cold water before pouring in the jelly, and when turning out dip the mould in hot water for an instant. A jelly should be just stiff enough to turn out of the mould without breaking, and in warm or sultry weather more isinglass may be required than in cold.

Clear Lemon Jelly.

One oz. packet of Swinborne's isinglass, 6 oz. loaf sugar, 3 lemons, the whites and shells of 2 eggs, 1 quart of water. Soak the isinglass in ½ pint of cold water, pour over it 1½ pints of boiling water, and stir till dissolved; put it into a saucepan with 6 oz. of loaf sugar, the peel of 2 lemons, and the juice of 3. Whisk the whites and shells of 2 eggs with a wineglassful of cold water, and stir them well into the whole; then boil five minutes without stirring; let it stand ten minutes near the fire, and then pass through a jelly bag till quite clear. This delicious jelly is very refreshing in hot weather, is easily made, and requiring no wine is very inexpensive.

Ornamental Jelly

is made by placing alternate layers of jelly and any suitable kind of fruit, such as strawberries, cherries, etc., either fresh or preserved. First pour into the mould a layer of jelly, and when set, place on it a layer of fruit, and then another layer of jelly, and so on till the mould is filled. The different layers of jelly may be of various colours, according to taste. To turn out without breaking, dip the mould in hot water for an instant, and see that it is well wetted before pouring in the first layer of jelly.

Fruit Jelly.

One oz. packet of Swinborne's isinglass, 4 oz. loaf sugar, ½ pint red currant jelly, 1 lemon, 1½ pints of water. Soak a packet of isinglass for five minutes or longer in a pint of cold water, add ½ pint red jelly dissolved in ½ pint of hot water, with 4 oz. of loaf sugar, and the juice and peel of a lemon, and stir over the fire till dissolved; strain through muslin, and pour into a mould. Instead of the currant jelly and water, a pint of any fruit syrup, without sugar, or a pint of any sweetened juice of fresh fruit may be used.

NOTE: Porcelain moulds are better than tin for all fruit jellies, as the acid acting on the tin discolours the jelly. If no porcelain mould is at hand, use cups or a pudding basin.

Dutch Flummery.

One oz. packet of Swinborne's isinglass, 8 oz. loaf sugar, yolks of 4 eggs, ¾ pint of sherry, 2 lemons, ¾ pint of water. Soak the packet of isinglass in ¾ pint of cold water; beat up the yolks of 4 eggs with ¾ pint of sherry or raisin wine, and add the juice and rind of 2 lemons with 8 oz. of loaf sugar. Place the soaked isinglass in a saucepan, and as soon as it dissolves add all the other ingredients; mix well together, and boil one minute; strain through muslin, stir occasionally till nearly cold, and then pour into moulds.

NOTE: This jelly, being very strengthening, is especially recommended for invalids. It is soon made, and if acids are forbidden the lemons may be omitted without spoiling the flavour. The whites of the eggs left in making Dutch flummery can be used in the following recipe.

Lemon Sponge.

Half a packet of Swinborne's isinglass, 5 oz. loaf sugar, ¾ pint of cold water, 2 lemons, and whites of 2 eggs. Soak the isinglass in ¾ pint of cold water, then dissolve over the fire with the rind of 2 lemons thinly pared, add the sugar and juice of 2 lemons. Boil all together two or three minutes, strain and let it remain till nearly cold and beginning to set; then add the whites of 2 eggs well beaten, and whisk ten minutes, when it will become the consistency of sponge; put it lightly into a glass dish immediately, leaving it in appearance as rocky as possible.

Isinglass Fruit Pudding.

Half a packet of Swinborne's isinglass, 5 oz. loaf sugar, ½ pint of cold water, and 1½ pints of cherries or any other small fruit. Soak the isinglass in ¼ pint of cold water, and boil the fruit in the other ¼ pint of water, adding the sugar according to taste. After boiling two or three minutes, as soon as it is tender, add the soaked isinglass, and stir till it is dissolved; pour into a basin, and when nearly cold turn it into a porcelain mould, cups, or a pudding basin.

Note: This pudding is much liked, being easily made in a few minutes at a trifling cost, and can be had all the year round by using any fruit in season-apples, rhubarb, etc.

Cream Blanc Mange.

One oz. packet of Swinborne's isinglass, 6 oz. of loaf sugar, a little flavouring, 1 wineglassful of brandy, 1 pint of new milk, and 1 pint of cream, or 2 pints of milk. Soak the packet of isinglass in 1 pint of new milk; add 1 pint of cream with flavouring, and 5 or 6 oz. of loaf sugar, and boil for five minutes; strain through muslin, stir occasionally till nearly cold, add a little brandy, and pour into moulds. This makes a very rich blanc mange, but all milk in place of the cream will also answer very well.

Fruit Blanc Mange.

One oz. packet of Swinbornes isinglass, 6 oz. loaf sugar, 2 pint of new milk, 1 pint of fresh fruit, and 4 pint of water. Soak half the packet of isinglass in the milk and the other half in the water. Boil 1 pint of strawberries, or any other fruit, with half the sugar (acid fruit will require more sugar); add the isinglass which has been soaked in water, and when dissolved pour into a mould. Then make a blanc mange of the milk with the remaining loaf sugar, and when the fruit which is in the mould is set, pour in the blanc mange, which should be nearly cold when turned out. This makes a very pretty dish.

Coffee Cream.

Half a packet of Swinborne's isinglass, ¾ pint of milk, ½ pint of cream, the yolk of 1 egg, 3 oz. raw coffee, 3 oz. sugar. Put the coffee into a saucepan, with a little butter to prevent it from burning; keep shaking it about till it is a light brown colour; pour on it ¼ pint of milk, and when it boils strain it to the

Isinglass, which has been previously soaked in ¼ pint of milk; add the sugar, dissolve it over the fire, and set aside to cool. Make a custard with the remaining ¼ pint of milk and the yolk of 1 egg; add it to the coffee. Whisk the cream, and pour the coffee to it, stirring all the time. Pour into a mould.

Strawberry Cream.

Half a packet of Swinborne's isinglass, a little sugar, 1 lemon, ¾ pint of cream, ¼ pint of strawberry syrup, 1½ wineglassfuls of cold water. Soak the isinglass in the water, add the rind and juice of the lemon with the sugar, and stir over the fire till dissolved; remove the lemon peel and pour into a basin, adding the strawberry syrup. Whisk the cream, and pour it into the other ingredients, gently stirring all the time. Colour with cochineal, and pour into a mould. Raspberry may be substituted for strawberry, and any suitable jam rubbed through a hair sieve, with a little water, will take the place of syrup.

N.B. Bottled fruits, such as usually imported into the colony, will answer the purpose of some of these recipes, if strained from their water or syrup.

Boiled Custard.

Beat 3 eggs well, take 1 pint of milk and 1 dessertspoonful of white sugar. Put the above into a jug, stand it into a saucepan of boiling water over the fire, and stir until it nearly reaches boiling point. 4 teaspoonful of mixed maizena will thicken it more. Flavour with essence, and serve in cups with nutmeg grated on the top.

NOTE: Condensed milk can be used for either custards or blanc manges successfully if none other be at hand. It is usual then to dissolve about ½ tin of milk in 1 pint of water.

Lemon Cheese.

Three eggs, the rind grated, and the juice of 4 lemons, ¼ lb. butter, and 1 lb. white sugar. Put the butter at the bottom of the pan, then stir in the sugar and other ingredients slowly, and stir over a gentle fire until it thickens well. It will keep a length of time if covered over well in small dry pots.

Apricot Cream.

Take a tin of preserved apricots, put them through a clean hair sieve, mix with it 1 pint of whipped cream, 1½ oz. of clarified isinglass; pour the cream into an oiled mould, and set in the usual way. This sort of cream may be prepared with other tinned fruits.

Cleghorn and Harris' Recipes.

Fruit Blanc Mange.

Stew nice fresh fruit; canned will do (whatever you may please, cherries and raspberries being the best); strain off the juice and sweeten to taste; place it over the fire until it boils. While boiling stir in maizena mixed with a little cold water, allowing 2 tablespoonfuls of maizena to each pint of juice. Continue stirring until sufficiently cooked, then pour into moulds wet with cold water; set them away to cool. This, eaten with cream and sugar, makes a delightful dessert.

Duryea's Maizena Recipes.

Ice Cream.

One pint of milk, yolks of 2 eggs, 6 oz. sugar, 1 tablespoonful maizena. Scald until it thickens. When cool add 1 pint of whipped cream and the whites of 2 eggs beaten stiff. Sweeten, flavour, and freeze.

Duryea's Maizena Recipes.

Stewed Apples and Custard.

Pare, quarter, and stew the apples with sugar and a few cloves, pour off the syrup, and place the fruit in the bottom of a pie dish. Pour a rice custard over them, and bake until nicely set. The dried colonial apples answer well where no others are obtainable.

Lemon Creams.

Pare 4 lemons very thinly, and throw the peel into 12 tablespoonfuls of water, squeeze juice of the lemons over 8 oz. fine white or castor sugar, well beat the yolks of 10 eggs, and add the peel water and juice gradually. Strain it through muslin into a stew pan, stir it one way over a gentle fire till it becomes rather thick, but it must not boil, Serve in custard cups.

Tapioca Blanc Mange.

Soak ½ lb. tapioca for one hour in 1 pint of milk, boil until tender; sweeten to taste, pour it then into a mould. When cold, turn it out and serve with stewed fruit.

Strawberry Compote.

Boil for ten minutes ¼ pint of water, with 6 oz. lump sugar, over 1½ pints of ripe strawberries, freed from their stalks. Turn them into a basin, cover, and let stand a few hours; boil the syrup up again a few minutes, pour it over the fruit, and serve when cold.

Stewed Prunes.

Buy box prunes, as they are of better quality than the loose or barrelled sort. Soak for one hour in cold water, put in a porcelain lined saucepan, and add a little sugar. Let them stew an hour or more slowly, or until they are soft. This fruit is good in small pox, measles, scarlet fever, and the like cases, not only as food but as medicine also, being particularly wholesome at such times.

Royal Baker and Pastrycook.

Apple Jelly.

Pare, core, and cut up the apples quickly, put them into stone vessels, with a little cold water; put the vessels into a potful of water; boil until the fruit is quite soft. Add 1 tablespoonful dissolved isinglass, and pass the whole through a jelly bag; weigh it and add 1 lb. sugar to 1 pint of juice; boil twenty minutes, removing the scum. Add the juice of 1 lemon to every 2 lb. jelly. Pour into shallow jars, from which the jelly should turn out firm. In cold weather it is not necessary to add any isinglass.

Apples in Pink Jelly.

Take several apples, say 6, pare and scoop out the cores, fill them up with white sugar and a few cloves, then place them in a pie dish side by side, with more sugar, juice of 1 lemon, and ½ pint of water, and cover the pie dish with a meat dish. Let the apples bake slowly until tender; take out separately, and place them in a glass fruit dish. The liquor they have been cooked in is then strained, and a tablespoonful of gelatine, which has been already dissolved in cold water, is added, also a little essence of lemon. This must be boiled till quite clear, then coloured with a drop or two of prepared cochineal. Strain this liquor again through muslin into a vessel, and after cooling awhile it can be poured around the apples. The tops of the apples can be made to look more pretty by having a little light apricot or Cape gooseberry jam or the white of an egg, beaten to a stiff froth, spread over them.

Orange Cheesecakes.

Blanch ¼ lb. almonds, beat them very fine with orange flour water, and ¼ lb. fine sugar pounded and sifted, ½ lb. butter that has been melted carefully without oiling, and which must be nearly cold before you use it; then beat the yolks of 5 eggs and the whites of 4, pound thoroughly in a mortar 2 candied oranges and 1 fresh one, which has been boiled for three hours. Beat the whole together, and bake in patty pans, lined with puff paste.

Ordinary Maizena Blanc Mange (White).

Place 1 quart of milk, or milk and water, over the fire. When it is nearly boiling, put into it 2 tablespoonfuls white sugar, the beaten white of 1 egg, and 3 heaped tablespoonfuls maizena, mixed smoothly with a little milk; also a few drops of any essence. Stir the whole quickly until it boils and thickens, and continue to do so for about two minutes longer to cook the maizena in it. If part of the blanc mange is to be coloured, remove a little from the pan into a basin, and colour it with not more than 1 or 2 drops of prepared cochineal; stir it well, and place it at the bottom of the mould. With a clean spoon then proceed gently to fill the mould, let it stand until cold, loosen the edge, place a plate on the top, and turn it over, and the blanc mange on the hottest day will turn out firmly and well. Serve with or without preserve or jam.

Grape Jelly.

Put grapes into preserving pan, with just enough water to prevent their burning. When hot rub them through a fine sieve, to get out the seeds and skins. Weigh the pulps, and to each 1 lb. put ¾ lb. white sugar. Boil three-quarters of an hour, then pour into pots, and cover in the usual way.

A Simple Jelly.

Dissolve 1 oz. packet of gelatine in 6 cups of water, add 1½ cups sherry, ½ cup brandy, ¾ cup lemon juice, rind and juice of 1 lemon, and 1 orange. Have the whites of 3 eggs well beaten, and add with 1 cup of white sugar. Boil for three-quarters of an hour, strain gently through a flannel jelly bag, and put into a mould to cool.

Snow Eggs.

Take 6 eggs, separate the yolks from the whites of them, and whisk the latter to a stiff froth with a tablespoonful of castor sugar. Put 1 quart of new milk into a saucepan, sweeten it to taste, bring it nearly to the boil; then take 2 dessert spoons, and shape the white of egg, dropping it one by one into the milk, when set on one side turn over; a few seconds are sufficient, then take out and drain on a sieve. When all the egg froth has been used, strain the milk into another saucepan, and let it get cold, then gradually mix with it the yolks of the eggs, and simmer gently over the fire to make a custard, flavour with vanilla, pour into a glass dish, and when cold lay the snow eggs on the top.

Swinborne's Pastrycook and Confectioner.

Tapioca Custard.

Boil 2 tablespoonfuls of tapioca very slowly in 1 pint of milk until soft, stirring it all the time. Add 2 tablespoonfuls of sugar and a small piece of butter. Thoroughly mix all, and then draw the saucepan to one side, so that the mixture may cool a little. Whisk well 4 fresh eggs, mix gradually part of the tapioca, then pour them into the saucepan with the rest of the tapioca. Stir all well over the fire, but do not let the custard boil. Flavour to taste, and turn out into a glass dish. Powdered cinnamon sprinkled on the top is an improvement.

Floating Island of Apples.

Bake 8 or 9 apples; when cold, pare and pulp through a sieve, beat this up with fine sugar, add the whites of 5 eggs beaten up with rose water; mix gradually till light, then heap on rich cold custard or jelly.

A New Way to Serve Strawberries.

It has been suggested more than once that the proper way to serve the strawberry is to smother it with cream. This is a very good scheme, but a far better plan is to place the berries in a dish, at the bottom of which has been strewn some freshly cut lemon peel. Put some more lemon peel on top of the berries. Cover the dish and let it stand in an ice-box for ten or fifteen minutes. Put on some sugar at the end of that time, and then put on enough red wine to saturate the berries about three-fourths of the way up. Let the dish stand in an ice-box sufficiently long to get the wine thoroughly cold. Then serve. The taste is something which cannot be described, but it is far superior to the taste of berries and cream.

Garlick's Gazette of Fashion.

Strawberry Soufflé.

Spread strawberry jam about ½ inch thick at the bottom of a tart dish. Make a custard in the following manner : Pour on the yolks of 5 eggs, ½ pint of boiling cream or milk, stir it over a slow fire until it becomes thick, taking care it does not curdle; sweeten and flavour with almonds; put the custard over the jam, and on the top of it the whites of the eggs whisked to a froth. Sift some fine sugar over the souffle, and put it in a slow oven until it assumes a pretty golden colour. Serve cold.

Quince Jelly, No 1.

Slice the quinces without either paring or coring. Put them in an enamelled saucepan and just cover with water; put over the fire, and boil until soft. Remove from the stove and strain off the liquor. To every gallon of it allow 4 lb. white sugar, and boil very fast, stirring the while quickly, until it becomes a thick jelly.

Quince Jelly, No 2.

Boil the quinces not peeled but cut into quarters, in water sufficient to cover them, quickly for about one hour. To about 3 quarts of liquid add 3 lb, of white sugar, and boil this together for another hour, stirring well the while. To ascertain when ready place a little in a saucer; when it cools thickly and is of a bright red colour it is done sufficiently. Remove at once.

Butterscotch.

Put into a very clean pan 1½ lb. of soft brown sugar, 2 oz. of butter, ½ teaspoonful of cream of tartar, ½ teacupful of cold water. Let the whole boil for ten minutes without stirring, then dip a spoon in cold water, pop it into the pan, and back again with its contents into the cold water, when if the mixture hardens it will do. Essence or powdered ginger may be added before pouring it out. Cut into squares when cool.

Toffee.

Take ½ cupful of cream or milk, 2 oz. of butter, and 1 lb. of brown sugar, and put these into a pan to boil for twenty minutes. At the end of that time drop a little into some cold water; if it sets it is done, and should be poured into a buttered dish. A few drops of essence improve the flavour of it. It need not be stirred whilst boiling.

Almond Toffee

is prepared as that above; but 4 oz. of almonds split and blanched can be thrown in to boil, but no essence. The almonds should he perfectly dry before using them.

Honey Toffee.

Take 1 lb. honey, same quantity of moist sugar, ½ lb. butter. Put them in a saucepan large enough to allow of fast boiling over a clear fire. Put in the butter first, and rub it well over the bottom of the saucepan, then add the honey and sugar, stirring together gently with a knife. After the mixture has boiled for about ten minutes, ascertain if it be done in the following way: have ready a basin of cold water, and drop a little into it from the point of a knife. If it be sufficiently done when you take it from the water it will be quite crisp. Now prepare a large shallow dish, rubbed all over with butter, and pour on the toffee to get cool.

Cocoanut Tablet.

Get a small fresh cocoanut, open it, and pour the milk into a cup, pare all the skin from the kernel, and grate about half of it. Dissolve ½ lb. loaf sugar in a large cupful of cold water; when dissolved put on a moderate fire to boil. Some of the milk may be added. Boil it for five or six minutes, removing all scum. When the sugar resembles a thick white cream add the grated cocoanut, and let it boil a few minutes longer, stirring it continually with a wooden spoon. When sufficiently boiled pour it on a buttered dish or paper, and when almost cool cut it into shaped blocks.

Lemon Drops.

Half lb. loaf sugar. Squeeze the juice of four lemons over it, mix well with a bone spoon until it makes a thickish paste, then drop it on writing paper in lumps about the size of a sixpence.

Chocolate Creams.

Take 1 lb. of loaf sugar, put it into a saucepan, and pour some good milk or cream over it, as much as the sugar will absorb. It can then be boiled gently for a time, how long can be ascertained by dropping a little into cold water. If it candies. it is ready. Be careful not to boil it too long, or it will stick to the pan. It need not be stirred till it is taken off; but then it has to be continually stirred until it creams. Beat it until cool, when it has to be rolled into little balls. Into a jar put ½ lb. vanilla chocolate, and place it into a saucepan of boiling water to dissolve; when melted dip the creams into it, and place them on a buttered paper to get cool.

Part XIX. Pickles, etc.

To Pickle Cucumbers.

These are generally pickled small and green. Both ends are to be cut off, and they must be soaked in fresh water for some hours. They are then to be drained until quite dry, and put into stone jars. They must then have sufficient boiling vinegar poured over them to cover them. When the pickle is quite cold the jar should be covered up for three days; then the vinegar is to be turned out, boiled again, and poured over the cucumbers. After three days it must be done again, but this time the spices best liked are to be added. Garlic, cloves, whole pepper, and salt to be used. The repeated boiling is to restore the green colour. It can be done again if the colour be not quite satisfactory.

To Pickle Peaches.

Take ripe but not too soft peaches, put a clove into the end of each peach. Take 2 lb. brown sugar to 1 gallon of vinegar, skim, and boil up twice; pour it hot over the peaches, and cover close. In a week or two pour off, and scald the vinegar again. After this they will, if well covered, keep any length of time

Royal Baker and Pastrycoak.

To Pickle Cauliflowers.

Take whitest and closest cauliflowers in bunches; spread on earthen dish, cover them with salt, and let stand three days to draw out all the water. Then put in jars, pour boiling salt and water over them; let stand over night. Thern drain with a hair sieve, and put in glass jars or bottles; fill these with vinegar, cork and seal tightly.

Royal Baker and Pastrycook.

To Pickle Tomatoes, No. 1.

Always use those that are thoroughly ripe. The small round ones are decidedly the best. Do not prick them as most books direct. Let them lie in strong brine three or four days, then put down in layers in jars, mixing with small onions. Then pour on the vinegar cold, which should be first spiced. Let there be a spice bag to throw into every pot. Cover carefully, and set by in a cellar or cool place one month before using.

Royal Baker and Pastrycook.

Pickled Tomatoes, No. 2.

This is a very good pickle for hot or cold roast meat. Take 2 dozen small ripe tomatoes, prick each one in two or three places, carefully preserve the juice that flows from them, and keep it in a covered dish until wanted. Put the tomatoes in layers in a deep earthen jar, and sprinkle a little salt between each layer. Cover the jar, and let the tomatoes remain undisturbed for three days. At the end of that time wash them well from the brine and dry them carefully. Put them into jars, and cover them with vinegar which has been boiled and allowed to get cold. Add the juice which flowed from the fruit in the first instance. The following spices should be boiled with the vinegar for this quantity of tomatoes: ½ oz. each of pepper and cloves, and a heaped tablespoonful of mustard seeds. Sometimes minced onions or celery, or both , are put into the jars with the tomatoes. Time, four days.

To Pickle Red Cabbage.

Cut off the coarse outside leaves, wipe the inside ones clean, cut them up into long thin pieces, lay them in a sieve, sprinkle well with salt, and let them drain all night. Have enough vinegar with 1 oz. whole pepper to each quart to cover the cabbage; cover it well over, and set aside for use. In pickling be careful that only the very best vinegar is used.

Lemon Pickle.

Cut up 6 lemons into quarters, remove the pips, spread the pieces on a flat dish, and sprinkle them thickly with salt. After they have remained twenty-four hours in the salt, put all into a large jug or earthenware jar, with 2 oz. of mustard seed, 6 shallots, as much cayenne pepper as will fill a salt spoon (more if liked very hot), and well cover with boiling vinegar. Place the jar or jug in a saucepan of boiling water, and let the pickle simmer till the lemons are quite tender. When cool, put into ajar, and tie down. The pickle will be ready to eat next day, but improves with keeping.

Mixed Pickles, No. 1.

Well rub several large marrows, remove all the seeds, and cut up, without paring, into convenient-sized pieces. Sprinkle liberally with salt, and spread out on a well dish if one is at hand; if not, a large fish drainer is a good substitute. A quantity of water will run off before next morning; this should be carefully drained away, and a little more salt strewn over the marrow. The same process must be repeated each day, but after the first two or three times no more salt need be added. When the marrows seem pretty dry, which will be in four or five days, they are ready to pickle, and if still too moist, dry them slightly in a cloth. Put a sufficient quantity of good brown vinegar into an enamelled stew pan with a little whole ginger, mace, allspice, and whole pepper, black and white; these latter tied up in muslin bags. Bring the vinegar almost, but not quite, to the boil, then pour it into a jug or pan, cover with a cloth and a plate above it, and let it stand till quite cold; the marrow can then be added, and should be covered tightly with a piece of bladder. Common garden cucumbers, which can be bought cheaply enough, may be treated in the same way, except that the seeds need not be removed. Gherkins are more expensive, but make a good addition to the pickle jar; they should be laid in salt and water to prepare. Cauliflowers, again, are excellent; they should be cut or pulled apart, all green carefully removed, as well as the little sprouting leaves which will be found in the flower. Salt in the same way as the marrows, and in each case the vinegar should not be added until quite cold. Onions should be peeled, either by hand or with a silver knife, then laid in salt and water for four or five days, changing the water, and adding fresh salt once during that time. When ready wash them in a very little cold vinegar, and pour on the pickling vinegar as soon as it is taken from the fire. These can be kept separate altogether if preferred, but are very good added to the others, though they will impart a strong flavour. It is a good plan to have a separate jar for each sort of pickle, allowing them to stand for about a year, then mixing altogether in one large jar kept for the purpose, but entirely fresh vinegar should be added, reboiling the spices, and adding a little more if necessary, as the first lot of vinegar is sure to be very salt. Of course, when once the pickle jar is started, it may be added to year after year, only taking the precaution occasionally to look it over, reboil the same vinegar, and add a little more when wanted. This is really very little trouble, and the home-made pickle will generally be much appreciated.

Mixed Pickles, No. 2.

Into 2 gallon vinegar put 2 oz. bruised ginger, 2 oz. allspice, 1 oz. chillies, 1 oz. white pepper, 2 oz. turmeric, ½ lb. mustard seed, ¼ lb. shallots, ½ oz. garlic, and ¼ lb. bay-salt. Boil all together, leaving out the mustard seed, which is to be added afterwards. When the vinegar is cold mix very smoothly 2 oz. made mustard with a little of it in a basin, then add to the remainder with the seed. Now take some French beans, radish pods, broccoli, cauliflower, or any other vegetables; blanch the vegetables, lay them on a sieve, and sprinkle a little salt over them to draw out the water. Let them be in the sun till quite dry, then pour the boiling vinegar over them in the jars.

Part XX. Preserves, etc.

As a general rule, jam should boil fast for three-quarters of an hour, cover off, stirring the whole time with a wooden spoon; when done, it will thicken at the side of the saucepan; the best test is to put a little on a plate to cool; it should stiffen. Jam should be placed in dry jars and left to stand a day, then covered with brandy paper. Keep it in a dry cool place; if hot it will be liable to ferment, and if damp to mould. Preserve differs from jam in being boiled slowly to prevent the fruit from breaking, and the time depends on the fruit; when transparent it is done.

Swinborne's Pastry cook and Confectioner.

To Cover Jam and Preserve Pots, etc.

Where bladders are not procurable, a piece of writing paper well-dipped into milk and tied down whilst damp over the tops of the pots, in one or two thicknesses, will become quite hard and air-tight when dry. A piece of oiled paper, or a piece dipped into brandy, is generally found advantageous to place inside the pot, under the top cover or lid of any home-made preserves. A well enamelled pan is the best article to use in making preserves, etc.

Simple Syrup, To Make.

Simple syrup is made in the proportion of about 2½ lb. sugar to 1 pint of water.

Clear Syrup, To Make.

Boil 1 lb. white sugar a few minutes in ½ pint of water, and skim it well, add ½ of the white of an egg well beaten. Skim carefully, and boil rather fast.

Clarified Sugar.

Dissolve 4 lb. white sugar (lump, if possible) in 2 quarts of water; when warm, add the whites of 3 eggs previously beaten up with ½ pint of water. Let the mixture boil, and while boiling take off all the scum which arises. When it is perfectly clear, pass it through muslin.

Apricots in Brandy.

Prick and blanch them. Lay them a short time in water. Drain them on a sieve until quite dry. Boil in sufficient clear syrup until tender. Place them in pots or glasses, and pour over them two parts good French brandy, mixed with one part boiling clear syrup, made of loaf sugar, which has previously been boiled, until the syrup could be pulled out in long strings. Cover the pots closely.

Grapes in Brandy.

Take some close bunches, black or white, not over ripe, and without any decayed or withered grapes among them; lay them in a jar first, pricking each grape two or three times with a bone, gold, or silver pin; well cover them with pounded white sugar candy (it can be procured at a confectioner's), and then fill the jar with brandy. Tie close down, and keep them in a dry place. They make a pretty dish for dessert.

Syrup of Quince.

Take 3 pints of clear quince juice and 1 lb. white sugar. Boil together to a syrup.

Preserved Cucumbers.

Select the smallest and best, lay them in a jar, cover with brine, and place a cabbage leaf over them for an hour or two. Then simmer them over the fire in water, which has a little salt dissolved in it; remove them from the salt and water, slice each into two parts, take out the seed, and place the cucumbers in cold water two or three days to take out the salt. Make a syrup with 1 lb. white sugar to ½ pint of water, boil and skim it; then put in the thin rind of 1 lemon and 1 oz. white ginger from which the outside has been scraped. The cucumbers must be nicely wiped, and put into the syrup when it is cold. Boil them up once, and give them a similar boiling once a day for a fortnight. They will then keep as long as required. Cover up as other preserves.

Citron Preserves.

Prepare rind into any form you desire, boil very hard thirty or forty minutes in alum water tolerably strong; take from alum water and put into clear cold water; allow them to stand overnight; in the morning change water, and put them to boil; let them cook until they have entirely changed colour and are quite soft; then make syrup, allowing 1½ lb. white sugar to 1 lb. fruit; then add fruit which wants but little more cooking. Mace, ginger, or lemon flavours nicely.

Royal Baker and Pastrycook.

Oranges Preserved Whole.

Twelve oranges not too ripe, with thick clear skins, 4 lb. white sugar, 4 quarts of water. Take the outer skin off the oranges very lightly with a sharp knife or grater; lay them in cold water for twenty-four hours, changing it several times; cut the oranges slightly in three or four parts to get the pips out; press them a little, put them on the fire in cold water and boil until tender, but then do not let them break. put Take them out, let them cool, then remove more of the pips. Now put on the sugar, and when dissolved, strain. Place this on the fire again, and when it begins to simmer drop in the oranges, and let them boil gently until you see the fruit is well preserved through and the syrup has well thickened. Be careful in putting into pots to have the fruit well covered with syrup, and keep the pots in a cool place, and air-tight.

Ripe Figs, To Preserve Whole.

Pare them thinly, not long before required. For the syrup use 1 lb. sugar to each 1 lb. fruit. Dissolve in a little water, and when it has boiled awhile drop in the fruit, and boil until they become quite transparent. The flavour is improved by sticking a clove in the end of each fig. Dried figs can be prepared the same way, but with less sugar.

Citron, To Preserve Whole.

Follow the same directions as in the oranges preserved whole.

Water Melon Convyt[26].

Pare the water melon, lay the rind one night in lime water, or in salt water. Wash it well, dry it; boil in water until nearly tender; remove and drain, then boil until transparent in a syrup made of 1 lb. white sugar to each 1 lb. fruit, with or without any approved flavouring. Cover in pots as other preserves.

Apricots, To Candy.

Slit the fruit on one side of the stone, dry them separately on a dish, and cover them with crushed loaf sugar. Bake them in a hot oven, and then dry them in a warm place for a few days.

Apricot Preserve.

Choose nearly ripe fruit; if too ripe it will break up. For each pound take 1 lb. loaf sugar which should be first boiled over the fire with a very little water to make a syrup, remove the scum, then put in the fruit and boil slowly till it becomes

---

[26] Convyt: *konfyt,* or preserve. This works well with old-fashioned melons, with a thick, white rind

transparent, gently shaking it occasionally in the saucepan instead of stirring.

Peaches, cherries, white *magnum bonum* plums, and some other fruits can be preserved in the same way.

Swinborne's Pastrycook and Confectioner.

Orange Marmalade, No. 1.

To every 1 lb. oranges put 1 lemon, 2 quarts of water; boil them for two hours; then change the water and boil them until quite soft; cut them in half, take out the pulp carefully, and remove the seeds; cut the peel into very thin slices, and return it to the pulp. To every 1 lb. fruit allow 2 lb. sugar. Put 1 pint of water the oranges were first boiled in to the sugar. Mix the whole together, and boil twenty minutes, or until the marmalade is clear.

Orange Marmalade, No. 2.

First weigh your fruit, and put the same weight of sugar aside. Peel and cut the oranges in half and take out all the insides; take away the pips and skins that separate the quills, leaving only the pulp and juice. Wash the inside of the skins in a little water, and put it to your pulp. The rinds must be boiled about four hours in plenty of water, changing it once, or it will be bitter. When the rinds are sufficiently cooked, cut them in thin slices; boil the pulp and sugar together for half an hour, then throw in the peel, cut up and let it boil four or five minutes. When this is done it is ready to be put into jars.

Orange Marmalade, No. 3.

Take 12 or 14 oranges, not over ripe; cut them into thin slices, taking out all the pips, which pips put into a separate basin. Pour over the oranges 5 quarts of cold water, and over the pips 1 quart of boiling water. Next day put the oranges on to boil, and let them boil rapidly for two hours. Then add the water from the pips, taking care to rub off all the jelly which adheres to them; also add 8 lb. white sugar. Boil all together quickly, from one and a quarter to one and a half hours, till a little of it poured into a saucer becomes firm. These quantities will make from eleven to thirteen pounds of marmalade, according to the size of the oranges.

Apricot Jam.

Cut the fruit open and remove the stones. Keep some of the kernels. Weigh the apricots, and use 1 lb. white sugar to each 1 lb. fruit. To dissolve the sugar put about ½ pint of water to 4 lb. of it. Boil the jam, stirring and skimming well for one and a half hours; when it is cold cover well in pots, and keep in a cool place. The kernels are to be put into the jam whilst cooking.

Guava Jam.

Pare the guavas, add ½ lb. sugar to each 1 lb. fruit, and follow directions of apricot jam as to boiling.

Apple Jam.

Pare and core the apples, cut them into thin slices, put them into an enamelled saucepan, and to every 1 lb. fruit use ¾ lb sugar. In a piece of coarse muslin tie up a few cloves, ginger, and the rind of a lemon. Stir the jam over a rather quick fire for twenty minutes if the apples are juicy. When sufficiently boiled the jam will cling to the spoon; it is then ready when cooled for the jam pots.

Tomato Jam.

Select small round tomatoes, wipe them dry, cut them in halves, and squeeze the pulp out of them; then boil all together for half an hour. Next pass them through a colander, leaving the skins behind. Having previously weighed your can, you may now weigh the whole together, and add ¾ lb. sugar to each pound of tomatoes. Flavour with essence of almonds. This jam can be boiled afresh with the sugar for another half-hour, then put into hot vessels, after skimming, and left to get quite cold before sealing up. Instead of almond flavour lemon juice may be used, and tomato jam made with lemon juice, not essence of lemon, tastes very much like strawberry, and is more delicious, and about the cheapest jam that can be made in this country.

Apple Chutney.

Pare, core, and cut up very small 2 lb. hard, green apples. Cut also very small ½ lb. stoned raisins, take 1 lb. brown sugar, 4 oz. table salt, ½ lb. ground ginger, and 4 lb. dried chillies; mix all in a brown jar, add boiling vinegar (good) sufficient to mix the chutney into a thick pulp; keep in a warm corner, stir every day for a month; if necessary put into smaller warm jars or bottles, cork tightly, seal or cover with bladder.

Quince Chutney.

Two lb. quinces, 2 oz. chillies, ¼ lb. sugar, ¼ lb. salt, 2 oz. ground ginger, ¼ lb. raisins cut small and stoned, 2 oz. coriander stamped, 2 oz. garlic fine, and 2 bottles vinegar. Boil until the chutney looks like jam and it is cooked nearly dry, then vinegar is added, but not enough to make it sloppy. Reboil it another quarter of an hour, and bottle ready for use. Watch well, stir frequently, and boil very slowly. When cool secure in bottles or small pots.

Mushroom Catchup.

Take some large mushrooms, and cut them to pieces, after they are pared. Put them into a large pan, sprinkle well with salt and let them stand for eight or ten days, then strain through ~ sieve, and after boiling and skimming the liquor well, let it stand to cool. Add to it 2 oz. whole pepper and mace to each gallon of juice, boil it up about half an hour, skim well, bottle when cold, and seal the corks to keep them air-tight.

Strawberry Jam.

Choose strawberries not too ripe, of a firm sort and good colour; allow ¾ lb. sugar to every 1 lb. fruit; put them into the preserving pan with sugar, and stir very gently (over a slow fire), so that it will not break the fruit. Boil for half an hour, and put in pots. Cover them in the usual way. Sometimes the strawberries are covered overnight with the sugar, which then becomes dissolved ready for the preserving pan.

Peaches, To Preserve, No. 1.

Take ripe but not soft peaches. Pour boiling water over them, to take off skins, which will peel off easily. Weigh equal quantities of fruit and white sugar, put them together in earthen pan overnight. In the morning pour off syrup, boil few minutes, remove preserving pan from fire, and skim the top; then put pan back on fire, and when the syrup boils up put in the peaches. Boil them slowly three-quarters of an hour, take out the peaches, and put into jars. Boil syrup quarter of an hour more, and pour over them. Cover the jars well.

Royal Baker and Pastrycook

Peach Preserve, No. 2.

Prick the peaches well with a fork before putting them into lime water, where they should remain for four hours. Use 2 lb. sugar less than the weight of the fruit. Boil for two hours. Skim it well, and pot.

Preserved Quinces.

Pare, quarter, and core small quinces, saving skins and cores. Put quinces over fire with just water enough to cover them, and simmer till soft, but do not let them cook till they break. Take out fruit and spread on dishes to cool, add parings and cores to water in which quinces were boiled, stew it an hour, then strain through jelly bag or a sieve. To each pint of this liquor add 1 lb. sugar, then boil and skim this, put in the fruit, and boil quarter of an hour. Take all off the fire and let stand in deep dish for twenty-four hours. Then drain off syrup, let it boil, put in quinces, and boil fifteen minutes. Take out fruit again, spread on dishes; boil syrup down nearly to a jelly. Put the fruit into jars two-thirds full and cover with the syrup. Tie up tightly. The quinces will be of a fine, deep-red colour.

Royal Baker and Pastrycook

Quince Jam.

Pare and core the quinces, saving all the pips. Cut the quinces into thin slices, removing any hard parts around the cores. Weigh the fruit, using 1 lb. white sugar to each 1 lb. of it. Boil the fruit until nearly tender in just sufficient water to cover it, then remove and strain through a hair sieve. Have ready a syrup of sugar dissolved with a cupful of water to each 4 lb. of it; then put in the fruit, also the pips tied in a piece of coarse muslin, and boil, stirring and skimming until the syrup thickens, and the quince is of a good, deep-red colour, and well-preserved. Remove the muslin, and when cooled put in small pots and cover well.

Green Apricot Convyt.

Prick the apricots and lay them one day and night in salt and water, then put them for half an hour in warm water, after which strain them. For each 100 apricots take 3 lb. sugar, boil, and let the syrup get lukewarm; then throw it over the apricots. The second day cook the apricots slowly in the syrup, stirring them well until they are well preserved and the syrup has become thick.

Green Spanspek Convyt.

Pare the spanspek thinly, cut it into pieces, remove the seeds, and lay it one night in lime water. Next day put it in salt water, then drain it well. Take as much sugar as the fruit weighs, make clear syrup of it with water, then put in the spanspek, and boil slowly until it is transparent and the syrup thickened.

Tomato Preserve, No. 2.

Make 3 cuts in the sides of each, pare; squeeze out the seeds, then lay them one whole night in lime water. Use ½ lb. less sugar than the weight of the fruit. When the syrup has boiled rather thick, add the fruit, and boil slowly until tender. Skim it well.

Naartje[27], Whole, To Preserve.

Rasp off the rough parts of the skin, cut into several divisions, but not too deeply into the naartje, press them rather flat and weigh them, using white sugar in an equal weight to the fruit, then lay them one night in lime water, or two days in fresh water after which boil them (after removing all the pips) in water for about a half-hour; then drain them and boil them in the syrup until they are quite tender and the syrup well thickened. In the small, large-necked pots cover them well with syrup.

Baked Apple Preserve.

Stew thoroughly as many apples as will half fill a middle-sized pie dish; add about 3 tablespoonfuls of yellow sugar and 2 or 3 cloves; beat well 5 eggs, and add to them ½ pint of cream or good milk; then make the apples perfectly boiling. Mix the whole together, and bake for half-hour.

Peaches in Brandy, To Preserve.

Wipe and prick the fruit with a silver pin; have ready ¼ of the weight of them in fine white sugar. Put the fruit into a small pot with a tight, close-fitting lid, or into a well-covered

---

[27] Naartje: clementine or small orange

jar, or into the empty imported fruit bottles which have large necks; if in the latter, cut down the corks and seal when preserved. Now stand either the pots or bottles which have been filled with brandy and sugar into a saucepan of water over the fire until the brandy without boiling is as hot as you can bear your finger in. When cool, secure the vessels well, and air-tight.

Lemons, To Preserve Whole.

Follow the directions given in preserving naartjes whole.

Lemons will keep good for months by simply putting them into a jug of buttermilk, changing the buttermilk about every three weeks. When the lemons are required for use they should be well dried with a cloth.

Lemon Rind Preserve.

Pare a quantity of lemons very thinly, cut into small pieces, weigh them, and add to them the juice of the lemons strained well through muslin. Place juice and rind in a stew pan of syrup, the sugar of which was an equal weight with the fruit, and boil until the rind is quite transparent and the syrup has thickened. Skim well, and cover in pots as other preserves.

Vegetable Marrow Preserve (Cornish).

Weigh a vegetable marrow after paring it, cut it up (removing the seeds) into small pieces of about one inch square; cover it over for the night with its weight of white sugar. Next day place it in a stew pan, putting 1 oz. ground ginger in a muslin bag, then continue to boil the marrow in the syrup until it has well preserved and the syrup thickened. Skim well, and cover in pots as other preserves.

Lettuce Preserve.

Take the tender stalks of lettuces that are running to seed, peel and cut them into lengths of one and a half inches;

put these into spring water for six days, changing the water daily. Take them out, and boil for a few minutes in fresh water, but not so as to render them quite soft. To every pound of stalk allow 1 lb. sugar, 1 pint of water, 1 oz. ginger root which has been previously soaked. Boil and skim till this syrup is clear, adding, while boiling, the rind of a lemon pared very thin and cut into small pieces. Dry the lettuce stalks in a cloth, and, when the syrup is cool, pour it over them. Drain off the syrup, and repeat the boiling process on alternate days for a fortnight, allowing it just to boil up and no more, and adding more ginger and lemon if required. There should be sufficient syrup to quite cover the lettuce when finished.

Gooseberry Jam[28], Cape.

Weigh the fruit, pick them over, and prick the skins here and there with a needle. Lay them one night in a large earthen vessel, covered with their weight in white sugar. Next day put them into a stew pan, and stew slowly from three-quarters to one hour. Add no water to the syrup.

Blackberry Jam.

Fine blackberries are obtained in some parts of the colony. Gather them in dry weather, pick them over, removing any stalks or red, unripe berries. Lay them aside overnight in a large basin sprinkled with their own weight in sugar. Next day boil them in their syrup for three-quarters or one hour until the syrup has nicely thickened.

In using blackberries for pies add some thin sliced cooking apples, which will much improve the flavour. Cream is often served with fruit pies. In the West of England it is prepared in the following way: the milk is brought into the

---

[28] This recipe refers to Cape Gooseberries, known in Europe as physalis

dairy after milking, strained, and turned out into large pans; it is then left to stand for about one day and a half; then it is placed over a steady fire, until a firm skin covers the top of the milk, but it is not allowed to boil. It is then removed and left in the vessel in which it has been scalded (as it is called), and is allowed to stand another day and a half. Then it is skimmed off carefully, and churned into butter. In warm weather the butter is made two or three times a week. The cream is there often spread on bread instead of butter, and sometimes syrup, honey, or any sweet preserve is eaten with it.

Mulberry Preserve.

Boil ½ lb. sugar with a little water until it becomes a thick syrup; then pour the boiling syrup over 3 lb. of mulberries. Leave them in the syrup a little while, then take them out, and put them gently into jars. Return the syrup to the pot to boil two or three minutes more, and when boiling pour it over the mulberries in the jars. It is then ready for use.

To Bottle Fruit, No. 1.

To 3 lb, fruit allow 1 lb. sugar; use bottles with wide necks. Put some hot cinders into an old saucepan, with a piece of stone brimstone. Let this burn for about ten minutes before you require it. Put the fruit and sugar into a preserving pan and let it boil for five minutes. To carry out this recipe easily and quickly three persons should do it. Hold the bottles over the brimstone until they are full of vapour, pour in the fruit at once, and tie down lightly with bladder. Will keep any length of time.

Bottling Small Fruit, No. 2.

Apricots, peaches, plums, and other fruits can be bottled in this way whole without sugar.

Get some clean, dry-necked bottles, fill them with sound fruit, picked and wiped, but not washed, which fruit should be gathered in dry weather; wrap each bottle around with straw or cloths; stand them upright without corks in a large vessel. A soap pot could be used if something be put in the bottom for the bottles to stand evenly; if so, tie a muslin over the neck of each bottle first, in case of any dust. Proceed to fill the pot with sufficient cold water as will reach the necks of the bottles, and with a slow fire bring it to a boil. Whilst doing so let another person get ready as much boiling water as will fill all the bottles, which must be carefully done as soon as the skin of the fruit begins to crack. If the bottles are not so full of fruit, fill them up with a spare bottle, and cork and seal firmly as soon as possible, and if left lying down in a cool place, the fruit will keep any length of time. Use good water.

Part XXI. Recipes for Invalids.

Lemon Drink.

Pare the rind off a small lemon, and cut it into a few thick slices, removing as much of the white of the lemon as possible; put it into a jug with 2 dessertspoonfuls white sugar; pour about 1 pint boiling water over it, cover closely, and in an hour or two it is fit to drink. Strain it through coarse muslin.

Toast Water.

This makes a cooling and wholesome drink. It is easily made. A piece of bread is well toasted brown and dropped into 1 pint jug of boiling water; sometimes a slice of lemon is added. When cold, strain, and it is ready for use.

Barley Water Drink, No. 1.

Boil ¼ lb. pearl barley in 1 pint of water, whilst still boiling stir in a few slices of lemon peeled, and sweeten to taste.

Barley Water Drink, No. 2.

Wash a tablespoonful of pearl barley, put this in a jug with a small piece of thinly pared lemon rind and sugar to taste (about one teaspoonful is generally enough); then pour on it rather more than a tumbler of boiling water, cover up the jug, and let it stand till cool, when it can be poured off quite clear. The barley can be used again.

Apple Water.

A pleasant drink is also made thus: two or three roasted apples are placed in a jug, which is filled up with boiling water, to which a little sugar is added.

Gruel.

One tablespoonful of patent groats is to be boiled in 1 pint of water for ten minutes, stirring the whole while. Sometimes a piece of thin lemon peel is boiled with it, or a little nutmeg grated in. Some invalids take wine with it; if so, add 2 tablespoonfuls of port or sherry. If the gruel is for a person suffering with a severe cold, some few drops of sweet spirits of nitre are added, or spirits are substituted instead of wine. It should for a cold be taken after retiring to bed.

Beef Tea.

Cut the beef into small pieces, remove the fat and skin, and put it into an earthenware jar; fill with water, and add a little pepper and salt. Cover the jar with a saucer or something, and let it remain in a moderately hot oven for two or three hours. If the beef tea be wanted quickly, shred the meat up fine, sprinkle lightly with pepper and salt, and stew awhile until it is strong enough, then pour it off, skim off any fat, and serve, after ascertaining if it be sufficiently seasoned.

Arrowroot.

Mix a dessertspoonful of the best arrowroot with a little cold water; pour 1½ pints of boiling water on it, adding a little sugar and lemon peel.

Strengthening Bread Jelly.

Toast a few slices of bread, remove the crusts, and boil the toast in about 1 quart of water until it is like a jelly; strain and squeeze a lemon into this, adding a little white sugar. Serve in a glass.

Port Wine Jelly.

One oz. isinglass, 1 teacupful of water, 1 dessertspoonful of sugar. Dissolve the isinglass and sugar in the water over the fire, then set it aside covered over in a basin till required; then melt a teaspoonful of it, and add it to a wineglassful of port wine in a tumbler with a little more sugar. It can be served hot if required. Isinglass is very strengthening, and should be given to an invalid as often as possible. It can be dissolved in tea or in other ways.

Strengthening Recipe, Excellent.

Take a pint of port wine, 2 oz. of isinglass, 2 oz. of white sugar candy, 1 oz. of gum arabic, and ½ a nutmeg grated. Put these ingredients into a jar, tie over with bladder, and put the jar into a saucepan of warm water. Allow it to boil gently till all is dissolved. It must be stirred continually. When cold it will be a firm jelly. Give a piece the size of a nutmeg at any time, or dissolve it in warm tea or otherwise.

Minced Chicken or Mutton with Poached Egg.

Take, if chicken, some of the white meat from the breast, and remove all skin and outside parts; if mutton, take an underdone slice from the leg, saddle, or loin; mince it very finely; put it into a stew pan with a little very good, strong gravy or beef tea, free from fat; flavour it if liked with a few herbs, 2 or 3 tiny pieces of good ham, and simmer gently until it boils; then thicken it with a little maizena, and if you have no ham, add a tiny lump of butter; season to taste with pepper and salt. Let it boil a. few minutes, and serve with a nicely poached egg on the top of it.

Family Herald.

Chicken Jelly.

Take the leg of a fowl, and after skinning and scalding it, remove all fat, and wash it clean in cold water; then put it into a saucepan with 1 breakfastcupful of water. Add a little salt and pepper to taste; boil slowly to pieces, strain into a cup, or let it stand till jellied.

Chicken, Boiled (Invalid's).

Procure quite a young chicken of two or three months, pluck, singe, and draw it; wash it well; put it on the fire with just sufficient water to cover it; add a very small knuckle of sweet ham, or a few slices of it; a little pepper, a little fine parsley, and boil gently for about half an hour or rather longer until the meat is quite tender. Add then a little salt if necessary. Serve with or without a little melted butter, and after removing any fat from the top of the soup, add to it a teaspoonful of milk, or dissolve a pinch of isinglass into it, and serve with a thin toasted slice of bread.

Child's Breakfast or Supper.

Squeeze a couple of large baked potatoes out of their skins on to a large soup plate; mash them with a fork until they are fine and free from lumps. Break over it a lightly boiled egg, add a little pepper and salt, and some fine bread crumbs. Pour over it when well mixed a cupful of good gravy or beef tea.

Apples and Rice.

Some apples gently stewed, served with a dish of boiled rice, is a wholesome dish for children.

Maccaroni with Mincemeat.

Stew the maccaroni with water, salt, and milk until it is swollen large and tender. Drain it. In the bottom of a pie dish place some meat which has been finely minced, seasoned, and a rich gravy thickened with maizena poured over it. Place the maccaroni over the meat, and brown slightly in a moderately warm over. Serve hot. Maccaroni must be plunged into boiling water.

Part XXII. Useful Knowledge, Recipes, etc.[29]

Chimney on Fire.

Throw salt or water on it, or, if possible, dip sacks in water, and push them firmly inside the top of the chimney. Keep doors shut, as the current of air spreads the fire; in case of a house being on fire, remember this too. Keep yourself cool, and use all the water at hand, or stifle small flames with thick cloths or blankets, remembering what help is nearest at hand.

Inquire Within.

Burning Oil.

This cannot be extinguished with water, it only serves to spread the flame further. Stifle it with thick cloths, or throw plenty of loose earth upon it.

To Stain Wood Mahogany Colour.

A small bottle, costing in the colony about 9d., of mahogany dye (Judson's) will stain to a nice colour any pieces of wood, and they may be further improved by being varnished when dry. The stain is simply made by pouring boiling water over it.

To Remove Ink Stains from Linen, etc.

As soon as possible rub a piece of the inside of a lemon well over the part; sprinkle well with salt; rub again with the lemon, rinse the part, and the stain will generally disappear.

---

[29] The advice and recipes given in this section should be viewed in an historical context; some recipes contain poisonous or hazardous ingredients or procedures and should not be followed

The juice of the tomato will also remove ink, wine, and fruit stains from linen.

To Mend Broken Knife and Umbrella Handles, etc.

Take a small lump of alum, melt it in an iron kitchen spoon in the fire. Remove any grease or grit from the article to be mended, pour the alum into the cavity, and press the parts together firmly, and it will become as firm as a rock.

To Mend China, Glass, etc.

These articles may be easily mended with coaguline, or Derby cement, procured in small bottles at the bookseller's or chemist's, but it does not answer where hot water has to be used on the articles, for it dissolves then and the parts loosen; but where only cold water is used, it mends the articles firmly and well, if the instructions given with the bottles are followed.

To Destroy Ants.

Pour some tobacco water or camphor dissolved in spirits of wine into their holes, for they dislike a strong smell. It is no good doing it for a day or two; but the remedy chosen should be applied steadily for three or four nights, then again after an interval of three or four days, and so until they cease to reappear. The same rule applies to ants as to black beetles and other creatures of the same kind. You must, if you really wish to exterminate them, not only destroy the present swarms, but also those which are bound to hatch off later, otherwise you will have no peace. It is said that if ants can be induced into a tree infested with the Australian bug the latter will soon disappear. Meat bones and other tempting food for ants laid on the trunks of the trees will cause their presence.

Antidote for Ants.

"I tried several methods to prevent ants molesting bees," (writes Professor A. J. Cook), "and found the following far the most satisfactory: by use of a crowbar make a hole in the middle of the anthill down to the bottom, which is easily found by the more open or less compact earth. Then turn into this hole a gill of bisulphide of carbon, and fill and crowd down with earth. As the liquor is very volatile, and cannot pass out of the now compactly filled hole, it quickly evaporates and kills all the ants. If clay be near, always use this to crowd into the hole, as it is more impervious than is sand, though by firmly pressing with the foot the sand can be made to hold the liquid. Kerosene may be used instead of the carbon, but it is far less effective. So, too, is carbolic acid. By means of syrup, so covered by gauze that bees are excluded, the ants can be trapped in great numbers and destroyed. I have often done this, and by adding Paris green have poisoned the ants."

To Destroy Moths.

Place some of Keating's insect powder among the woollen articles or clothes they are likely to get at, or place among them a good-sized piece of Boer tobacco. A piece of wax candle is sometimes used also for the same purpose. Camphor keeps the moths from ostrich feathers; and if they are rolled into a new piece of unbleached calico, and stitched up firmly, it is said they will keep untouched by moth for any length of time. Blankets and furs put away well sprinkled with borax and done up air-tight will never be troubled with moths.

Destructive to Household Pests.

No insect which crawls can live under the application of hot alum water. It will destroy red and black ants, cockroaches, spiders, bed bugs, and all the myriads of crawling pests which infest our houses during the heated term. Take 2 lb. of alum, and dissolve it in 3 or 4 quarts of boiling water, let it stand on the stove until the alum is all melted, then apply it with a brush while nearly boiling hot to every joint or crevice in your closets, bedsteads, pantry shelves, and the like; brush the cracks in the floor and the crevices in the skirting if you suspect that they harbour vermin.

To Remove Candle Grease from Table Cloths, Carpets, etc.

Lay a piece of blotting paper over the part, then hold a warm iron over the paper, and it will absorb the grease at once.

To Remove Insect Stings.

To get at the sting, which should be extracted, if it be small, press the barrel of a watch key over it, then give 15 drops of hartshorn, *sal volatile*, or a few drops of liquid ammonia in half a glassful of water, and place a piece of lint or linen covered with zinc ointment over the wound.

To allay the smarting of the stings of small insects, bathe the part in a mixture of brandy and salt. A bee sting is relieved by rubbing the blue-bag or some damp earth over it.

To Remove Odour of Painted Room

Keep a bucket of water constantly changed in the room so long as required.

Good Disinfectants.

The odour of coffee whilst it is being roasted.

Condy's Fluid is one of the best disinfectants, but it is expensive to buy, and it is much better to make it yourself. Get a small quantity of permanganate of potash at the chemist's, and put it in a large medicine bottle. Fill up with water, and put a tablespoonful of the mixture in each pail of water with which you flush your drains. A very good preventive against infection is to use carbolic soap for all scrubbing. Oil of peppermint is a strong disinfectant and germicide, and it is said that one part in a hundred thousand of water will kill roaches.

Mildew.

To remove mildew dip the goods in soft water, then rub the spot with soap and chalk, lay it on the grass for two or three days; rub it each day with soap and chalk until the mildew is removed.

Pomade, To Make.

Quarter lb. marrow, 2 oz. sweet oil, 20 drops Omar or other sweet scent, a little palm oil or yellow colouring, obtainable from the chemist. Melt altogether, save the scent, which add after it is strained. Add rather less oil in summer than in winter. Pink pomade is made by adding a drop of prepared cochineal instead of the other colouring.

Remedy for Tainted Meat.

A lump of charcoal boiled in the water when meat is slightly tainted benefits the meat. Charcoal can be obtained by dropping into water a piece of wood well burnt in the fire. Another remedy is to dip the meat into water for about ten minutes in which a little Condy's Fluid has been put. Butter, poultry, and fish are also said to be remedied from taint in the same way.

To Wash Small Bottles.

To wash castor bottles put them ¼ full of rice, and fill up with water; shake thoroughly.

To Stone Raisins.

Hold raisins under water while stoning; this prevents a stickiness to the hands, and cleanses the raisins. Put the quantity of raisins needed in a dish with water to cover. Stone them before removing from water.

Washing Paint.

The best method to wash paint is to rub some bath-brick fine, and when you have some soap on the flannel dip it in the brick. This will remove the grease and dirt speedily without injury.

White and pale shades of paint may be beautifully cleaned by using whiting in the water.

To Remove Paint from Window Glass.

Clean them with a strong solution of washing soda dissolved in warm water, assisting the process with an old knife, or by using diluted spirits of salts.

Mixture for Destroying Flies.

Infusion of quassia, 1 pint; brown sugar, 4 oz., ground pepper, 2 oz. To be well mixed together, and put in small dishes when required.

Condy's Fluid, or, as it is otherwise called, permanganate of potash, put into water in soup plates will also drive away flies and other insects.

Mosquito Bites, To Prevent.

Make a mixture of cocoanut oil and eau-de-Cologne, and rub it over exposed parts before retiring to rest. The smell of it keeps them at a safe distance. Vinegar will also sometimes answer the purpose.

Spirit Lamps for Heating Water, etc.

Many persons are not aware that these lamps, provided with a small kettle, saucepan, and frying pan, can be very cheaply procured all over the colony. They are called "Kitcheners". They are invaluable where there is sickness, or a hot cup of tea or coffee may be quickly required. A little spirits of wine (obtained at the chemist's or the wine stores) is put in the burner, which stands safely on a plate, and the water will boil in five minutes. Alcock of Port Elizabeth supplies the kettle and burner for 2s. 6d.

Save-alls for Candlesticks.

In a house there is often great waste in allowing candles to burn quite out in candlesticks which are not made to slide up and down. To prevent this, save-alls for candlesticks can be bought at many crockery shops; they are made of alabaster or other composition, and look like a piece of candle. A pointed wire is fixed on the top, the short end of the candle has to be placed on this, and it will burn itself quite out. The save-all also protects the candlestick from being burnt or cracked. Candlesticks are now also made with upright points on which to fix small pieces of candle.

Canvas Water Coolers.

In hot country parts bags are made of canvas, neatly sewn, and provided with the neck of a bottle in one corner to pour the water out. The bag is then put awhile into soak, filled, then hung in a shady place, and on the hottest day the water is delightfully cool. Other bags have open tops, and milk or other articles are put in them in suitable vessels, and they remain fresh and cool.

Passengers by train find them useful, and hang them outside the doors of the carriages.

Cow Dung Wash.

Where tents, kitchens, or other rooms have earthen floors, they are greatly improved and hardened, if after being damped and swept they are now and again washed or "smeared", as it is termed, with cow dung. It has to be immersed, well softened and mixed into a thin wash with water. An old bucket or tin answers the purpose well to hold it, and an old American broom will, without soiling the hands, do it quickly and well. If the soil be loose outside the house it saves a lot of sand being trodden in, only it will be necessary to do it again after each shower of rain.

To Clarify Water.

Place some alum in muslin, pour boiling water upon it, let it cool, then bottle it. A small quantity put into thick, discoloured water will soon clear it.

To Remove Fruit Stains from Knives.

Vinegar or fruit stains can be removed by rubbing the knives with a raw potato before cleaning.

To Remove Fruit Stains from Linen.

To take fruit stains out of white napkins let them, as soon as taken from the table, be thrown into a large vessel of clean, hot water, and let them soak for six or seven hours. Take out and dry them, and it will generally be found that the stains have disappeared. If any remain, wet the stains with hot water and rub on some lemon juice or salt of lemon powder, washing it off as soon as it has removed the stain. It is very difficult to get a stain out of any sort of napkin after it has been previously washed with soap.

To Remove Ink Stains from Table Cloths.

To remove the ink stains from your coloured table cloth dissolve 1 teaspoonful of oxalic acid in 1 teacupful of hot water, and rub the stained part well with the solution.

To Remove Grease Spots from Silk.

A sure and safe way to remove grease spots from silk is to rub the spot quickly with brown paper. The friction will soon draw out the grease.

Ammonia, Uses of.

Ammonia will remove finger marks from paint. It will save much rubbing, which would otherwise wear off the paint. A teaspoonful in a basin of warm water will cleanse hair brushes well; but be careful not to let the backs of the brushes remain in the water. After washing them rinse in clean water, and let them drain in the wind to dry. A little ammonia water used with a sponge will remove spots or stains from dresses, etc. Before applying it, place a folded towel under the parts to be cleansed. Turpentine also cleanses grease spots or the soiled necks of coats and dresses; after applying it place the article in the air awhile to carry off the odour of the turpentine.

To Clean Marble.

Take ½ lb. soda, and 1 lb. whiting; mix this with warm water, and stir till it reaches the consistency of cream. Stand this in a jar in the oven overnight, just to keep it warm; in the morning the mixture will stir into a thick paste. Wash the marble well with soap and water, then lay the paste smoothly over it about half an inch thick; leave this on the marble for twenty-four hours, then wash again, and polish with a soft cloth. For very bad stains this process may halve to be repeated twice.

Furniture Polish, No. 1.

Here is a good recipe for cleaning and polishing furniture: mix 2 tablespoonfuls of vinegar, 2 of spirits of wine, 2 of linseed oil, and 4 of cold water; put into a bottle, and shake well before using. This gives a beautiful polish, without much labour.

Furniture Polish, No. 2.

A polish for furniture may be made from ½ pint of linseed oil, ½ pint of old ale, the white of an egg, 1 oz. spirits of wine, and 1 oz. spirits of salts. Shake well before using. Remove spots from furniture with kerosene.

Spermaceti Ointment, To Make.

Take 2 oz. white wax, 1 oz. spermaceti, 2 oz. almond oil, put together in a basin before the fire to dissolve, and when it is cold it is ready for use.

Court Plaster, To Make.

Soak bruised isinglass in a little warm water for twenty-four hours, then evaporate nearly all the water by placing it in a slow oven. Dissolve the sediment in a little spirits of wine, and strain the whole through a piece of muslin. The strained mass should be a stiff jelly. When cold extend a piece of silk on a wooden frame, melt the jelly, and apply to the silk with a fine brush. When the first coating is dry, apply a second, and when both coatings are dry cover the whole surface with coatings of balsam of Peru.

Sticking Plaster, To Make.

To make sticking plaster, put 2 spoonfuls of balsam of Peru to 6 of isinglass, melted with very little water, and strained. Mix these well together in a small stone jar over the fire. Pin out some black Persian or sarcenet on a board, and, dipping a brush into the mixture, pass it over the silk five or six times, then hold it to the fire, but not very near, and it will soon become black and shining.

To Clean Engravings.

It frequently happens that fine engravings, despite the care taken of them, will in some unaccountable way become stained and soiled to such an extent as to seriously impair their beauty. To those of our readers who own engravings that have been injured in this way, a recipe for cleaning them will prove of value. Put the engraving on a smooth board, and cover it with a thin layer of common salt, finely pulverized; then squeeze lemon juice upon the salt until a considerable portion of it is dissolved. After every part of the picture has been subjected to this treatment, elevate one end of the board so that it will form an angle of about forty-five degrees with the horizon. From any suitable vessel pour on the engraving boiling water until the salt and lemon juice are well washed off. It will then be perfectly free from stain. It must be dried on the board, or on some smooth surface gradually. If dried by the fire or sun it will be tinged with a dingy, yellowish colour.

To Restore Scorched Linen.

To restore scorched linen take 2 onions, peel and slice them, and extract the juice by squeezing or pounding. Cut up ½ oz, of white soap, and add 2 oz. of Fuller's earth; mix with them the onion juice and ½ pint of vinegar. Boil the composition well, and spread it, when cool, over the scorched part of the linen, leaving it to dry thereon. Afterwards wash out the linen.

Watercresses, Use of.

Why do not colonial people consume more watercresses with their food? Often they are growing in profusion near farms, and yet the inmates seem unaware of their existence, or if so do not know of their wholesomeness or medicinal properties. Those farmers who have families, and plenty of watercresses growing in good fresh water, should encourage their children to eat them with their bread and butter. Watercress tea is said to be useful in erysipelas.

Milk, Boil before Using.

Scarlet fever and other infectious diseases are often transmitted to persons by the cows being diseased, from whence milk has been obtained. In all cases it is much better to boil the milk before using, for although its quality then may not be so good, the germs of any disease will be destroyed. If there are any cases of fever in your neighbourhood, it is better to use condensed milk, taking care to mix it only with boiled water. This milk is prepared from the best milk of cows fed on sweet, pure food, in healthy country places. Where water is stagnant or bad it is much safer to use it after being boiled and allowed to grow cold.

Vaseline, Uses of.

This useful preparation, which should be in every home, is considered to be an invaluable remedy for burns, wounds, sprains, rheumatism, sunburn, chilblains, catarrh, and for every purpose where a liniment is needed. Taken internally it is said to cure coughs, colds, sore throats, croup, diphtheria, whooping cough, etc. It is often used instead of the old remedy of buck-fat in smearing over a child's chest suffering from hoarseness, or for the stuffing of an infant's nostrils. Vaseline is sold in bottles by all chemists at various prices.

Part XXIII. Hints and Recipes for Farmers.[30]

Colonial-cured Hams.

Remove the ham from the pork when the meat is cold, then rub it with ½ lb. saltpetre. Leave it on the table till next day, meanwhile preparing this brine: boil in say 3 gallons of water, 1 bucket of salt, 1 oz. cloves, 2 lb. brown sugar, and 2 tablespoonfuls potash. Immerse the pork in the brine when it is cold for three weeks, turning it over often, and keeping it well under the liquor; then hang it in the air in a shady place for some days. In England as much common soda as saltpetre is used to keep the rust away, and the lean part soft, and many of the hams are, when cured, smoked by being hung over smouldering sawdust and wood ashes.

Egg Tests.

There are several tests of good eggs. When placed in water, a good egg lies flat at the bottom; a poor one floats either wholly or partially. Frame the egg in the hollow of the hand, and look at the sun through it with the naked eye; or hold it close to a bright light in a room. If it looks clear and transparent, the chances are that it is good. When an egg is addled, if you shake it gently at your ear, it will gurgle like water; if there be a chicken inside, there will be a slight thud as it hits the shell.

To Keep Eggs, No. 1.

To 4 quarts air-slacked lime put 2 teaspoonfuls cream of tartar, 2 of salt, and 2 quarts of cold water. Put fresh eggs into

---

[30] The advice and recipes given in this section should be viewed in an historical context; some recipes contain poisonous or hazardous ingredients or procedures and should not be followed

stone jars, pour this mixture over them. This quantity of liquid will keep nine dozen, and if fresh when laid down, they will keep many months. If water settles away, so as to leave upper layer uncovered, add more water. Cover close, and keep in a cool place.

Royal Baker and Pastrycook.

To Keep Eggs, No. 2.

Dip the eggs in a cold solution of 2 oz. gum arabic in 1 pint of water; let them dry, and pack in powdered, well-burnt charcoal,

Mrs. Winslow's Family Almanac.

To Keep Eggs, No. 3.

Add salt at the rate of 1 lb. to the gallon of water, and mix lime with it, just as if you were going to make a very strong lime-wash.

Let it stand a few days to get properly cooled, then cover the eggs with it—in a butter barrel, or anything that will hold water. Keep them in the coolest possible place.

A Scotch Recipe for Keeping Eggs.

As the eggs are brought in rub them all over with butter (or oil), and lay them in a large jar, with common salt to cover them.

They will keep six months. The butter is used to close the pores.

Soap, To Make—Dutch Method.

One bucket of Boer ash, 5 buckets of water, ½ bucket of lime. Boil this together for two hours. Strain the liquid off clear, add 2 lb. fat, and boil together ten to twelve hours in the pot. Stir well, then let stand till quite cold for cutting up.

Soap, To Make—English Method.

Three lb. caustic soda, 3 gallons water, and 2 lb. limewater, 6 lb. liquid tallow. Boil the caustic soda with the water for half an hour, then add the fat into the same liquid, after which boil the whole for six hours.

To Make Soft Soap.

Three lb. washing soda, 1¾ lb. unslaked lime, 3 lb. common refuse grease, ¼ lb. borax, 2 gallons of soft water. Put the lime, soda, and water on the fire; boil until the soda is melted and the lime all powder; pour this into a pail, and let it stand until settled and the water clear; then pour off the water into the kettle you intend boiling the soap in; add the borax and grease, and let it boil slowly from one and a half to two hours; then pour into a small tub, adding from two to three gallons of cold water, slowly stirring the mixture all the time until it gets thick and ropy and almost white. The next day it will be thick as a firm jelly.

Caustic Soda.

The Greenbank caustic soda can be obtained at Messrs. B. G. Lennon & Co.'s in Port Elizabeth, and doubtless in other parts of the colony, in cans containing ½ lb., 3 lb., 5 lb., and 10 lb., with full directions for use. The makers state that it makes the best and purest household soap by simply mixing it with tallow or grease. The same makers also supply "Pure Caustic Potash" for making the finest possible "Wool Scouring Soap". They also recommend this for making a sheep dip, when it is mixed with tobacco juice, adding that it destroys the lice, ticks, and scab, and it washes as well in cold as with hot water.

Skins, To Poison.

To 25 gallons of water, and when the water is warm, add 7 lb. of potash, and when boiling, add 10 lb. arsenic, and let the whole boil until the arsenic runs over, then add a little cold water to cool the poison. For use, 2 quarts to 1 bucket of water.

Sheep Farming.

It may interest some of our farmers to read the following paper on "Sheep Farming", as supplied by Mr. J. C. Rippon at a Farmers' Meeting Association, held in the colony some time since:

"The subject `sheep farming' refers to one of our most important industries, one which I am sorry to say has been very much neglected during some years past, but which I hope will again become one of the most flourishing pastoral pursuits of this colony. To make sheep farming a success many points ought to be considered, among the most important of which is, what kind of sheep are best adapted to our different farms ? The kind of which I have had most experience in is the French merino, which I think, for wool and carcase combined, is the most suitable for the farms, in this neighbourhood. Last year I tried crossing the merino with the common Cape sheep, but, while I find that the carcase is no better, the wool is worth considerably less, besides being much lighter in weight than merino wool. I should strongly advise the introduction of new blood into our flocks, say every three or four years, by importing rams of the best breeds of merino sheep, or getting them from farmers in the colony, who have already imported these breeds, and who are known to be very particular in the selection of their breeding ewes. In selecting rams I should always look for those of the largest carcase, with heavy thick-set wool. Another very important point is, in my opinion, the fencing of our farms, as I am thoroughly convinced that sheep farming can never be the success it should be until we can do without, in a great measure, the constant driving backwards and forwards of our flocks, the animals requiring a certain amount of time for rest, most of which they are deprived of by the old system of sheep farming. Of course many difficulties lie in the way of letting sheep sleep out at present, such as attacks of wild animals, and theft by natives; both of which evils, I think, would be considerably modified by fencing. Another most important point is always to have our flocks completely free from scab, both with regard to the condition and health of the sheep, and also to get a good, sound, heavy, and whole fleece of wool; as, from my experience, the Port Elizabeth buyer will give from 2d. to 3d. per lb. more for a really good article than for wool which has been scratched off from different parts of the animal's body; and my decided opinion is, that the sooner the Scab Act is put in force in this colony the better, both for the benefit of the farmer himself and also for the general prosperity of the country. Surely, if the thousands of sheep in Australia can be kept perfectly free of scab, the comparative half dozens in this colony can. With regard to shearing only once a year, I certainly am in favour of it, say in November, as by this practice the sheep have no weight to carry during the summer months, and have a good warm coat for winter, tending both to keep the animals in good condition, and enabling the ewe to rear her lamb better, to say nothing of the increased value of the wool, and only one expense of shearing. I should also advise the farmer to be careful in sorting his wool from locks and pieces, thereby ensuring a far better price for his wool. With regard to the lambing season, my experience has been that the months of June and July are the best for the lambs to come on, as I find that lambs born during these months are not so liable to tapeworm as those born in March, and also that it is only a short time before the spring of the year, when the young grass, by giving the ewes more milk, causes the lamb to develop more rapidly. I have also found that a patch of burnt grass is of advantage, although I do not hold with burning, as I think that small paddocks, where the grass can be eaten down, and then allowed to rest, would benefit the farm far more. I have found it best to keep ewes and lambs in flocks of not more than two hundred each, as the older lambs, by running about a good deal, are liable to knock up the young ones, thereby retarding their growth. I have always found that sheep which can sleep on a high and dry piece of ground are far more healthy than those that have to lie in damp, low places, especially during a hot, damp summer; and I should always advise the adopting of this plan where practicable. Hammels that are fattened for the butcher should, I think, be kept in flocks of not more than five hundred each, to be allowed, as far as possible, to do as they please; they ought also to be run on a piece of veldt that has been well rested. With regard to the different diseases of sheep, the tapeworm in the lamb I find to be the most destructive, attacking the animal when about three or four months old; the best remedy for which is about ½ wineglassful of turpentine, in about ½ cup of milk, given after the lamb has been fasting about eight hours. I have also found some of my lambs scoured a good deal, but put it down to want of more milk. Amongst diseases in big sheep there is gall sickness, of which I have had little or no experience, but which I have been told can be prevented by driving the sheep rather fast when coming home in the evening, thereby benefiting their digestive organs.

"The best remedy for gall sickness is Epsom Salts, 4 lb., as soon as possible after noticing the sheep is ill. Heart water is another very troublesome disease, caused by poorness of blood, from having a large quantity of a very small parasite or threadworm in the milk paunch, the remedy for which, I believe, is salt and half copperas—about 2 teaspoonfuls of salt, and ½ teaspoonful of copperas in ½ pint of water. We have also the tongue sickness or fever in summer to contend with. This, I find, can be generally cured by a little salt being put into the mouth, and keeping the sheep in a cool place until better. This disease is also the cause of footrot, which can be cured by keeping the feet clean and applying a little Stockholm tar.

"As a cure for scab I have generally dipped the sheep with sulphur and lime, about a month after shearing, but have a decided objection to dipping in this mixture after the wool has grown, it being very liable to spoil the colour of the wool. For washing, a mixture of glycerine or Little's Dip, about 1 lb. to every gallon of water for hand dressing is, with a little elbow grease, a certain cure. "

Another gentleman, speaking from experience, said his lambs in March did very well. He agreed with shearing once a year, and separating wool into locks and pieces. He fully agreed with Mr. Rippon in paddocking sheep, but he did not believe in overstocking. He did not agree with Mr. Rippon that driving was a cure for gall sickness. He thought it would rather tend to kill them, from his own knowledge.

Mortality among Sheep.

The Friend some time past gave the following remedy of Mr. J. H. Kingsley's for a disease which appeared among sheep, when on being opened their intestines were found to be infested with worms and the heart covered with water. Here it is: one bottle of Stockholm tar to 3 of water; boil for ten minutes; when boiling add 1¼ lb. Boer tobacco, broken up; when pot is taken off fire cover it up; liquid to be used when cold; dose; 2 pint. The tar water dissolves the slime in which the worms burrow, and the tobacco kills them.

Remedy for Potato Disease.

The Paris correspondent of the Daily Telegraph states that M. Prilleux has just discovered an infallible remedy for potato disease. This is the recipe : Put 13 lb. sulphate of copper and the same quantity of chalk into 22 gallons of water, and souse the plants with the mixture. An experiment made from the 5th to the 16th inst. saved the diseased plants thus treated, while thirty-two per cent. of those which were left to themselves went to the wall; but the disease must be taken in hand as soon as the first black spots have been perceived on the leaves. The remedy is simple enough, and so is the application, which has been favourably received by the Academy of Science.

Uitenhage Chronicle.

Potatoes Preserved in a Silo.

Last year, when the prices of potatoes was so exceedingly low that many farmers used them for feeding purposes, a farmer near Dundee resolved to make an experiment with the view of ascertaining whether potatoes can be preserved in a silo. He cut a quantity of potatoes, and placed them among chaff at the bottom of a silo, which was opened the other day, when it was found that the potatoes were as fresh as the day on which they were cut. The potatoes are now being used for feeding purposes, and the cattle are eating them greedily.

New Use for the Potato.

That useful tuber the potato can, it seems, be turned to new account, so there is an opportunity for Paddy to set up a fresh industry. A composition of the nature of paint, it is asserted, can be made by taking 2 lb. of peeled potatoes and boiling them in water, mashing them, and then diluting them with 1½ pints of water, and passing them through a hair sieve. Then dilute 4 lb. of Spanish white with about 6 pints of water, and add to the potatoes. The result is a milk-white colour. The mixture can be made of various colours by using different ochres, etc., and dries so rapidly that two coats may be applied immediately one over the other.

To Destroy Tigers.[31]

The Agricultural journal publishes the following remedy from "Neef Hendrik": take a leg of sheep or goat mutton, insert the requisite quantity of strychnine, and hang it on a bush or tree three or four feet from the ground. Care must be taken in handling; the use of gloves is advised. Tigers and leopards are often very wary in regard to taking bait in a trap, but meat in a hanging position has an irresistible attraction. Where tigers are destroyed in an open or mountainous country where there is no bush baboons increase rapidly; the man, therefore, who can devise a means for their destruction will confer a boon on many farmers. They are great pests, killing lambs, and have been known even to attack large sheep. Wild ostrich nests do not come amiss to them, as they break the eggs and eat them.

Uitenhage Chronicle.

Raisins and other Dried Fruits.

It is surprising that those farmers who grow so many grapes, apricots, apples, etc., do not prepare and dry more for later use. A farmer, although often very poor, has raisins to buy continually at a store.

Drink for a Tired Horse.

One of the best things to give a horse after he has been driven far (as is often the case in this country), and he is hot and exhausted, is a bucket of water with one quart of oatmeal

---

[31] 'Tiger' here almost certainly refers to the serval cat (*Leptailurus serval*)

stirred into it. It refreshes him and prepares the stomach for more solid food; but let the horse cool down awhile first.

Horses Killed by Administering Drenches through the Nose.

The *Friend of the Free State* says;

"Mr. H. J. Oertel, of Lower Tempe, has had the misfortune to lose thirteen well-seasoned and trained horses at the end of last week, by injudiciously administering a drench to them. He had, it seems, lost two horses from what he assumed to be bots. He therefore prepared a drench, by mixing a pound of brown sugar with a bottle of water, and gave this as a dose to each animal, by placing the neck of the bottle in the nostrils. Out of fifteen horses so treated thirteen have died from congestion and inflammation of the lungs. The lungs of one of the horses which died shortly after being treated were brought into town, and Dr. Stollreither pronounced them to be very much congested and inflamed. We believe Veterinary Surgeon Hutcheons, of the Cape Colony, warns all people from administering medicine by the nostrils, as the farmer of this country is apt to do it. We publish this as a warning to others not to give a drench in this way. "

Dishorning of Cattle.

The dishorning of cattle, says the *Herald*, is a subject much discussed just now among European farmers. The arguments in favour of dishorning are (1) That it improves the temper of the beasts, (2) That it prevents them inflicting injury on each other or their herds, (3) That dishorned stock grow bigger. The opponents of dishorning do not dispute the advantages, but urge that the pain inflicted is quite out of proportion to the good gained. On the question of pain it seems that young cattle may be polled close to the skull with but little pain, while with full-grown cattle the horn should be cut further from the head, and a meeting of five hundred farmers at Perth have decided to adopt the practice. In this country where the ox grows horns of such enormous size, the polling of cattle is a subject worth consideration. The trek ox would, at any rate, travel the lighter without his horns.

Remedy for Distemper.

The following remedy, which has been repeatedly and successfully tried, is an almost certain cure for distemper in dogs, and is simple and easy of application, is given by a correspondent to the Agricultural journal. Take a piece of camphor about the size of a pea, put it into a piece of meat, and give it to the dog. If the dog is too weak to swallow it, put it down behind the tongue with a smooth bit of wood, and make the dog swallow it. I have cured dogs that were so weak they could not stand, with one dose, repeatedly. I do not remember a single failure when the medicine is given early.

Cure for Mange in Dogs.

A quarter lb. shag tobacco should be boiled in about 4 pint of water, and allowed after boiling to simmer; it should then stand for four-and-twenty hours. Paint the animals afflicted every day or two with the mixture. A correspondent says that he has often seen it successfully used on cats and dogs.

Larva and Grub on Pear Trees.

Some time since Mr. J. L. Frost gave us some of the larva and grub of an insect infesting his pear trees. They were forwarded to the Agricultural Department, and Mr. Peringuey, the entomologist, reports: "The insect is pretty well known, and is always found in dead wood, seldom in wood full of sap." Moral: cut out all the dead wood from your trees. Mr. Peringuey also says the grub takes about ten years to go through all its changes. Since this we have seen several other trees thickly infested and dying slowly.

Uitenhage Chronicle.

A Certain Destroyer of the Prickly Pear.

To the Editor, *Somerset East Budget*:

"SIR,—Will you please allow me a little space for the following letter.

I have been for the last three years trying to discover something that will kill the prickly pear tree, and I am glad to say that I have at last succeeded. Your readers will be glad to know that Cooper's Dipping Powder inserted in small quantities in the tops of the highest leaves will completely destroy them in a very short time. One teaspoonful divided into small quantities and put into three or four leaves round the tree will kill it in a month. At the time of the year when the sap rises I think it would be best to put the powder into the trunk; but at this time of the season it is best put into the leaves as the sap is now drawing towards the trunk. A tree 3 feet high can be destroyed in a fortnight's time with 4 teaspoonful of the powder. About two weeks after the large trees have been poisoned the fruit drops off, and there is no doubt that it is poisonous; so this is a warning to all prickly pear eaters not to eat any on the farm "Thorn Grove". I may mention that the remedies I have tried are arsenic, Little's chemical fluid, carbolic acid, besides many others; but none have proved effectual. The arsenic I inserted into the trunk of the tree about 5 inches from the ground, consequently the tree rotted off, and all the fallen leaves shot out again, so I did more harm than good. Chemical fluid has no effect whatever.

"Let us take into consideration what a valuable discovery this is for farmers-what a saving compared to the old style of eradicating the prickly pear; one man can now do more in one day than six could do in a month.

"I have poisoned about five or six hundred trees within the last three days, and I will write again and let you know the result.

"I remain, etc., T. S. LEPPAN."

The Editor writes :

"We have to thank Mr. Leppan for his interesting communication. After the last meeting of the Divisional Council one of the members informed us how efficacious "Cooper's Dip" appeared to be in killing the prickly pear, and we hope this new method of ridding the land of a pest which is fast spreading all over the colony to the serious loss of farmers will be generally adopted. We have been told that if the plants cannot be got at conveniently the leaves may be syringed with a strong solution of the Dip, which will be found quite as effectual as the insertion of the powder in the leaves and trunks of prickly pear.—Editor."

Another farmer writes :

"Some time ago I heard a talk of Cooper's Sheep Dip being the right thing to poison prickly pears with, but wouldn't believe it. However, some of the farmers in this part have tried it lately, and I can assure you that every tree seems to be dying. Some of them are positively dead from the top to bottom. I have given mine thirteen days, but I think one month will complete the destruction of a large tree, that is, from the day the dip is put in. The way I did it was to give each tree or plant 1 teaspoonful; but they seem to tumble over too soon for the poison to penetrate the whole tree. So I think we ought to put the same quantity, only in different places. Say a tree has three branches; split with a large knife one leaf on each branch and put in the poison. The dry powder has been used by some; but I should say if given in a liquid state it would produce the desired effect sooner."

Regarding prickly pear plants, the following extract of a letter to the Tines from Deputy-Surgeon T. G. Hewell, late Sanitary Commissioner for the Government of Bombay, says:

"Mr. Reinold, I believe, first tried burning, as Professor MacOwan did, and with a similar experience. He was then led to try burial under at least 2 feet of earth, and he has found this method to be perfectly effectual. He now, I believe, recommends 3 feet of earth as safer, the object being to insure as much as possible the exclusion of light. This plan has now been in operation for at least three or four years, and it has been followed with the greatest success; and it cannot be too widely known, for no one who has not seen the rapidity with which this plant advances would believe in its power of propagation. The unrestricted growth of prickly pear in the immediate vicinity of villages in India is one of the chief insanitary conditions which so largely prevail in them; and the Government of India would effect the greatest possible good if it were pleased to order, or, if necessary, to pass a law enacting, that all prickly pear growing in the vicinity of inhabited areas is to be cut down and buried under at least 3 feet of earth. "

The Milking of Cows.

Slow milkers gradually dry up a cow, the faster and more gently a cow is milked the better. Many milkers draw the milk with a strong downward pull-indeed with a jerk; but this is injurious to the cow. The teat should be filled, and with a firm pressure of the last three fingers it should be emptied, drawing slightly on the teat and udder at the same time; so proceed alternately with each hand, until the supply of milk is exhausted. Five minutes is about the time that should be allowed for milking a cow, and they should be milked at as near the same hour each day as possible, for undue distention of the udder is most injurious.

In our colonial bred cows it is noted that they will not, as a rule, allow any one to milk them until the calf has had a short drink; and, in some instances, cows will not allow a white person to milk them, whilst other cows will not let a native do so.

Extract on Milking, from English Newspaper.

In learning to milk, the student should start at an early age. It is always considered that a woman makes a better milker than a man, principally because her fingers are more supple. When the fingers, then, are young and pliable the owner is certain to make a better use of them than when he gets old and stiff. An "easy" cow should be selected for the student to commence upon; by which I mean a cow which gives up her milk with a very little pressure. The milker approaches the cow with his pail in his right hand, and the stool in the left, and takes up his position on the right side of the animal; looking from the tail to the head. A cow which, from long experience, understands what it is to be milked, quickly places herself in position by putting the left hind leg forward, and the right one back, thus giving a space underneath for the pail. The pail may either be held between the knees and rest on the foot of the milker, or it may stand on the ground and be kept in position by the knees. The higher, however, it can be held the better, as it is not so liable to be upset by the cow putting her foot in it. The milker, having seated himself, takes one of the front teats gently in the right hand, and with the left clasps one of the hind ones, giving each a little pressure in turn. This causes the milk to flow, and until the whole of it has been drawn from the udder, milk should be falling into the pail from one teat while it is being collected in the other. When two of the four teats have been milked for a minute or two the hands should be changed to the other pair, in order to relieve the pressure. The hands should not be wetted, although it is the custom to do so by many milkers. As a rule, however, it will be found that more or less milk finds its way into the hands during the operation, so that after the first cow has been milked the operator's hands will not be dry until the milking is over. The question is sometimes asked whether it is best to milk the two teats on the same side at the same time, or milk one on the right side and one on the left together. This, I think, is a question for the milker himself to decide. When I was a boy and learnt to milk I was taught to milk "cross-wise" but, as I grew older, and had more experience, I found it better to change my hand according to the shape of the cow's udder, for some cows could be milked more easily by one plan than by the other. Whichever plan be adopted, I advocate the complete milking of the cow at one operation; I do not believe in the system of sitting a second time under the same cow at the same milking, although this plan is sometimes followed. The young milker must not overtax his wrists at first, but milk as rapidly as he can, and not "strip" between the finger and thumb too much. The best milkers draw as much milk as possible by the firm clasp of the full hand. When the milker can operate on ten cows an hour in the height of the season he will be in the front rank; but eight cows per hour is very good work.

MASONIC HOTEL,
CAPE TOWN.

The New Proprietor, while thanking his Patrons for their liberal support at his late Hotel, the St. George's, begs leave to solicit a fair share of Public favours in his New Venture.

ALF. PITTMAN,
PROPRIETOR.

LATE OF THE ST. GEORGE'S HOTEL,

Part XXIV. Newspaper Gleanings, etc.[32]

Fever.

In the tropics the country is a hot-bed of fever. Summer and winter fever reigns; in the marshes and swamps, on the rivers, on the hills, and on the mountains. A contributor to the *Natal Mercury* says he has observed as much fever in the Lower Shire, on the top of Mount Morambala, 4,000 feet high, with a cold climate for the tropics, as in the low-lying country. In a fever country, if one remains long enough in it, one must take fever : the only way of escaping it is to leave the country. Some constitutions are, of course, more susceptible to fever than others; but it is not uncommon for a person during the second year's residence in the country to average five days a month down with an attack. In East Central Africa there is hardly any ailment but fever, and a little diarrhoea and dysentery. If quinine is taken regularly, as a preventative, it may do good or may not. The system gets used to it, and its value as a curative is diminished.

The following is the late Dr. Livingstone's remedy, which is to be obtained at any chemist's : 8 grs. resin of jalap, 8 grs. calomel, 6 grs. rhubarb, 6 grs. quinine. Make into powders or pills, and 10 grs. is a dose, to be taken immediately on fever attacking. When nature has been relieved, 6 or 8 grs. quinine, dissolved in the usual manner, may be taken, to be repeated, but no quinine must be taken before. Sweating between blankets as soon as attacked is part of the treatment. If the fever is not got under in twenty-four hours it ought to be. If it be not

---

[32] The advice and recipes given in this section should be viewed in an historical context; some recipes contain poisonous or hazardous ingredients or procedures and should not be followed

subdued in three days the patient's life may be in danger. Disease is rapid in the tropics, and treatment must be strict to be of any use. Fever combined with dysentery is very difficult to manage, and requires great skill; but English doctors are of little use in dealing with Central Africa fever.

To Procure Ice.

Fill a gallon stone bottle with hot spring water (leaving room for about 1 pint), and put in 2 oz. of refined nitre. The bottle must be stoppered very close, and let down into a deep well. After three or four hours it will be completely frozen; the bottle must be broken to procure the ice. If the bottle is moved up and down, so as to be sometimes in and sometimes out of the water, the consequent evaporation will hasten the process.

Diphtheria or Sore Throat Gargle.

Cover with best vinegar 1 egg entire with its shell, and leave it until the shell dissolves; beat all up, and add 1 tablespoonful honey, 1 tablespoonful good brown sugar, and ½ teaspoonful borax. Make the whole up into 1 pint with water. Well shake this mixture, and gargle the throat.

Specifics for Diphtheria.

We know that the doctors are "down" on the publication of "household" cures for diseases, but the following extract is sent to us by an esteemed correspondent, who thinks, with good show of reason, that as so orthodox a paper as the Medical Times has been the first to give it publicity, the specifics mentioned are worthy of some attention. With regard to the "Sulphuric Acid Cure" the *Medical Times* says: "A few years ago, in view of the fatal scourges of diphtheria in Australia, the Government offered a reward of £5,000 for any certain method of cure. The sulphuric acid cure of Dr. Greathead was found the simplest and most successful. It is simply to take 4 drops of sulphuric acid in 3 parts of a tumbler of water, of which let the patient sip every few minutes. The result is coagulation of the diphtheric membrane and its removal by vomiting and coughing." The second method of cure is called the "Turpentine Tar Cure", as to which the same high medical authority says: "Dr. Deithill, of the French Academy of Medicine, is sponsor for the curative effects of vapours of a mixture of tar and turpentine in cases of diphtheria. He says: take equal parts, say 2 tablespoonfuls each of tar and turpentine in cases of diphtheria; put them into a tin pan, or cup, and set fire to the mixture (taking due precautions against fire). A dense smoke arises, and the patient obtains instant relief, falls into a slumber, and seems to inhale the smoke with pleasure. The fibrinous membrane soon becomes detached, and the patient coughs it up. Convalescence may be expected in three days from the first use of this remedy. "

These two remedies, approved by high medical authority, are within the immediate reach of every mother, whether on the farm or in town, and no home should be without them both. A bottle of Stockholm tar, 1s.; a bottle of turpentine, 1s.; a small phial (glass stoppered) of sulphuric acid, 1s. 6d.

Will any of you mothers, who read this, run the risk of your child losing its life through neglect to spend 3s. 6d.? Will your medical men continue to refuse to apply these remedies because they are so simple, and not in the Pharmacopoeia?

Diamond Fields Advertiser.

A correspondent of a Victoria paper writes: "Should you or any of your family be attacked with diphtheria do not be alarmed, as it is easily cured without a doctor. When it was raging in England a few years ago I accompanied Dr. Friend on his rounds to witness the so-called "wonderful cures" he performed, while the patients of others were drooping on all sides. The remedy to be so rapid must be simple. All he took with him was powder of sulphur and a quill, and with these he cured every patient without exception. He put a teaspoonful of flower of brimstone into a wine glass of water, and stirred it with his finger, instead of a spoon, as the sulphur does not readily amalgamate with water. When the sulphur was well mixed he gave it as a gargle, and in ten minutes the patient was out of danger. Brimstone kills every species of fungus in man, beast, and plant in a few minutes. Instead of spitting out the gargle, he recommended the swallowing of it. In extreme cases in which he had been called just in the nick of time, when the fungus was too nearly closing to allow the gargling, he blew the sulphur through a quill into the throat, and after the fungus had shrunk to allow it, then the gargling. He has never lost a patient from diphtheria. If a patient cannot gargle, take a live coal, put on a shovel, and sprinkle a spoonful or 2 of flower of brimstone at a time upon it, holding the head over it, and the fungus will die. If plentifully used the whole room may be filled almost to suffocation; the patient can walk about in it, inhaling the fume, with doors and windows shut. This mode of fumigating a room with sulphur has often cured most violent attacks of cold in the head, chest, etc., at any time, and is recommended in cases of consumption and asthma.

Fevers.

A Quaker magazine reports that many cases of malarial, typhoid, and scarlet fever, along with typhoid pneumonia and diphtheria, have been quickly cured by the application to the soles of the feet of a poultice of mashed raw onions. In a number of instances the cases had been pronounced hopeless by the medical attendants. The remedy is simple and harmless, so should be tried, for the testimony from Maryland is authentic, and from a Quaker gentleman named John R. Cox.

Ammonia and Alcohol in Snake Bites.

Writing to the *Medical Times* from the Delaware Water Gats, where poisonous snakes abound, Dr. J. B. Shaw says that he was called to see a child, aged ten, female. She was bitten by a copperhead on the foot, about one inch above the middle toes. He saw her in four hours from the time she was bitten. Her symptoms then were: extreme prostration, with nausea; respiration very slow; pulse weak; eyes fully dilated, with a wild look. The foot and leg were very much swollen and purple, and very painful. He gave her 60 minims of spirit of ammonia aromat. hypodermically, ordered 1 oz. whisky every two hours, and a large poultice of linseed and raw onions to be applied to the foot and to be renewed every hour. The whisky and onions were kept up until the child was well, which was on the third day. The above has been his treatment for the last six years, and he has never lost a case; nor has he heard of a death from snake bite when the treatment has been carried out.

N.B. Croft's Tincture for Snake Bite is also generally successfully applied, and in the colony "Jesse Shaw's Sure Cure" has been much used.

Small-pox, Remedy for.

Dr. J. T. Miller, of Stockton, California, in a communication to the *Kimberley Independent*, recommends the following as a preventative of small-pox: "Place 1 oz. cream of tartar in 16 oz. of water, and take 1 tablespoonful three times a day, and you may sleep with a small-pox patient with perfect impunity. Let each citizen do the same thing, and in fifteen days it may be the end of small-pox in this or any other city."

How to Prevent Typhoid.

A lady correspondent writes to the *Sydney Herald*: "Will you publish a simple but almost certain preventive for typhoid, which seems, unfortunately, to be on the increase? Let all mothers of families give their children rectified spirits of turpentine, in the following quantities, every night going to bed: Three to twelve years old, 4 to 8 drops, in ½ teaspoonful of sugar; above twelve years, 8 to 10 drops. It destroys the typhoid germ, and much suffering may be prevented by this simple and cheap remedy. If a child be seized with typhoid, repeat the dose 5 or 6 times a day, and let no solids or meat in any form be given. I speak from certain knowledge, and hope this little information may prove of use to some one."

Onions, Use of.

Whatever may be one's prejudices against the odour of onions, there seem to be so many arguments in their favour as possessing marked healthful advantages as food that prejudice yields to judgment in the minds of most people. Many authorities go still further, and claim for this homely vegetable medicinal qualities of a high order. A medical writer recently advocated the giving of raw onions to young children at least three times a week until the onions become too strong to eat raw, when they should be roasted or boiled, but part of the regular diet must be onions.

Another writer in the *Lancet* says :

"During unhealthy seasons, when diphtheria and like contagious diseases prevail, onions ought to be eaten in the spring of the year at least once a week. Onions are invigorating and prophylactic beyond description. Further, I challenge the medical fraternity or any mother to point out a place where children have died from diphtheria or scarlatina anginosa, etc., where onions were freely used so." Do not miss treating children to raw onions three or four times a week. When they get too large or too strong to be eaten raw, then boil or roast them.

Celery, etc., Uses of.

Celery acts upon the nervous system, and it is a cure for rheumatism and neuralgia. Tomatoes stimulate the liver, and spinach and common dandelion, prepared in the same way, have a direct effect on the diseases of the kidneys. Onions, garlic, and olives promote digestion, by stimulating the circulatory system, with the consequent increase of the saliva and gastric juice. Raw onions are also regarded as a remedy for sleeplessness, and the French believe that onion soup is an excellent tonic in cases of debility of the digestive organs.

Hot-water Remedies.

A strip of flannel or a napkin dipped in hot water and wrung out, and then applied around the neck of a child that has croup, and then covered over with a larger and thicker towel, will usually bring relief in ten minutes. A towel folded several times dipped in hot water, wrung out, and then applied over the seat of the pain in toothache or neuralgia, will generally afford prompt relief. This treatment in colic works like magic. There is nothing that will so promptly cut short congestion of the lungs, sore throat, or rheumatism, as hot water when applied promptly and thoroughly. Pieces of cotton batting dipped in hot water and kept applied to old sores, new cuts, bruises, and sprains, is a treatment now adopted in hospitals. Sprained ankle has been cured in an hour by showering it with hot water, poured from a height of 3 feet. Hot water taken freely half an hour before bedtime is the best of cathartics in case of constipation. This treatment, continued for a few months with proper attention to diet, will alleviate any case of dyspepsia.

To Cure a Cold.

Before retiring soak the feet in mustard water as hot as can be borne. The feet should at first be plunged in a pail half full of lukewarm water, adding by degrees very hot water until the desired heat is attained, protecting the body and knees with blankets, so as to dissect the vapour from the water as to induce a good sweat. Next, to 2 tablespoonfuls of white sugar add 14 drops of strong spirits of camphor. Drink the whole, and go to bed under plenty of bedclothes, and sleep it off.

Colds, Remedy for.

Here are two fairly good recipes: "Tincture of benzoin may be used with beneficial results in influenza and for the relief of 'cold in the head'. The tincture should be inhaled from the bottle containing it. Long inspirations of the vapour should be drawn into each nostril, the other nostril being meanwhile kept closed." If the "tincture of benzoin" does not find favour, the following recipe from the *Cincinnati Lancet* is described by Dr. J. L. Davies as having been used by him for colds in the head with complete success: "Half grain of tartar emetic is dissolved in 4 oz. water, and 1 teaspoonful of this is given every fifteen minutes for 4 doses, and then hourly, and after that, every three or four hours." The disease is thus often cured in the course of one day.

Things worth Knowing.

To cure and heal a running sore apply alum water twice a day.

It is essential that a wound be kept clean, and the bandages changed at least every other day.

For canker sore mouth, 1 tablespoonful of borax dissolved in ½ pint of water is excellent used as a wash.

There is nothing better for a cut than powdered rosin. Pound it until fine, and put it in an empty, clean pepper-box with perforated top; then you can easily sift it out on the cut, and put a soft cloth around the injured member, and wet it with cold water once in a while. It will prevent inflammation and soreness.

A little saltpetre or carbonate of soda mixed with water in which flowers are placed will keep them fresh for two weeks.

When feet are tender and painful after long walking or standing, great relief can be had by bathing them in salt and water, a handful of salt to a gallon of water. Have the water as hot as can be comfortably borne; immerse the feet, and throw water up over the knees with the hands. When the water grows cool, rub feet and limbs briskly with a dry towel.

A half teaspoonful of carbonate soda in ½ cup of water will relieve sick headache caused by indigestion.

A fever patient is cooled and made comfortable by frequent sponging with warm soda water.

Warm mustard water should be given to one who has accidentally swallowed poison. This will cause vomiting. After that give a cup of strong coffee; that will counteract the remaining effects.

When going from a warm room into the cold air, close your mouth and breathe through your nose, to prevent taking cold.

A hard cold is oftentimes cured by a cup of hot lemonade taken at bedtime, as it produces perspiration.

Consumptive night sweats may be arrested by sponging the body at night with salt and water.

For croup or pneumonia, bruise raw onions, lay on a cloth with powdered gum camphor sprinkled over it, and apply to chest and lung, and cover with hot flannel. This is a sure cure if taken in time.

For nervous headache, when the pain is over the eyes and the temples are throbbing, apply cloths wet with cold water to the head and hot baths to the feet.

A neuralgic headache is also sometimes relieved by sponging around the hair of the head with vinegar and water, then gently brushing the hair for a while.

The Secret of Longevity.

A French medical man, who has just died at the age of one hundred and seven, pledged his word to reveal the secret of his longevity, when no more, for the benefit of others. It was stipulated, however, that the precious envelope containing the recipe for long life was not to be opened until he had been buried. The doctor's prescription, now made known, is simple enough, and easy to follow; but whether it is as valuable as he pretends is extremely doubtful. He tells his fellow-men that, if they wish to live for a century or more, they have but to pay attention to the position of their beds. "Let the head of the bed be placed to the north, the feet to the south; and the electric current, which is stronger during the night in the direction of the north, will work wonders on their constitutions, insure them healthful rest, strengthen their nervous system, and prolong their days." It is, he adds, to scrupulous attention to the position of his bed that he ascribes his longevity, the enjoyment of perfect health, and the absence of infirmity.

Never sleep opposite a window which will throw a flood of strong light on your eyes when you wake in the morning.

If you wake in the morning with headache and lassitude try whether ventilating your bedroom will not remedy the trouble.

In every room where human beings live—either sitting-room or bed-room—the window should always be open at least two inches at the top. This allows the escape of the foul air which is always in the upper part of the room. You will soon see, if you stand on a table so that your head is near the ceiling, how much hotter and closer it is there. All that hot air wants to get out, and you should let it do so by opening the window; and fresh pure air will come in under the door or by the fireplace.

A Simple Method for Ventilating Sleeping and Living Rooms.

Cut a piece of wood three inches high, and exactly as long as the breadth of the window. Raise the sash, place the slip of wood on the sill, and draw the sash closely over it. If the slip has been well fitted, there will be no draught in consequence of the displacement of the sash at its lower part; but the top of the lower sash will overlap the bottom of the upper one, and between the two bars perpendicular currents of air, not felt as a draught, will enter and leave the room, and the atmosphere will be kept fresh and wholesome.

Part XXV. Medical Hints, Recipes, etc.[33]

Burns and Scalds.

If severe send at once for a doctor. In the meantime cover the part over well with flour, and wrap it up quickly in cotton wool, wadding, soft thick calico, or anything else to keep out the air. So long as the blisters are not broken, there is but little danger. Be careful in removing clothing then not to break the blisters, rather cut the clothing away to get at the burn more readily. If the person be much exhausted, give a glass of brandy and water.

Milk and lime water in equal proportions may be applied as a lotion. When necessary, if flour has been used, it can be gently washed off, and other flour be put on again. Scalds can be treated in the same way. Should a person be in flames, tell him to lie on the floor, cover him up as quickly as possible with a blanket, big coat, tablecloth, or the nearest suitable thing, and roll him over and over gently till the flames be extinguished.

Lime in the Eye.

Syringe the eye with warm vinegar and water—one-eighth part of vinegar with the water. Dirt in the eye may often be easily removed with the edge of a piece of writing paper or handkerchief.

---

[33] The advice and recipes given in this section should be viewed in an historical context; some recipes contain poisonous or hazardous ingredients or procedures and should not be followed

Bleeding of an Artery.

A large coin folded well up into a piece of calico, and then tied tightly and firmly over the artery, taking care it is situated between the wound and the heart, will generally be sufficient to remember to do before the doctor arrives.

Bleeding from the Nose.

A plug of lint or cotton wool placed in the nostril will often stop it, or a cold lotion to the forehead, holding the arms above the head. Another remedy is to roll up a small piece of blotting paper, and chew it well for some time, without swallowing. The continual action of the jaws will often stop it; or a plug of lint or wool dipped into Friar's Balsam may answer the purpose, or thrusting a cold key, or pouring a little cold water, down a person's back may do so.

Constipation of the bowels will often produce bleeding from the nose. Do not excite the person or child by showing yourself greatly concerned.

Fainting, or being Stunned.

Unloose the person's clothes, raise the head, moisten the face and palms of the hands with water, and open the window, doing all quietly; then see if there is any wound or bleeding. Send for a doctor if it seems at all necessary.

Choking.

Press your forefinger upon the back of the tongue to make the person vomit, if possible. If this does not succeed, let him swallow a piece of soft potato, soft bread, or any such article; if this fails, give some mustard and warm water, mixed, to cause vomiting, or send for a doctor. An infant apparently choking is often relieved by a sharp blow given between his shoulders.

Drowning.

In this country especially, where we have so many rivers suddenly swollen, and so much loss of life by drowning, it is the duty of all persons to acquaint themselves with the following prescribed remedies to restore animation and life. Such knowledge may be required at any moment. Youth is the time to commit them to memory.

Carry the person to the nearest house or place of shelter, with the face downwards. Send at once for a medical man; meantime

1. Strip the body, rub it dry, wrap it in hot blankets, place it in a warm bed.

2. Wipe cleanly the nostrils and mouth.

3. Apply warm bricks, bottles, or anything suitable wrapped in flannel, to the armpits, between the thighs, and soles of the feet.

4. Rub the body with your hands, covered over in socks, keeping the body well covered with warm blankets.

5. If it can be done quickly place body in a warm bath.

6. Warm cloths frequently placed under the spine assist.

7. To restore the breathing get the kitchen bellows, place the pipe of it close to the person's nostril, press finger on the other nostril, and keep the mouth closed; then draw gently down and press rather backwards the windpipe in the throat. Now blow bellows gently till the breast be raised a little, then set nostril and mouth free, and continue to do this till signs of life appear, even should it not do so for several hours.

Inquire Within.

Sprains.

If the sprain has been severe keep the part at perfect rest by means of a roller, applying at the same time rags saturated with tincture of arnica lotion, which is made with 10 to 20 drops of the strong tincture of arnica and ½ teacupful of water. Arnica, as prepared for internal use, should be taken at the same time. If promptly attended to, this remedy has a most striking and rapid effect

Suffocation.

Remove the person into the fresh air, bathe with vinegar and water, keep the body warm, and, if necessary, apply warm mustard or onion poultices to the soles of the feet.

Toothache.

A simple remedy to afford temporary relief is to put a piece of camphor into it, or a small piece of wool with the "Toothache Jelly" sold at most chemists. In country parts keep this always at hand. A warm poultice on the face, of any sort, often gives relief, so does also an aperient medicine.

Drink for Heartburn.

Juice of 1 orange, with water and white sugar to taste, to be mixed together first; then nearly 2 teaspoonful of carbonate of soda should be mixed in. Drink while effervescing.

Earache.

A little oiled cotton wool placed in the ears of children, when travelling or exposed to unusual draughts, will often prevent earache. When the pain is severe the centre of a roasted onion applied warm in a piece of soft muslin to the ear will often give relief.

Eye Lotion.

For inflamed eyes, take a lump of sulphate of zinc, the size of a pea, put it into ¼ pint of water, or if for a child's use dilute it rather more; put a little into a small bottle; shake well; remove the cork, press the bottle tightly over the eye, and pour in a drop or two, which will easily make its way under the lid through the inside corner. Use once or twice a week on retiring to bed. Keep the eye closed awhile after applying.

Wash for Weak Eyes.

To 6 oz. soft water add 1 oz. brandy; bathe the eyes with it every night and morning. This is an excellent wash, although from its simplicity it is often disregarded.

Effectual Cure for Corns.

In ¼ pint bottle of water get a chemist to place six pennyworth of nitrate of silver, then with a feather, or the wet cork, moisten the corn two or three times a week, taking care it does not touch any other part of the foot. Although the corn will at first become painful and tender, if applied long enough it will gradually waste away.

Warts.

The milk of a green fig occasionally applied, or acetic acid, will after several applications remove them.

Treatment of the Hair.

Wash the head once or twice a week in warm water, in which is thoroughly beaten up an egg. Before adding the egg to the water, dissolve in the latter ½ spoonful of carbonate of soda. Soap should not be used, as it makes the hair sticky, while ammonia, soda, or borax causes it to become brittle or coarse. Washing the hair, however, in the manner that I have recommended will make it soft in texture and lovely in hue. After the egg water, rinse the head well with warm rain water, to which add a little eau-de-Cologne; this will prevent the person from catching cold.

Blackheads.

This disfigurement is a form of skin complaint known as acne, and consists of concretions of fatty matter in the natural pores of the skin. They should be removed as soon as they appear by squeezing them out, either with the tops of the fingers or by pressing a watch key over them. The face should then be washed with a lotion of equal parts of glycerine and vinegar, or there should be a nightly anointing with glycerine of tannin, to be washed off next morning. Goulard water may also be used for the purpose. Plenty of towel friction and a free use of soap will generally keep them away.

Medicine for Boils.

According to the British Pharmacopeia the medicines for boils are:

1. *Cerevisiae Fermentum*, beer or brewers' yeast. Dose, ½ to 1oz., i.e. a tablespoonful every morning. It is very useful in low states of the system, and said to prevent the formation of boils and carbuncles. 2. Sulphide of lime, 24 grs.; sugar of milk, ½ oz., mix thoroughly. Dose, 5 grains of the mixture every 4 hours. Any chemist can make this mixture in the form of pills, which are more convenient to take. 3. Iodide of potassium is also used. It may be taken in something like the following mixture: Iodide potass., 1 drachm; spts. ammonia aromatic, 2 drachms; tinct. cinchona, 2 oz.; water to make up 8 oz. Dose, a tablespoonful in water three times a day. The hygienic treatment for boils is, as soon as the boil makes its appearance, to bathe the place with repeated and continuous applications of ice-cold water, and apply carbolic camphor, tr. iodine or solution of lunar caustic, because it has been noticed that applications of poultices and hot fermentations favour the development of the germ which causes boils, and often produce a plentiful crop after the first one has burst and discharged. The sulphide of lime pills are considered the best remedy for boils and gumboils.

Splendid Indian Remedy for Dysentery.

In country parts, the Diamond and Gold Fields, and other places where you may be attacked by it, keep ready for use a bottle well corked, containing 6d. or 1s. each of laudanum and essence of peppermint procured from a chemist. Dose : For a child 10 drops, for an adult 20 drops, in water, every four hours until relieved. Attention must be paid to the diet. Many cases have been cured by this remedy. Only a short time since a cured native offered £1 for a bottle of this mixture.

Cough Mixture.

Mix well together 6d. each of pure glycerine, paregoric, Ipecacuanha wine, syrup of squills, syrup of Tolu, with 2 tablespoonfuls honey and ¾ pint of good vinegar. For a dose, take 1 teaspoonful every three hours.

Linseed Cough Mixture.

To 1 lb. linseed (not the meal) add 1 pint cold water.. Put on the fire in an enamelled saucepan, watch it well, and when nearly boiling, strain, keeping the liquid. Pour the liquid again into the saucepan, adding to it ¼ lb. good liquorice procured from a chemist, which is to be cut into small pieces. Add to it also 2 tablespoonfuls of brown sugar and the peel and juice of 1 lemon if in season. Stew the mixture gently until the liquorice is quite dissolved. It can be taken either cold or warm, and should be kept ready for use in a bottle. Take from a teaspoonful to a tablespoonful for a dose.

Remedy for Sea-sickness.

Mix 20 grains potass. bromide with ½ oz. water. Dose: one tablespoonful, say when going on board, and the other doses occasionally.

A Cooling Medicine.

Two oz. Epsom salts, 2 oz. carbonate soda, 2 oz. cream tartar, 1 oz. tartaric acid, ½ lb. white sugar, and 6d. essence of lemon. Mix this well together, bottle, and cork tightly. Dose: 1 dessertspoonful to half tumbler of water, children rather less.

Hooping Cough Mixture.

Mix 3d. cochineal with ½ lb. white sugar and 1 pint of water. Boil it down to ½ pint slowly, and covered. Dose: for an adult a dessertspoonful, for a child a teaspoonful, every three hours.

Sore Throat Gargle.

Carbonate of soda and water is a handy and simple gargle, and 1 teaspoonful of Condy's Fluid to 1 cupful of water is another excellent one. See also the "Goonah Gargle" in the article "Sore Throats" later on.

To Allay Pain of Small Burns.

Dip the part into a solution of 1 teaspoonful of Condy's Fluid to 1 pint of water, or into a solution of carbonate soda and water.

Part XXVI. Hints and Advice to Isolated Mothers.[34]

Food for New-born Infant.

To a new-born infant, until the mother gives nourishment with her own milk, give every two hours (not oftener) 1 tablespoonful of milk mixed with 2 tablespoonfuls of hot water, and a little sugar.

Soap for Infant's Use.

Castile Soap or Pears', both obtained from the chemist, are the best for washing a young infant.

Indications of a Child's Illness.

A cold or hoarseness in a child should be attended to at once, for if neglected it often leads to croup, bronchitis, and inflammation of the lungs.

If a child is hoarse keep it indoors out of any draught for a day or two, and rub the throat with the following liniment well with the hand. The liniment: Whisk an egg thoroughly, then mix well with it 1 wineglassful of spirits of turpentine, and the same quantity of vinegar; cork tightly in a small jar, and in a day or two it will become thick, so it is well to make it before one wants it, and keep it always ready in the house. (The empty pots of Liebig's Extract of Meat are suitable for keeping it in.)

The little patient's feet should be bathed in hot water with a tablespoonful of mustard stirred into it, and then he should be comfortably tucked into bed, and a flannel nightdress

---

[34] The advice and recipes given in this section should be viewed in an historical context; some recipes contain poisonous or hazardous ingredients or procedures and should not be followed

with long sleeves will further check the chill he may have taken, whilst 3 drops of spirit of nitre in a tumbler of water, or a basin of gruel, will help to allay any feverish symptoms there may be.

Give light food until the hoarseness has ceased. Should the symptoms of croup appear, be guided by the directions given in that article later on in the book.

A shivering fit should also be attended to at once; it is often a sign of coming illness. Put the child to bed, cover him extra warmly, give some hot tea or gruel, and when the patient is well warm take the extra clothing away gradually. Give no spirits or opening medicine. If other illness follows, send for a medical man, for, if taken in time, a serious illness is often prevented, as shivering fits may precede an attack of inflammation in some part.

Adapted from Sylvia's Home Journal.

Medicines Necessary to Keep on Hand in Country Parts.

I would advise all mothers, living far from a doctor, to purchase a book called *Advice to a Mother*, by the late Dr. Chavasse, published by Messrs. J. & A. Churchill, 11, New Burlington Street, London. It is a most useful work, and can be procured in the colony at most of the booksellers of the large towns. It will guide them in many ways, and particularly show by stating the symptoms of each disease when it is necessary to send off for medical aid, or what to do if such cannot be obtained for some hours. I am unable to do more than make a few extracts from the book (with the permission of the proprietors); I have therefore only done so in the most urgent cases of illness, which might prove serious or fatal, if not early attended to; but there is so much information in the book I refer to, that I strongly recommend our colonial mothers to procure it for themselves. The chapters on accidents are most invaluable.

A mother thus isolated should keep a stock of simple medicines always at hand, such as rhubarb and magnesia, castor and sweet oil, a 4 oz. bottle of Ipecacuanha wine (but be sure of its good quality; it should be quite clear), honey, borax, essence of peppermint, ground ginger, a lance for infants' gums, obtained from a chemist, cotton wool and lint, old linen for cuts, etc., sticking plaster, sweet spirits of nitre, dysentery mixture, linseed meal and mustard, syrup of squills, balsam aniseed, toothache jelly, Vaseline, and teething powders.

If a mother remains long in the country she will at times find one and all of them most serviceable.

Hiccoughs of a Babe.

These are sometimes stopped by giving it a bit of sugar or a teaspoonful of water. Indigestion often produces them, in which case a few drops of pepsine wine give relief.

Stuffing of the Nose of an Infant.

If an infant labours hard in breathing through the nose, smear it well over the outside with a little lard, oil, or vaseline, or bathe the nose with a sponge of warm water, then when the mucus of the nose is within reach, gently remove it from the inside.

Washing the Head of an Infant.

This does not injure the child in the least, as many of our country people think it does; but it must be regularly performed, or the child will take cold. If the head be not regularly washed, the scalp will become quite dirty; in which case, if it has been neglected, choose a fine warm day, and oil well all such parts with cocoanut oil, then gently remove the thick dirt with a fine comb, after which wash the head, rinsing the soap well off, and continue to do the same daily. A little eau-de-Cologne after washing a babe's head prevents it getting a cold in the winter.

Infant Crying Violently.

A drop or two of essence of peppermint, or gin, if peppermint be not handy, will often relieve a babe when it cries violently. Put the peppermint into a little sweetened hot water, when sufficiently cool administer gently; it may relieve any windy spasms causing pain after a few moments.

Woodward's Gripe Water will often relieve a child of much pain, and assist in the digestion of its food, and it is perfectly harmless, and free from laudanum.

Food for Infants.

After the first four or five months begin to feed the child a little, either with bread well boiled in water, and slightly sweetened with sugar, or later on with the boiled inside of the flour, which has been tied in a cloth, and boiled four or five hours, then reduced to powder; or use the inside of baked flour which has been moulded by the hand into balls, and baked till a light brown, and powdered; or take dried bread crumbs, reduced also to powder. Use the one for the child which it seems to thrive upon best. Many kinds of prepared foods for infants are sold by chemists and grocers, which sometimes are very helpful, when the one most suitable is selected. Some children deprived at an early age of the breast thrive on cows' milk, others on goats' milk, or it may be necessary where the digestion is very weak to obtain asses' milk; others thrive better on the condensed milk, but all agree when using this that the milkmaid brand, prepared in Switzerland, or the unsweetened condensed milk with the pink label is the best. For some months the milk must be well diluted with water, and a grain or two of salt added.

Before weaning accustom the child if old enough to a little gravy or other food, farinaceous-puddings, bread and butter, and so on. The child does not then feel the absence of the mother's milk so much.

250

After weaning, if the child begins wasting away, give it small doses of "Maltine" three times a day. It is prepared at Hart Street, Bloomsbury, London, and is extracted from malted barley, wheat, and oats. I can vouch from my own observation that it has the elements necessary for bone and fat production; moreover, it aids digestion, has an agreeable flavour, is readily taken, and the result is most surprising. It is also recommended for other delicate thin children, and for mothers whilst suckling.

When about from fifteen to eighteen months give it meat very finely minced, with mashed potatoes, other vegetables, rice, and the like, until it is old enough to partake of the food usually served to the other children. An infant learns to drink from a glass through which it can see the milk sooner than from anything else; always teach it when you know it to be thirsty. Never give young children tea that has been made strong, although you may well dilute it afterwards, and it should never be very warm. A regular glass of good stout night and morning will greatly increase the quantity of the mother's milk, and support her strength during the period of suckling.

If an infant has to be brought up by hand (which should never be where it is possible to be avoided), cows' or goats' milk is the best to use, but it must be well diluted with lime water, about 3 oz. to 1 pint of the milk, and then sweetened with a little sugar of milk, not ordinary sugar; and this diluted milk must be only used until the child is about six months old. If the quantity of lime water produces constipation, use less of it. Pure water mixed with the milk is not so wholesome. Take care all feeding bottles, etc., are kept scrupulously clean, or the infant will soon get a sore mouth, and become otherwise diseased, and do not overfeed the infant-they are more likely to be overfed than otherwise. Do not give it farinaceous food too early before it can digest it.

Carrying a child in the arms, well wrapped up especially, in cold weather, is much better for it than propelling it through the cold air in a modern perambulator; it can see about it better, too, then, and its blood circulates better.

Walking of an Infant.

It is generally thought that an infant should not be allowed to stand on its legs until twelve months old; but this is proved to be a mistake, even with my own children, for unless the child be particularly heavy it rather tends to strengthen its legs than otherwise if it be put early upon them, and, in consequence, the child runs alone much earlier. If a child be likely to have bandy legs give it "Maltine" in doses, or some similar preparation, to strengthen its system, as this fact proves it to be naturally weak in bone formation.

Clothing.

Clothe your children with light but warm clothing in the winter, for clothes made of heavy materials are not so healthy. Be at much pains to keep your children's feet dry and warm. Do not bury their bodies in warm flannels and wools, and leave their knees and legs naked.

Benefit of Wearing Flannel.

In a climate like this, where there are such sudden changes of the weather, all children from their babyhood should wear flannel even in the hottest weather next to their bodies; for a cold wind may suddenly blow after great heat. Then many children catch severe colds if unprotected by flannel, and children wearing it are not so uncomfortable with perspiration in the hottest season, for then their linen clothes do not cling so tightly around their bodies.

Teething of an Infant.

An infant when teething may suffer greatly, and often just from the want of the gum being lanced, which being done saves it a great deal of misery, and the upset to its system is often prevented if, when no doctor is near, the mother can do it herself.

I have often lanced the gums of my children, and also those of my neighbours in the country; it is very simple, as *Advice to a Mother* explains. "Let the child lie on his back, and keep the hands firmly held. Then if it be the upper gum that requires lancing, let the child's head be on your own lap, and look over the head into the lap, another person holding the child. Hold the lance firmly, and steady the gum with the forefinger of the left hand. Cut the gum, where it is so much swollen and inflamed, down to the tooth, which you will feel grate the edge of the lance, and the incision should be about the length of the expected tooth. If it be the lower gum that requires lancing, go to the side of the child and steady the outside of the jaw with the left hand and the gum with the left-hand thumb, and then lance it as before directed."

My own observation has shown me that a child may at the time cry more from fright than from the pain it causes; and very soon after the gum is lanced you can observe the relief it has given, as the child will often commence to play at once, and the new tooth appear in a day or two. The lancing, then, is not so cruel as to be continually rubbing it, and letting the child have continual pain when eating, until each tooth has forced its way tediously through the gum; but the part must be lanced only when the gum is very red and swollen. The first set of a child's teeth numbers twenty, many of which they shed when about seven years of age.

Convulsions.

An infant may have convulsions whilst teething if the process be very painful and tedious. Lancing the gums will often prevent them. At other times they are produced by its having eaten some food, such as currants, peas, or grapes, which they have swallowed whole, and remained undigested. In this case administer an enema of soap and warm water, and if the food does not then come away give a dose of castor and sweet oil in equal parts. This dose will never do harm, and it often proves beneficial. Rhubarb and magnesia is a useful aperient medicine, as it never binds the bowels after a dose; it cleanses the stomach well, and may with safety be administered to the child of a few days' age.

It is said that a child always turns its thumbs inside the hand during convulsions.

Teething children may be relieved of convulsions by being immersed in a warm bath and cold water applied to the head.

Bathing.

In bathing a child be quick over it, and dry it briskly with the towel, or it will do it more harm than good if allowed to get chilly under the process; and this remark applies also to older persons.

Do not force your children into a cold bath, but when the weather is warm encourage them to use it, and if their constitution be strong enough they will naturally grow to like it. On no account should they be allowed to sit on the cold cement sides of a bath, for this will often give a cold, and predispose to kidney and other diseases. In taking a bath to cleanse the skin of the body properly, it (the body) should be well rubbed with a piece of flannel, or a flesh glove obtained from the chemist, or a rough bath towel cut up, shaped as a glove, can be used for the purpose.

To Prevent a Bruise.

Rub the part well, if the skin is not broken, where a child falls, to circulate the blood there again, and thus a bruise will be prevented. A bruised part should be well smeared with butter several times a day. Cold raw meat applied to the part will often help to remove the disfigurement of a bruise.

How to Prevent Accidents to Children.

Keep matches out of the reach of a young child, for besides their being often poisonous, a child is tempted to strike a light, and many children have lost their lives by being burnt.

See that wells of water are securely covered over; also remove as far as possible out of the way of a child any large tubs or vessels containing water.

Be careful, when there is a strong wind, to close one door behind you before opening another; this will prevent a sudden bang, and may save a child's fingers being cut or injured.

Never place a lighted candle so near a window or bed curtains that an unexpected current of air might cause them to set fire. Do not read in bed. Always see the lights out in your children's and servants' rooms before retiring to rest.

Never allow little children to play with marbles, thimbles, buttons, small coins, pins, needles, knives, or any sharp pointed articles, nor let them run about with a tin whistle or other such toy in their mouth.

Rub the soles well of a new pair of infant's boots before they begin to walk in them. By roughening them you may save a broken limb.

Caution your children against all dangerous places, and never let a little child wander out alone. Keep them from rambling where snakes, scorpions, and other poisonous things are likely to be found.

Place jugs of hot water, hot tea and coffee pots, on the table far enough from the reach of little hands; and place bottles containing liniments and poisons out of their reach altogether. In hot weather keep the children's heads well protected from the sun, and do not allow them to drink much cold water when they are very hot, or have partaken plentifully of apricots, loquats, and some other fruits.

If a child has climbed to a dangerous height or place, do not shout out or appear frightened, but quietly see in what way you can rescue it.

Always encourage your nurse-girl or your other children to speak the truth, and tell you fully if an infant or little child has had a fall, or been injured in any way, for if a thing be known early, and prompt measures are taken for relief, much mischief and danger may be prevented.

The Use of an Enema.

Rather than relieve an infant's bowels by giving aperient medicine, use a small enema, which can be procured for the purpose (made of indiarubber) from any chemist. To use it have ready a quantity of warm water, but see it does not become too cold before it is passed into the bowels. Fill the enema in this way: squeeze the indiarubber part firmly in the hand whilst you place the nose of bone in the warm water, then by gradually letting the indiarubber resume its shape, the inside will become filled. Squirt the water from it once or more to see that it acts well, then refill it, oil the nose, and insert it gently into the bowels; press the water gradually from the enema, letting the enema remain in the bowels a moment or two, then remove it gently, and usually the bowels are quickly relieved; but should this not be the case, administer another after a short time in the same way. It does not hurt the child in the least, nor even a very young infant, but if a very small enema be required, a syringe will answer the purpose instead.

A pair of tweezers is very useful to keep in a house in this country where there are so many thorns. You can extract them and splinters much more readily from the flesh with tweezers.

Diarrhoea.

It is not always wise to try to stop the looseness of an infant's bowels whilst teething; for such looseness assists in relieving the child of its pain; but should it have, say more than six motions in a day, some attention should be paid to it, as it then assumes the form of diarrhoea, in which case administer a dose of castor oil, or rhubarb and magnesia. In such cases these medicines are more efficacious than teething powders, which weaken the child, especially when often administered. It is better to give these only when the child seems particularly hot and feverish, and then but seldom. After this treatment, if the relaxation still continues, send for a medical man, but if such cannot be obtained, use the following mixture, prescribed in *Advice to a Mother*, which I would recommend being kept at hand in the country. A chemist will mix it for you. "Aromatic powder of chalk and opium, 10 grains; oil of dill, 5 drops; simple syrup, 3 drachms; water, 9 drachms; make a mixture. Dose: Half a teaspoonful to be given to an infant of six months and under, 1 teaspoonful to a child above that age every four hours. Shake the bottle."

If an infant is at the breast keep it without other food for the time.

Dysentery.

This is neglected diarrhoea, and must be attended to by a medical man at once, when the motion is mixed with blood, and slimy. A child wastes away very quickly without proper attention, and its pitiful face is heartrending to see. If a child has to be conveyed some distance to a doctor, wrap him in warm light clothing, and if in a cart over a rough road, rest him on a pillow placed on the lap.

Measles.

This complaint is not so dangerous in this country as in England, especially if proper precaution is taken to keep the child in bed whilst the eruption is coming out, and after, when the rash is disappearing, to keep him in a warm room, and not exposed to any draught. The measles come on generally after a severe cold, and a peculiar ringing cough, and they are first observed usually about the face and neck, which previously has been looking rather red.

The measles can be felt by the finger to be raised above the surface of the body, and are of a crescent shape.

Give the child light food, and keep him warm until the measles have developed, after which from chills and draughts awhile, and he will be able to go outside in about ten or twelve days if the weather is warm, but should any signs of bronchitis set in, or there be very much inflammation, call in a medical man, meanwhile giving a little Ipecacuanha wine.

In letting a child after an illness go out of doors again wait until the morning is well advanced, and the air warm, to prevent a relapse of the illness, and see that the child comes inside again before the air begins to cool.

Children who are delicate should at any time, when the weather is chilly, be inside the house at sundown, for they generally catch colds and get coughs after that time when they are out.

Scarlet Fever.

This is something like measles, only the skin is a brighter red, and the whites of the eyes become reddish too, after the child has been feverish and poorly for two or three days. When such is the case, do not give any opening medicine, but send for a medical man as soon as possible, meanwhile keeping all persons from the one affected, for the disease is contagious, as it also is in measles. Keep the child warm, not hot. In scarlet fever the eruption cannot be felt above the skin as in measles. A child must not leave the house after scarlet fever until the new skin, which appears after the other has peeled off, be well formed and hardened.

Hooping Cough.

This also is a contagious disease. Spring is the most favourable season of the year for a child to have it. To an infant it is very trying whilst teething. It often lasts from six weeks to three months, or even longer if it comes on at the beginning of winter. Hooping cough commences as an ordinary cold and cough, but the cough increases each day until the child begins to hoop, then brings up after each fit of coughing some slime, which a little child should be encouraged to spit out. Between each fit of coughing the child seems to be well enough. Do not excite it, and keep it in from cold and draughts. Let him stand whilst you support him in coughing. Should it be only a mild attack of hooping cough, you may manage it yourself, but if likely to be a severe attack consult the doctor. After the cough has fairly set in, give the child plenty of air, and when recovering take him if possible somewhere for a change, if living in the country to the seaside, or vice versa. If he becomes very weak give a teaspoonful of cod-liver oil three times a day, directly after meals, in a little orange juice if you can. A tasteless cod-liver oil is now sold.

Garlic, steeped in brandy, rubbed on the spine at night, or rum and turpentine mixed in equal parts, applied with a feather, or sometimes a poultice of raw mashed onions to the soles of the feet will assist the recovery.

Sore Throats.

A little child should, when well, be encouraged to learn to gargle the throat; other children are the best to teach them, they can do so all together with water, and consider it fun; then the little one tries, and often succeeds, after which, although young, if it gets a sore throat, a gargle will greatly relieve it, and often in a severe case help to save its life. Do not allow your children to get into the habit of wearing scarves round the neck; they are far more liable to get sore throats. A disordered stomach will often cause a sore throat, therefore an aperient medicine given whilst a gargle is used for the throat often assists a cure. A splendid gargle, especially if there is any indication of what is called a white sore throat, and contagious, is prepared from the "Goonah" plant, which trails wild along the ground freely in country parts[35]. The thick narrow leaves are full of juice, which can be pressed out, through a muslin, if the plant is beaten with something heavy; this green juice is to be mixed with small quantities of honey, vinegar, alum, and borax. It has a rough, unpleasant flavour, but it is very efficacious. Sometimes country people will, when they find their throat commence to get sore, suck the juice from the leaves of the plant, and thus effect a cure.

Mumps.

Rub the throat well with hartshorn and oil, tie it up in flannel. Give a little aperient medicine and low diet for a few days. Keep the other children away, and the patient indoors a few days, and recovery may be speedy.

Coughs.

Do not try to stop a cough suddenly, as they arise from several causes. In an infant a cough will often come on whilst a tooth is being cut; the only thing necessary to do generally is to give a little syrup of squills, a little honey, or if there be a tightness of the chest, apply a linseed poultice at night. The poultice can be put into thin muslin or flannel, and tied around the neck with tapes, or it will slip from the chest when the child is asleep. When the poultice is removed in the morning, place a piece of thin flannel for that day on the chest, or a piece of oiled linen.

---

[35] The "Goonah" plant is *Carpobrotus edulis* or Sour Fig, a ground-hugging succulent used by the Khoikhoi people as a traditional medicine plant.

If coughs in an older person, from a cold, give doses from a mixture of the following: 2 tablespoonfuls syrup of squills, 1 teaspoonful Ipecacuanha wine, and 2 teaspoonfuls of Powell's Balsam of Aniseed. Shake well together, and give a child 1 teaspoonful, and an adult 1 dessertspoonful in a little water, after coughing. It will loosen the phlegm, and the cough will in consequence gradually disappear. Linseed poultices, with a little mustard mixed in them, give relief to the chest at night. If the cough proceeds from consumption, or other causes, consult a medical man for a remedy.

Worms.

A child sometimes, without any apparent reason, becomes very thin and wasting; this is very often due to the presence of worms in the system. At times a child will scream, or talk much in his sleep; this is sometimes caused by teething, but more often by the worms troubling it. Another sign of their presence is by the dark circles seen around the eyes, and the habit of constantly picking at the nose; the child is moreover sometimes ravenous, and at another time will scarcely be induced to take food; if so it is necessary to give medicine to expel the worms. Even should there be none the medicine will not affect the child. It is best to obtain suitable medicine from a doctor for the purpose, and follow his directions fully.

Children in the colony are troubled a great deal with worms, and especially those who are in the habit of eating unripe quinces and other fruit. Ripe fruit will not hurt a child; on the contrary, in moderation, it is good for him. Well flavour the children's food with salt.

Croup.

This, of all illnesses in the country, when far from medical aid, requires the most prompt attention. If the hoarseness of a child has not been attended to, croup will often suddenly follow, especially if there be a cold wind blowing, and the child should be living in a damp house or situation.

Advice to a Mother says: "After being hoarse his voice at length becomes gruff, he breathes as though it were through muslin, and the cough becomes crowing. These three symptoms prove that the disease is now fully formed. Sometimes the latter symptoms come on without any previous warning, the little fellow going to bed apparently quite well, until the mother is awakened, perplexed, and frightened in the middle of the night by finding him labouring under the characteristic cough, and the other symptoms of croup. If she delay in not giving instantly the proper medicines, in a few hours it will be of no avail, and the little sufferer will become a corpse. If a medical man is within reach, by all means send for him; otherwise give a teaspoonful of Ipecacuanha wine every five minutes until free vomiting be excited. In croup, then, before a child is safe, free vomiting must be established, and that without loss of time.

If, after the expiration of an hour (the Ipecacuanha wine having been given during that hour), 1 or 2 teaspoonfuls of it every five minutes have been found sufficient, then after the vomiting place the child in a warm bath, and wrap him when he is removed in a blanket without staying to dry him first. Rub him dry from the outside of the blanket, then shift him into another warmed one, and gradually put on his flannel night-dress (a child likely to suffer from croup should always wear such in cold weather), and continue to give him small doses occasionally of Ipecacuanha wine. It is not pleasant to a child's palate, but is necessary to administer in such cases; therefore always keep it in the house. Small bottles of it well sealed are better to keep than one large bottle. After croup be careful not to expose the child too suddenly to the cold air."

Bronchitis.

When a child is suffering from this he is fretful and feverish, breathes hurriedly, and has a hard, dry cough, and if you put your ear after removing the clothes between his shoulders, you will hear him wheezing. Inflammation of the lungs is more serious than bronchitis. In that case the skin is hot and dry, whilst although hot in bronchitis, it is moist. The cough also is feebler in inflammation of the lungs, and the breathing more short and panting. In such cases get a medical man if possible, or if such cannot be procured, in bronchitis put a poultice of linseed mixed with a little mustard both on the chest and back of the child, and on removing it sew a sheet of cotton wool all around the parts, which is to be left until another two plasters be put on, or the child has sufficiently recovered to let it be removed gradually from it. Keep the child to one room, and keep it ventilated by the door being left open now and again. Give very light food until the child has lost its feverishness, at the same time administering large doses of Ipecacuanha wine, say 1 teaspoonful every four hours, as *Advice to a Mother* directs.

Diphtheria.

In speaking of the advanced symptoms of this disease, *Advice to a Mother* observes: "On examining the throat, the tonsils will be found to be swollen and redder-more darkly red than usual. Slight specks will be noticed on them, and in a day or two they will be covered with an exudation; also the back of the swallow, the palate, the tongue, and sometimes the inside of the cheeks, and of the nostrils. The exudation of lymph gradually increases until it becomes a regular membrane which puts on the appearance of leather; hence its name, diphtheria. This membrane peels off in pieces; and if the child be old and strong enough, he will sometimes spit it up in quantities, the membrane again and again forming as before. The discharges from the throat are occasionally but not always offensive. There is danger of croup from the extension of the membrane into the windpipe. In some cases there is diarrhoea."

By all means, when the symptoms set in, send for a doctor, or use the specifics for diphtheria mentioned already in this book. Keep the rest of the family out of the way, and prevent their visiting other homes where this disease is known to be, for it is very contagious and dangerous.

Broken Limbs.

In case of broken limbs, while the doctor is being fetched, put the child on a mattress covered with blankets. If the leg be broken, tie it to the other, before moving the child. If the arm, let one hold it while the other lifts the child to bed. Wait the doctor's arrival before undressing the child. In conveying an adult or big child who is much injured, a light canvas stretcher, a light door removed from its hinges, or a shutter with small mattress and pillow on it will answer the purpose. In all cases of accidents and emergencies keep cool, and consider what is best to be done.

Babies and Mothers.

English children (says the *Daily Telegraph*) are the admiration of all foreigners, especially of Americans, who cannot understand how in this unequal climate they contrive to present a robust appearance, and to display "roses" on their cheeks. Take the average infant in the United States, and he—or she—is sallow. Possibly mistakes in diet account for this peculiarity. The American mother feeds her child on candy, and believes firmly in patent foods; she allows it to sit up to unearthly hours, and generally antedates its coming of age by about twenty-one years. We have a good deal of reason to take pride in the far-famed ruddiness of British-born infants; but at the same time it cannot be denied that in great towns the children look the reverse of healthy, or that parental laziness or ignorance leads to the substitution of ruinous dietetic compounds for the wholesome food which Nature suggests. Teetotallers are mistaken if they suppose that an addictedness to the immoderate use of "the bottle" is confined to adults. As civilization advances, the dieting of infants tends to become more and more artificial, and at the next census it would be useful, if it were possible, for a return to be presented showing the number of babies who are being brought up on natural nutriment and those which are expected to thrive on concoctions of man's devising. Infants nowadays suffer from the prevalent delusion that Art and Science together are much cleverer than Nature, and that a variety of patent foods are a good deal healthier than mother's milk. As the pessimistic philosopher Schopenhauer very truly observed, "Man no longer comprehends the language of Nature; it has become too simple for him." This is why babies "take to the bottle" in sober earnest almost as soon as they make their debut on the terrestrial boards. What is the result? When carefully used, under medical advice, and from absolute necessity, the feeding-bottle may be a blessing; but the vast majority of mothers are not careful, and simply follow a stupid custom without in the least degree comprehending the reason of it, or the precautions needed in order to prevent its abuse.

It would be an exaggeration to lay the whole blame of excessive infant mortality in summer-time at the door of errors of diet. Yet the experience on this head which Liverpool has recently gained is, without doubt, somewhat disquieting. Doctors tell us that in the hot months it is natural for dysentery and diarrhoea to prevail among infants; but the weather lately has been by no means sultry. In fact, in the announcement made as to the present state of Liverpool babyhood, the bad results are ascribed, not to heat, but to "cold and wet weather". The Health Committee of that city have had brought before them the fact that in a single week 340 children have succumbed, 200 of whom were under five years old. These numbers are very far in excess of the proper average for the time of the year; and it is not much consolation to the bereaved parents or those anxious for the salubrity of Liverpool to be assured by the Assistant

Medical Officer of Health that "the atmospheric conditions of summer and autumn promote fermentation of food, and induce diarrhoea". A flood of light, however, is thrown on these unfortunate circumstances by the subsequent statement that, out of 463 children under six months old, whose deaths have resulted from digestive ailments, "only 23 were fed from the breast alone, the remainder being wholly or partially reared on artificial diet." What does the Aesculapian professor in the Northern seaport say to these rather startling figures? It must occur to ordinary minds that the food which is spoken of as "fermenting", and so causing intestinal derangements, is the milk on which "bottled" infants are brought up. There is a good deal of indiarubber tubing about these articles, and, unless sedulously cleaned in the most thorough manner, they retain particles of milk which "go sour". Who can tell how many impurities, how many bacilli, a bottled baby is compelled to suck into its delicate digestive apparatus, owing to insufficient care in the manipulation of these mothers' aids, which might fairly be termed infants' terrors? The fact is that the mothers of England ought to be told that, if they can possibly nourish their infants, it is their bounden duty to do so.

If circumstances render this impossible, let them remember that on the care which they devote to the condition of the feeding bottle and the compound put into it their child's life depends. There are hundreds and thousands of women who give their babies, before they have cut a single tooth, starchy farinaceous foods which the poor little beings are utterly unable to digest. Others forget to dilute the cow's milk with water; others give it to the baby cold; and the simple rules which any medical man could lay down as to the necessity of keeping bottles and tubes absolutely clean are unknown or habitually neglected. In truth, the rearing of infant children is a fine art, in which ignorant parents blunder dreadfully, and even fatally, when once they abandon, or are forced to relinquish, the plain path of Nature. The miracle of provision which Providence makes for the new-born babe of the robust mother is full of exquisite devices for absolute health and safety. These are miserably imitated, or not imitated at all, by the machinery of the glass and rubber shops, and the consequence is this infant mortality which we witness. It is, perhaps, grimly true that, under the existing system, only the fittest of all the poor little mortals survive; but philosophers will approve of this more readily than young mothers and fathers. Besides, who can tell what intellectual capacities a weakly baby contains? Sir Isaac Newton was born two months before his proper time, and was so tiny that his nurse in derision popped him into a silver, quart flagon; yet he solved for the world the secrets- of the universe. But then he was nursed naturally, and not brought up on the bottle. It is not to be supposed that these sad bills of mortality from Liverpool enshrine the fate of many a budding Newton. We may be sure, however, that they record the loss of many a little one immeasurably dear to its home, and there is no getting over the stern significance of the figures, which tell us that only 23 out of the 463 children under six months of age, whose deaths are recorded, were nourished as Nature intended that they should be.

Everybody will admit that the temptation to mothers and nurses to use this artificial feeding-contrivance is immense. Baby is peevish and fretful; its attendants push an indiarubber apparatus into the little creature's mouth, and at once peace reigns over the establishment. In the still watches of the night the infant raises its voice in protest against what Americans call a feeling of "goneness" in its little interior, and a mother by just turning in bed can adjust the bottle to its lips, and can slumber again. The question of whether it is rational and healthy for the infantile lips to be engaged in sucking at nothing all night long does not occur to her. She knows that these bottles are on sale, that they look clean and comfortable, and that they are recommended-by their manufacturers and vendors-as panaceas for every babyish woe, and sure preventives of that bane of maternity-sleepless nights. But the use of nourishment is not to stop noise. Food is one thing, and a gag is another. The amount of trouble which is saved by the bottle is, no doubt, very great. It can be put away in a perambulator when baby takes its rides abroad, and can then be administered when required; or, if the parent of an infant wants a day's outing, or if the mother be called away to work, it is always possible to leave baby with a neighbour and a bottle, with the satisfactory feeling that at all events the little thing need not starve. What baby's own opinion may be on the subject of a glass and indiarubber machine as a substitute for mamma is unfortunately a matter which there is no means of ascertaining. When a child grows up to a sensible age it forgets these painful incidents of its helpless immaturity. Frequently—as we see has been the case at Liverpool—it fails to grow up at all, and then our climate gets the blame for what has happened. The lesson that requires to be learned in all nurseries, and especially in the homes of the poor, is the old-fashioned Stoic maxim, "Follow Nature". There are always as many breasts as babes, if some way could be found of utilizing the maternal assistance of those who have lost their own children. The natural mode of dieting infants is perfect; the science of artificially imitating this is in a wretched state of undevelopment. Mr. Toots, in the case of a motherless babe, wanted to know if "something temporary could not be done with a teapot", and that homely receptacle would really be a good deal less harmful than the more elaborate contrivances now in vogue.

269

Part XXVII. Household Work.

Introduction.

In doing this, avoid mere bustle and confusion, thus making a home more uncomfortable than is necessary. Always have one part of a house clean and tidy to go into at any time if possible.

Most persons who have resided for any length of time in South Africa prefer raw native servants. English-speaking ones are generally regarded as dangerously "slim", and as having lost native honesty, whilst acquiring the white man's vices without his virtues. The following from *Imvo*, a paper edited by a native, bears out this contention, and is therefore of peculiar interest as bearing on the important question of native labour, "There is this difference between the English and the native girl, that the one is utterly dependent and the other is the most independent of all human beings; for one must work for her living and the other need never do one stroke of work from birth to death. Any kraal is a home (and she will be cared for there) to a native girl, no matter where she may come from or why. This is a great evil which missionaries have to contend against, even when they try to educate them for domestic work; for it is not necessary for them to work. It is a question which will never be settled theoretically but by practice, and that practice must be by kindness and consideration on the part of the mistress—white or black. Educated and uneducated have the self-same feelings with regard to treatment. A good and kind mistress retains the services of her maids; on the other hand, there are some who will never be suited, not even if an angel came to serve them. In my experience 'the red, rude, and untutored Kafir' makes the better servant, not that she is 'rude and untutored', but because she has not learned any of the evils of civilization. Every class 'has its black sheep'; yes, European and native-taught and untaught-heathen or school Kafir, all have their proverbial exception. "

Why should so many of our colonial-born girls be ashamed to be seen performing any house cleaning? Even apart from it being perhaps necessary where means are limited, or when a servant is absent, it is well to practise it sometimes, for a bad servant well knows if her mistress understands what she may be about, and it is well to be able to direct, if no need to do it oneself. Girls of the Mother country are not ashamed to be seen when working; they rather pride themselves upon it, and dress according to their work, not in ragged and torn dresses, slipshod shoes, and untidy hair, but suitably; and such helpers at home certainly make the far better housewives later on.

To Clean a Window.

If it has short curtains, remove them for the time; if long ones, pin them aside; then proceed to wash the panes well with a small sponge dipped in water, in which there is a little dissolved washing soda. Wet only about two panes at a time; polish and dry them at once with a linen cloth, and finish off with a clean chamois leather, which can be obtained cheaply at any furnishing warehouse. Be careful to make the corners of the window clean; if they are very dirty, get a stick nicely pointed, which place inside a cloth in washing them.

To Sweep a Bedroom

Open the window, and if there are bed or window curtains, pin them up, turn up the valance of the bed, and cover the quilt well over with an old sheet or other large cover, cretonne ones being mostly used. Proceed then to dust and remove the articles from the toilet table, chests of drawers, brackets, etc., placing them on the cover of the bed, and turn the looking-glass with its face downwards on to it, to prevent its breaking, otherwise cover it over with a duster. Place all bottles on the washstand, and cover it with its ware over, after having seen that each article is perfectly clean. When all the small things are removed, and placed. on the bed, cover them over with another large cloth, which it is, well to keep handy for the purpose. Proceed then, after shifting any small articles left standing on the floor, with a soft hair or feather broom to brush the dust down from the pictures, hangings, and walls : in the latter case the hair-end of the broom should be first enveloped in a clean cloth. If the carpets are to be shaken fold them up neatly, and carry them outside, where they may hang awhile in the air in the shade, so that their colours will not fade. Before bringing them in let some person assist in carefully shaking them, not letting them trail in any dust outside, or get muddy. When sweeping, a good plan is to have ready some clean damp tea-leaves to sprinkle over the floor of the room; but they must not be too wet or slimy. If you are accustomed to use tea-leaves for sweeping your carpets, and find that they leave stains, you will do well to employ fresh-cut grass instead. It is better than tea-leaves for preventing dust, and gives the carpets a very bright, fresh look. Proceed then to sweep, not in an excitable manner, throwing the dust up into the air, but by keeping the broom steadily on the floor rather draw than push the dust along. Begin at the corner furthest from the door where you finish, and when you have completed the task look back to see if any dust or pieces still remain. Gather up with the hand any threads of cotton or feathers there may be still about, and always remember to do so from door mats and passages as you walk along, for a house never looks tidy with them about the floors.

Clean stair rods with a soft woollen cloth dipped in water, and then in finely sifted coal ashes. After the rods have been well rubbed in this way rub them with a dry flannel or woollen rag until they shine, and every particle of ashes has disappeared.

To Scrub a Room.

If the bedroom or any other room has to be scrubbed, after the small articles have all been removed from the floor, it being well swept, procure a bucket of clean water, in which a little washing soda is dissolved, a clean house flannel, and a good scrubbing brush, free from grease, and begin in this way, at furthest corner from the door. Wash with the cloth the piece you will scrub, then, with or without a soaped scrubbing brush (the best scrubbers never use soap, as they consider the fat of it discolours the boards), scrub the part well, using the brush as much as possible the way of the grain of the wood. When this is done, do not wipe it dry at once, but well wash off the dirt you have scrubbed up, after which wring the flannel well and dry it as much as you can. Be sure to get the corners of the room perfectly clean; if necessary, use a skewer of wood to bring out any dust from them. After scrubbing wait awhile until the room dries before putting down the carpets and tidying it. A scrubbed room will never look so well if it is much stepped over before it is dry.

To Sweep a Carpeted Room.

Remove and protect from the dust as far as you can all small articles which are about; pin up curtains, cover over furniture, or anything else which requires covering; then with a carpet broom brush the carpet firmly and steadily, beginning at the furthest corner from the door. Small hand carpet brushes are handy for getting at the corners; for collecting into a dustpan any small pieces there may be in a carpeted room, when a big sweep is not required, or for sweeping down carpeted stairs. Let the dust settle well before attempting to move any of the covers, or rearranging the room.

To Dust a Room.

Use a clean duster, and commence to do the highest things first; beginning at one side of the room, and going quite round it. Do not strike the dust off from one thing to another; but wipe it carefully away, then shake the duster well before using it for other articles in the room.

To Make a Bed.

Put a clean apron on. Always keep one handy for the purpose, as it saves the bed valance and quilt from getting dirty. As early as possible in the morning strip the bed of its clothes, one by one, remembering which is the top or bottom of its sheets, as they must be put back the same way; when this is done, if there be a feather bed remove it aside, whilst the mattress or palliasse is turned over to its other side. Then the bed can be put back and well shaken, the bulk of the feathers being brought up nearest the head of the bed, then flattened into a good shape, the four sides being nicely even. A feather bed requires to be well shaken each day, or it will become lumpy. After the bed is smooth and even, or in the absence of it, the mattress is neat and in order, the bed clothes are put back evenly one by one. A Kafir blanket or sheet next the mattress, or bed, under the usual sheet, makes the bed more comfortable, nor is the mattress or bed so likely to be soiled. Remember in putting on the top sheets and blankets to have them both high and also low enough to be comfortable, for although the blankets may be short, if there are two of them, you can give the benefit to the top part of the bed with one, and to the bottom of it with the other. Tuck the blankets well around the bed or mattress before putting on the quilt, which generally hangs loosely over the bedstead. This task completed, most people fold down quilt and sheets, neatly giving two or three turns' to them, until they rest across the bed just under the pillows, which are neatly arranged above, with their openings all turned to the inside of the bed. Feather beds and mattresses should now and again be exposed to the sun and air, for they get damp, as the rust on an iron bedstead plainly indicates. A piece of Hessian cloth, or canvas, protects a mattress from being spoilt by the rust of the bedstead. Those persons who travel find their bed and mattresses are greatly protected from dirt and injury if they make covers of gingham, or some other serviceable washing article, which can be made to slip off and on them, in the way of pillow slips. A clean wool-bag is one of the most convenient things to put a bed, pillows, or small mattresses, etc., in, for transit from one place to another.

To Make a Stove Fire of Coal.

See that all the ashes and cinders are well cleaned out from the bottom of the stove, save the cinders, and remove any soot from any accessible part of it-from over the top of the oven, and from around the damper and piping if possible; then place a few cinders loosely in the bottom of the stove, above them a little paper, over which put some wood, the first pieces being very thin, and gradually increasing in thickness; after which set light to it, and as it begins to burn well, put a few pieces of small-sized coal over the wood where the flames will reach them. As the fire begins to burn up well put more cinders and coal, until you have, a sufficient quantity in the stove,

A Wood Fire.

If the fire is to be made of wood only, clean out the ashes well first, and if there be a few half-burnt pieces of wood still remaining from the previous time, put them in lightly first, then some paper, next thin and thicker wood until the stove is sufficiently full. When the wood is damp (which a good housewife should always avoid, if possible) it is usual to pour a little paraffin over it, in which case do it before the wood is placed in the stove, and use it from a small quantity, as many accidents have happened from its being poured from a large quantity on to a fire, which will suddenly blaze up, and explode the whole possibly. Where much bacon or ham is used, the rind saved, and when necessary slipped into a sulky fire, it will often be the cause of its burning up quickly and well.

To Trim Lamps.

These should never have to be done just as they are required at night, or they may need the light of a candle to attend to them, and that should not be placed too near paraffin. Pour into the bowl of the lamp rather more than two-thirds full, if the remaining oil of the lamp is clean in it, otherwise pour out this oil over the stored firewood or coal; then remove the parts of the lamp around the wick, clean out dead flies, dust, etc., wipe the parts clean, and then attend to the wick. Either wipe or cut the top off of it evenly and well; see the bowl, glasses, globe, or shade of the lamp is also clean, then return it at once to its place.

A long experience has taught me that washed lamp chimneys break quicker than unwashed. When you want to clean them, take a very soft old newspaper, hold one hand over the top of the chimney and gently breathe in the other end. Then insert the paper and rub briskly. You will be surprised at the clear glass.

To Clean a Stove.

If other than the kitchen one, spread a mat or clean sack in front of it to kneel on and stand your requisites; sweep off any dust with a small hand hair broom, then with a round black lead brush cover the whole, or a part at a time, with black lead, which has been dissolved in water, in a cup or small basin. At once, before it commences to dry, proceed vigorously although lightly to polish it with the other brushes. It must not become white, but when well polished be a good shining black colour. A pair of housemaids' or other gloves save the hands from getting much soiled. Take care not to spill the black lead, or with your hands mark any door or furniture when you have finished, and carry out your mat, etc. A stove must be quite cold before it can be well cleaned. A kitchen stove should be cleaned each day if possible, and then thoroughly well now and again.

To Clean a Cemented Stoep.

Sweep and wash it well. As each portion is done, if you are able to obtain the English hearth-stone, rub it over the washed part, then with the house flannel wrung dry, with a smooth part turned outside, proceed to move it over the surface in a straight course backwards and forwards, so that the applied hearth-stone covers the whole of the cement, and remains to dry as the fine grain of a piece of wood, and not in round smears. In the absence of hearth-stone sifted white wood ashes answer the purpose well. They are when sifted mixed with a little water, and the smooth side of the flannel dipped into it and drawn over the washed stoep, one part at a time, neatly and evenly. If carefully done, the stoep dries beautifully white and clean, its only disadvantage (as is also the case with whiting) being that it treads off more. easily into the house than the hearth-stone does.

To Clean Knives and Forks.

Wash them as soon as they are removed from the table, but do not let their handles get into the water, then on a knife board covered with leather rub them backwards and forwards, after seeing there is sufficient knife polish there. The same powder will do for several times, if when finished with the board be wrapped in paper, and put aside instead of being hung up. Plain deal boards with bathbrick rubbed on them are sometimes used, but they cause the knifes to wear out more quickly; besides the noise of their being cleaned most people dislike to hear. Steel forks can be cleaned with a leather dipped into a little moistened bathbrick powder, and metal ones, if solid, and not plated, can be cleaned with a leather and Oakey's polish; but plated ones only need washing in soap and water, then dried with a clean chamois leather. In putting unused knives and forks away dry them well, and smear them over with a rust-protecting preparation by "Steel" sold in small tins, or by a mixture of oil and whiting.

To Polish Furniture.

There are several polishes prepared and sold for this purpose, but the one of sweet oil mixed with a little vinegar is much used. The article to be polished must be well dusted, fly spots or sticky places gently sponged clean, and the mixture applied with a small piece of flannel. Rub it well in, then dry the article thoroughly with a soft cloth.

To Clean Boots.

Remove any mud or dust from them, see they are well dried, when with a soft brush rub the blacking over them, and proceed quickly to brush them with the dry brush until they shine black and brightly. If they dry too rapidly, before being well polished, rub more blacking over the part, and polish again. A little vinegar added to the water improves some blackings. Day and Martin's is the best imported article; it is sold either in jars or tins.

Culinary Cleansing.

Copper utensils can be washed in very hot water with a little soda dissolved in it, a tablespoonful to a gallon or so of water, then scoured with soft soap and fine sand, or with sapolio rubbed on with a soft cloth. If verdigris has formed upon them it must be removed by vinegar and salt. Then the coppers must be thoroughly rinsed and dried. A mixture of salt, sand, and flour, made into a paste with milk or buttermilk, is used by some professional cooks to clean their copper utensils; brass should be scoured with vinegar and salt, and well rinsed. Tins can be scoured with sapolio, and rinsed in hot water, or with ashes, or yet with fine sand or whiting. After rinsing, dry well before putting away. Iron ware when new should have fresh hay boiled up in it. If it be washed the moment the food is emptied from it, in plenty of hot water with a little soap, it can be constantly kept in a good condition. An iron-linked dish cloth is the best for cleaning iron ware. A little soda should be boiled in any utensil which smells of fish or onions. Steel ware, knives, forks, etc., should be scoured with bathbrick, washed in hot water, and well dried. Sieves ought to be scrubbed with a soft brush in soft hot water, then thoroughly dried. Jelly bags must be thoroughly scalded, and perfectly dried. If kept in a drawer out of the dust they need never be touched, except when needed for use.

A Use for Lemons

The next time you think you have done with a lemon, just dip it in salt and rub your copper kettle or stew pan with it. You will be surprised to find what a brilliant surface you will obtain if you rub the article instantly with a dry, soft cloth. You can polish, all brass-work by the same means, every stain disappearing as. if by magic. A mouldy lemon put into a dirty saucepan half full of water and boiled for half an hour cleanses the utensil amazingly and removes any odour such as fish or onions.

FOR PRIVATE SALE,

60 CASES BASS'S ALE,
40 „ MARRIAN'S Do.
5 „ JEFFERY'S Do.
5 „ WHITEBREAD'S Do.
DRAUGHT ALE,
SALTS,
GINGER BRANDY,
20 CASES HENNESSY'S BRANDY,
30 RED CASES GIN,
ROUGH AND SWEET PONTAC
CAPE SHERRY,
„ BRANDY,

DRAUGHT ALE AND PORTER (in small barrels)
SOUCHONG TEA,
CAPER „
BISCUITS, IN TINS,
OVERCOATS,
RAILWAY RUGS,
SHIRTS,
20 DOZ. CUPS AND SAUCERS,
SPERM CANDLES,
BOTTLED FRUIT,
AND OTHER ARTICLES.

HERMANN PETERSEN,
AUCTIONEER AND AGENT.

Pniel, 26th May, 1871.

Part XXVIII. Washing, Starching, and Ironing.

Introduction.

This household task should always, if possible, be got over early in the week, and never left until Saturday, unless the weather prevents its being accomplished.

A husband, possibly employed from home all the week, does not care to see it about, when he is able to be home after the week's duties; it appears as if there is no room or welcome for him if much work of this sort is about then. A mother can always contrive to have some small article of needlework handy to do, if she must be busy whilst he is home, and but few men object to that. Where much needlework has to be done in a family, the mother generally finds it cheaper to pay for her washing than for sewing, nor is it in this climate such trying work for her. Washing by the English method can, to a greater extent, he dispensed with here, the climate is so bright, the clothes bleach beautifully, and if the native women are only made to understand how to be tender with the clothes they wash, their method saves much labour, and if they have plenty of clean water for rinsing, it answers the purpose well.

If some of the stains will not come out with their process, give them some washing soda, and a suitable pot, and instruct them how to boil such articles awhile. The way to blue the clothes they do not well understand; they make the water as dark with blue as they consider necessary, and plunge in all articles indiscriminately, even to the flannels, unless they are noticed, and if you are not particular in seeing them wash and shake these latter articles, putting them to dry at once, they will soon succeed in spoiling them all. This is the reason flannels are often washed at home with the stockings, which they seldom wash well either. Flannels are better when washed in warm water, the soap should not be rubbed upon them, but be lathered in the water. They must be well rinsed and shaken before being hung up. Clothes pegged on to lines dry better, and are not so liable to be torn, as upon the thorny bushes. If living in the country, and your clothes are spread upon bushes, take care the bucks, kids, or ostriches do not tear or devour them. As a rule, our native women are very careful to return all the clothes entrusted to them, and this is to their credit.

When the clothes come home (a coffee bag is a good thing to send them in, being light) they have to be sorted; the ones for the starch are set aside, and the rest of them damped and folded ready for smoothing over with an iron, for mangling, or for tramping under foot. If the latter they are laid in coarse sheets or bags, and thus protected from the dust, then they are placed in a doorway or other thoroughfare, where the feet of all may help, and it is surprising to see how well the clothes appear, if they are sufficiently damped and well folded. When taken up, they only require airing, perhaps repairing, and then put away ready for use. Sometimes clothes are very carelessly aired before they are put away; if so we need not wonder why so many families suffer with severe colds and coughs.

Raw Starch.

Starched clothes are more trouble; some, such as collars, shirt fronts, and wristbands, short curtains, lace, and other small articles, are put into raw starch. This is prepared in the following way: a sufficient quantity of starch is put into a muslin with a little fine salt, to prevent the sticking of the iron, or a clean tallow candle is stirred into it for the same purpose; a sufficient quantity of cold water is added, and the starch is squeezed gently through the muslin. The clothes are then dipped into it, after which they are rinsed in clean water, then folded up neatly and tightly in a clean cloth, where they are left until ironed. In starching a shirt dip in the wristbands, then the neck band or collar, and the front, but not more of the shirt than can be helped; these parts are then rinsed, the remainder of the shirt is damped if the weather be hot, the starched parts are folded inside, and the shirt is rolled up firmly and set aside (maybe with loose starched collars also inside) until the irons are ready. It is best to starch the shirt a few hours before ironing it.

Boiled Starch.

This is used for larger or coloured articles, dresses, etc., and often prepared from the blue starch, whilst the white starch is used for smaller fine articles. A quantity of starch with some salt is placed in a large basin—generally the toilet one—it is then mixed with a little cold water, as little as possible, then fast-boiling water is poured upon it whilst being stirred, and the starch will thicken. It is then allowed to get sufficiently cold to dip the clothes in—those of the lightest colour and those requiring to be the stiffest the first. These clothes are after this rinsed in clean cold water, shaken out, and hung up to dry, then they are brought in, sprinkled, thus damped, rolled up tightly, covered over with a thick cloth, and left ready for ironing.

Ironing.

Plain clothes, i.e., those that are not starched, are easily ironed. It is usual to smooth the sleeves, strings, and all the small parts first, then the larger or body parts. Embroidery should be ironed out from the inside; its pattern can be better seen. Where there is a double row of gathers, fold the article in half, so that the point of the iron turns to them, first on one side, then the other. Side fires on the hearth with the irons placed on a tin, over a trivet, generally heat the best, nor do they take so much firing as a stove. If a stove fire be used, the box irons answer well, those holding hot coal or wood are to be preferred to the other sort with iron heaters in them. Beeswax and salt will make rusty flat-irons as clean and smooth as glass. Tie a piece of wax in a rag, and keep it for that purpose. When the irons are hot, rub them first with the wax rag, then scour with a paper or cloth sprinkled with salt.

Starched clothes require more particular attention than the others, and only by practice a person succeeds in ironing them well; they get to know exactly how damp they should be—how much starch must be used—how hot the irons must be—so if you do not succeed the first time, try again; you soon will. Skirts of dresses and petticoats are more easily ironed on a board made for the purpose, broad one end, narrow the other. It is covered evenly with a blanket, whilst for ironing lace and fine articles, a piece of linen is fastened on too. It is well to have a little sponge, or a small piece of clean white rag, and a little water handy, to remove any smears the iron may sometimes produce, especially on a shirt front or wristband, which a nervous ironer is somehow sure to make. The bodies of shirts are first ironed, then the sleeves, after which the wristbands, and lastly the collar and front. The front of the neck is then pinned to keep the shirt in a good shape, the sleeves are laid in the back, and the shirt is folded to the width of the front, which should be the length of it also when ready to put away. In case of any dampness remaining, shirts when ironed are generally left to air awhile over a chair or clothes-horse before setting aside. Tucks of petticoats, etc., are first ironed, either at the back, or under each one, then over their tops. The easiest plan to have pinafores and small articles starched is to have ready cooled a quantity of boiled starch at the time of washing, then as soon as the article is rinsed and blued it is dipped in the starch and rinsed again before it is hung up at all. It only then requires damping, when the other clothes are brought in, before ironing.

Some kinds of lace, long muslin curtains, etc., are not always ironed, they are starched in raw starch, nearly dried, and drawn out straight with the hand; they are then placed under pressure, then aired, and put away.

Country people in some parts, instead of starch, use the gum which exudes from the willow and other trees. Borax can be used with starch; it stiffens the article better, and imparts a gloss.

To keep the colours of muslin bright dissolve a small lump of alum in the starch.

The Masonic Hotel,

CAPE TOWN,
ESTABLISHED 1859.

THIS First-class Family and Commercia Hotel is situateed in a central position facing the Parade and close to the Railway Station, with Tramway Cars passing from the Docks.

Private Sitting Rooms and Dinners; Wines of the choicest quality; Table d'Hote; Luncheons à la Carte; Billiards

TERMS MODERATE.

F. W. PRATT, Manager.

Index

The Rhodesia Medal Roll
Edited by David Saffery

Containing the names of over 12,000 recipients and revealing 1,700 previously unpublished decorations, this definitive book is the ultimate compendium of Rhodesian military and civilian honours and awards gazetted between 1970 and 1981. Fully indexed by surname, it is perfect for medal collectors and dealers, historians and genealogists—and a brilliant heirloom souvenir for recipients and their families. ISBN: 0-9553936-0-4

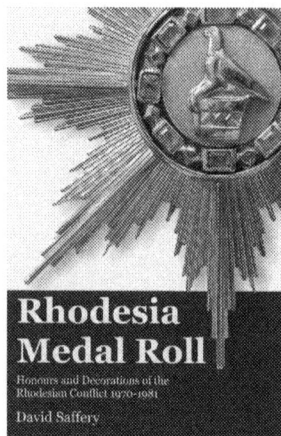

The Bulawayo Cookery Book and Household Guide
Edited by Mrs N. Chataway

This reprint of Zimbabwe's earliest cookery book is packed with recipes for Edwardian African delicacies: garnet-red tomato jam; fiery, home-made ginger beer and spicy bobotie. Packed with contemporary advertisements for companies like Puzey and Payne, Philpott and Collins and Haddon and Sly, the book even contains a section on veld cookery, contributed by Colonel Robert 'Boomerang' Gordon, D.S.O., O.B.E., who went on to raise and command the Northern Rhodesia Rifles at the outbreak of the First World War. ISBN: 0-9553936-2-0

For full details of our inventory, or to order direct, view our web site at **www.jeppestown.com**

JEPPESTOWN